The
GREAT STORY
— *of* —
ISRAEL

The GREAT STORY — *of* — ISRAEL

ELECTION, FREEDOM, HOLINESS

ROBERT BARRON

W☼RD *on* FIRE.

Published by Word on Fire, Park Ridge, IL 60068
© 2022 by Word on Fire Catholic Ministries
Printed in the United States of America
All rights reserved

Cover design, typesetting, and interior art direction
by Nicolas Fredrickson, Sandra Jurca, Cassie Bielak, and Rozann Lee

Excerpt from the English translation of the *Catechism of the Catholic Church*
for use in the United States of America Copyright © 1994, United States
Catholic Conference, Inc.—Libreria Editrice Vaticana. Used by permission.
English translation of the *Catechism of the Catholic Church*: Modifications
from the Editio Typica copyright © 1997, United States Conference
of Catholic Bishops—Libreria Editrice Vaticana.

Scripture quotations are from the New Revised Standard Version Bible:
Catholic Edition (copyright © 1989, 1993), used by permission of the
National Council of the Churches of Christ in the United States of America.
All rights reserved worldwide.

25 24 23 22   1 2 3 4

ISBN: 978-1-685780-19-7

Library of Congress Control Number: 2022907597

Contents

Introduction

When I was doing my university and seminary studies some forty years ago, the privileged, practically dominant approach to the Bible was the historical-critical method. The purpose of this technique—employed in the Catholic context by such weighty figures as Jerome Murphy-O'Connor, Roland Murphy, Joseph Fitzmyer, John Meier, and, most notably, Raymond E. Brown— was to uncover as fully as possible the intention of the human authors of the biblical books. Accordingly, it involved a number of subdisciplines, including redaction criticism (which sought to identify the theological assumptions of the final editor of a biblical text), source criticism (which traced the history of the development of a scriptural writing), literary criticism (which focused on the genre employed by the writer/editor), etc.

There are numerous virtues to this method. First and most importantly, it takes with utter seriousness the groundedness of biblical religion in history. Though it certainly contains poetry, legend, song, and philosophical musing, the Bible is primarily the account of how God acted in history, precisely through the people Israel. And the climax of the biblical narrative (at least from the Christian perspective) is a very particular Jew, Jesus from Nazareth, who fulfilled God's promises to Israel through his dying and rising from the dead. If we forget that the texts of the Bible were written by real human beings operating within definite historical contexts and with their own perspectives and limitations, the Scriptures can devolve rapidly into abstract philosophy or vague "spirituality."

The historical-critical method holds off this tendency. Secondly, it very effectively blocks the temptation to hermeneutical whimsy, by which I mean wildly imaginative or irresponsibly speculative interpretations of biblical texts. In this, it represents a reiteration of the patristic commonplace—sometimes, admittedly, honored by the Fathers themselves more in the breach—that the spiritual sense of a scriptural text must always be based upon the literal meaning of that text. Thirdly, by stressing the role of the human author so strongly, it holds off a naïve reading of inspiration as tantamount to divine dictation, as though God were working through automatons. And in this, it respects the incarnational principle, so central to Christianity, that God acts noncompetitively with his rational creatures, his proximity enhancing rather than diminishing their own activity.

However, there are a variety of limitations to this method, and the almost exclusive practice of historical criticism in biblical exegesis and preaching has led to problems galore. First, by stressing so completely the human authorship of the biblical books, the method effectively bracketed the reason the Bible is still read in the Church—namely, that God in some very real way is the principal author of the Scriptures. Thomas Aquinas gives voice to the mainstream of the classical Christian tradition when he insists, at the very beginning of the *Summa theologiae*, that *auctor sacrae Scripturae est Deus* (the author of Sacred Scripture is God).[1] That Thomas holds to the integrity of the human authors of the Scriptures is clear from a number of his observations, but he understands those writers as acting instrumentally in service of the ultimate author. I can vividly remember how in biblical classes in the seminary, I would ask my professors, after we had laboriously gone through a historical-critical analysis of a given text, "Yes, but what is God saying?" To which the answer was, "That's for your homiletics class or your spiritual direction." That

1. Thomas Aquinas, *Summa theologiae* 1.1.10, in Sancti Thomae de Aquino Opera Omnia, Leonine ed. (Rome, 1882), 4:25.

bifurcation between formal academic study of the texts on the one hand and spirituality, preaching, and prayer on the other was and is tragic, and it was bequeathed to us by a one-sided employment of the historical-critical method.

A related difficulty is that the historical-critical approach effectively atomizes the biblical writings, thereby eliminating the coherence of the Bible as, at least in a significant sense, one book. I have long argued against those who naïvely look for a single hermeneutical key to the Scriptures and insisted that the Bible is best construed as a library or a collection of books with different authors and audiences and written in a variety of literary genres. That said, given the uniqueness of the principal author of the Scriptures, we must see, even amidst all of this variety, a thematic coherence and a recognizable narrative arc. These features have been emphasized strongly in the so-called canonical approach, which focuses on the totality of the Bible as a finished product. N.T. Wright's exegesis, which highlights the history of salvation as a sort of five-act drama—stretching from creation and the fall, through the formation of a people Israel, to the coming of the Messiah and the age of the Church—represents a unified reading of the Bible as a whole.[2] If the stress, in the historical-critical manner, is on the particularities of each book and the peculiar emphasis of each author, one can easily lose the forest for the trees, and this is not a merely theoretical difficulty, for it leads to a radical undermining of Christian proclamation and preaching.

Still another difficulty is that the historical-critical method can effectively relegate the Bible to the past. Without gainsaying a bit of what I just argued regarding the basis in history of the Christian faith, it is crucial to see that the reflections of the authors of Genesis, Exodus, 1 Samuel, Ecclesiastes, and the Letter to the Romans do not have to do exclusively with their own times and

2. N.T. Wright, *The New Testament and the People of God* (Minneapolis: Fortress, 1992), 121–143; *Scripture and the Authority of God: How to Read the Bible Today* (San Francisco: HarperOne, 2013), 121–127.

circumstances. Rather, they are conveying something of universal and transtemporal value, indeed, a revelation of God that speaks as powerfully to a contemporary audience as it did to the original recipients of the text—perhaps even more so. A Bible that belongs only to the past will be of interest to historians of religion or literary specialists, but it will provide little foundation for preaching or pastoral work.

A final problem—massively on display in the years that I was going through school—is that historical critics of the strict observance almost invariably see the theological tradition as a distorting overlay rather than as a clarifying lens. James Kugel's book *The Bible As It Was* illustrates this problem with particular clarity.[3] A great writer and a gifted exegete, Kugel dissects every major text of the Bible using the tools of historical criticism and discovers that they typically have to do with relatively mundane events in the ancient Near East: tribal conflicts, ethnic disputes, the founding of tiny towns, etc. His rational approach results in an almost total demythologization of the biblical books. Running on a completely parallel track to this historicizing interpretation is the ancient and elaborate theological reading of the Bible as the story of God's dramatic involvement in the history of Israel. Kugel more or less suggests that one can practice the high, spiritualized exegesis of the Bible, but that this has nothing finally to do with what the human authors of these books were actually talking about. On his reading, the classical theology of the Christian Church is a fanciful overlay with little real connection to what amount to mildly interesting ancient texts. Thus, many of the practitioners of the historical-critical method wanted to scrape away the speculations of Origen, Augustine, Aquinas, Newman, and Rahner in order to get at what the Bible "really means," which, as we saw, typically amounts to what was in the minds of the human authors of the texts. However, this method is conditioned

3. James L. Kugel, *The Bible As It Was* (Cambridge, MA: The Belknap Press of Harvard University Press, 1997).

by a sort of Protestantizing, *sola scriptura* set of assumptions. Far more realistic and illuminating is the Newmanesque approach, which assumes that theology represents a development and clarification of themes and ideas present in the scriptural texts.[4] Thus, for example, Augustine's highly refined Trinitarian theology was certainly not in the minds of any of the New Testament authors, but it nevertheless serves to render explicit many motifs implicitly present in the Gospels and epistles.

The commentary you are about to read was written in light of these concerns. It is not a work of historical criticism, but it deeply respects the achievements of that method and in many cases draws upon its findings, even as it attempts to push beyond them. Perhaps the most accurate term for its nature and purpose is "theological interpretation." Though it fully acknowledges that the human writers of the biblical books were operating within their own historical and cultural frameworks and were pursuing their own particular theological agendas, it assumes throughout that the prime author of the Scriptures is the Holy Spirit, working noncompetitively through instrumental causes and with his own "agenda" and purpose. Consequently, it takes for granted a deep coherence between the various biblical texts. It recognizes patterns, themes, trajectories, rhymes, and rhythms that obtain throughout the entirety of the Bible, and therefore it does not hesitate to read the parts in light of the whole, and each of the parts in relation to one another. Furthermore, it respects the spiritual and theological tradition, from the ancient world until the present day, as the organic development of motifs and patterns implicit in the Scriptures, and hence it is eager to use that heritage in the project of interpretation. With Joseph Ratzinger, it assumes a mutually enhancing relationship between doctrine and exegesis. Finally, it endeavors to read the Old Testament consistently in light of Christ, who is the new Adam, the new Moses, the definitive son of David,

---

4. John Henry Newman, *An Essay on the Development of Christian Doctrine* (Park Ridge, IL: Word on Fire Classics, 2017), 27–44.

the yes to all the promises made of Israel, as St. Paul puts it (2 Cor. 1:20). It stands unapologetically in the Augustinian tradition that recognizes that "the New Testament lies hidden in the Old and the Old Testament is unveiled in the New."[5]

What you are about to read is the first of two volumes. The project is a theological reading of the entire Old Testament, this particular book covering the Pentateuch, the historical writings, and the biblical novellas. The second volume will treat of the prophets and the poetic writings of the first testament. The only two of the historical books that I do not consider are 1 and 2 Chronicles, and this is because they overlap narratively and theologically so thoroughly with 1 and 2 Samuel.

The Second Vatican Council called for a revival of biblical studies and a deepening of a biblical sensibility among the Catholic faithful. For a variety of reasons—not least the one-sided dominance of the historical-critical approach—this renaissance, in my judgment, has not happened. My hope is that this commentary can contribute, however modestly, to making that dream of the Council Fathers a reality.

5. See Augustine, *Quaestiones in Heptateuchum* 2.73; PL 34:623.

Genesis

CREATION NARRATIVE

It is, of course, with trepidation that one approaches these opening verses of the Bible, for they constitute one of the most famous and commented upon texts in the literature of the world. I would make this first general remark: these passages describing the creation of the cosmos are not intended to be either scientifically or philosophically precise. Their genre is theological poetry. That is to say, they are indeed making claims that have both scientific and philosophical implications, but their form and purpose are neither scientific nor philosophical.

Therefore, simply comparing this account to those offered by astrophysicists and cosmologists concerning the origins of the visible universe is to commit a category error. Similarly, to see in this story an original cosmic dualism of spirit and matter, along the lines of Aristotle's or Plato's philosophical cosmology, is also to miss the point. The purpose of this text is, first, theological and spiritual.

"In the beginning when God created the heavens and the earth" (Gen. 1:1). God creates everything, for "heavens and earth" is a kind of biblical code for the totality of the universe, both that which we can see and that which is less immediately available to us—in the language of the Nicene Creed, what is "visible and invisible."[1] And the creative activity of God obtains from the

---

1. "Nicene-Constantinopolitan Creed," in Heinrich Denzinger et al., *Compendium of Creeds, Definitions, and Declarations on Matters of Faith and Morals*, 43rd ed. (San Francisco: Ignatius, 2012), no. 150.

beginning—which is to say that no aspect of time is outside of his control or not under his aegis. As St. Augustine said, it is incorrect to think of time moving along and then God intervening to create at a certain moment.[2] On the contrary, time itself is a creature.

From this elemental claim, much of the spiritual dynamism of the Bible flows. To be in right relation to God is to acknowledge one's total dependence upon him; to be in sin is to seek to stand somewhere apart from him, to find some place where or some time when he is not. God's press is from the beginning, and he embraces the heavens and the earth. He cannot be avoided.

From the very fact that God is Creator, we learn a great deal about his nature. Since he brings the whole of finitude into being— the heavens and the earth—God is not himself ingredient in the universe. Unlike the accounts we find in both ancient mythology and philosophy, the supreme reality is not a prime instance alongside other basically similar beings. Think here of the Greek and Roman divinities, which are super-humans, massively impressive beings, quantitatively but not really qualitatively different from humans here below. This qualitative otherness, signaled by the fact that God creates, has led the theological tradition to refer to God in strange and distinctive ways. For example, St. Anselm famously describes God as "that than which nothing greater can be thought."[3] A moment's reflection reveals that this reality cannot be a supreme being at the top of the chain of beings, for such a being plus the rest of finite reality would be greater than that being alone. Though it is a high paradox, it is correct to say that God plus the world he makes is not greater than God alone.[4] After creation, there are indeed more beings, but not more perfection of being. Thomas Aquinas expressed this conviction in his account of God as *ipsum esse* (to-be itself) rather than *ens summum* (highest

2. Augustine, *Confessions* 11.11–11.13.

3. Anselm, *Proslogion* 2–5, in *Anselm: Monologion and Proslogion*, trans. Thomas Williams (Indianapolis, IN: Hackett, 1996), 99–102.

4. Robert Sokolowski, *The God of Faith and Reason: Foundations of Christian Theology* (Washington, DC: The Catholic University of America Press, 1995), 42.

being).[5] A key implication of this theology is that God and the world are not ontological rivals, competing, as it were, for space on the same metaphysical ground. Giving glory to God, therefore, is not tantamount to denying glory to creatures—just the contrary. I don't know if there is a theological principle in the Bible more important than this thesis of the noncompetitiveness of God vis-à-vis his creation—and we will trace it throughout this study.

Responsible for the to-be of his creatures, the Creator God is properly described as the uncaused cause, but in the most basic sense of this term—that is to say, God not only moves and affects finite things; he grounds them in their being. Existence as such is his proper effect. But this entails that, in the language of the scholastic theologians, God's very nature is to be.[6] If he received his act of existing from a source extraneous to himself, he would, quite obviously, not be the Creator, but rather a creature among others. Therefore, in God, essence (what he is) and existence (that he is) coincide. To be a creature is to be a type of being, or being according to some mode; but to be God is to be in an unrestricted way. "To be God is to be to-be," as David Burrell put it.[7]

And from this state of affairs, it follows that the Creator must be in possession of any and all perfection of being since his manner of existence is unrestricted or unconditioned. Thus, God must be all-powerful, all-knowing, all-benevolent, all-beautiful, etc. We will see these attributes assumed throughout the narrative sections of the Bible and sung in many of the poetic sections.

We hear that when he creates the heavens and the earth, "the earth was a formless void and darkness covered the face of the deep" (Gen. 1:2). If we are examining this from a purely philosophical perspective, we would have to accuse the author of committing an elementary error, for there is a strict contradiction between

5. Thomas Aquinas, *Summa contra Gentiles* 3.19; *Summa theologiae* 1.4.2, 1.11.4.

6. Thomas Aquinas, *Summa theologiae* 1.2.3, 1.3.4.

7. David B. Burrell, *Aquinas: God and Action* (Notre Dame, IN: University of Notre Dame Press, 1979), 26.

"creating the earth" and the earth being already in existence. What matters here is the phrase "formless void and darkness," the English rendering of the famous Hebrew phrase *tohu wabohu*. It is not advisable to think of this in metaphysical terms, as though it signals prime matter or the elemental stuff from which God creates. Rather, I would follow Karl Barth in seeing it as the "nonbeing," the chaos that stands opposed to God's creative intentions.[8] Once we understand this, we can see this "watery abyss" resurfacing throughout the biblical narrative—in the waters of the Red Sea, in the flood of Noah, even in the stormy waters on which Jesus walks.

God has lordship over this opposition and remains permanently capable of bringing order and harmony out of it. The agency by which he effects this creation—both in the beginning and throughout salvation history—is the *ruach* (breath or wind) described as sweeping, or in some translations, "brooding" over the *tohu wabohu*. This is none other than the Holy Spirit, which calls forth, inspires, and gives rise to life, as Gerard Manley Hopkins saw: "Because the Holy Ghost over the bent world broods with warm breast and with ah! bright wings."[9] Once more, as in an overture to an opera, one of the principal themes of the entire biblical drama is anticipated here: the *tohu wabohu* will not win, for the Spirit is brooding over it and bringing order out of the chaos. We will follow this motif in story after story in the Bible, until Jesus finally breathes the same Holy Spirit onto his Apostles, sending them out to bring order from the chaos of sin.

"Then God said, 'Let there be light'; and there was light" (Gen. 1:3). In practically all of the mythologies of the ancient world, creation comes through some primordial act of violence: one god conquering another; one army of divinities overwhelming another. And in the early philosophical accounts, the prime mover

8. Karl Barth, "God and Nothingness," in *Church Dogmatics*, ed. G.W. Bromiley and T.F. Torrance, vol. 3.3, *The Doctrine of Creation, Sections 50–51* (London: T&T Clark, 2010), 1–78.

9. Gerard Manley Hopkins, "God's Grandeur," in *Ignatian Collection*, ed. Holly Ordway and Daniel Seseske (Park Ridge, IL: Word on Fire Classics, 2020), 179.

or creator god imposes himself on recalcitrant matter. In short, both types of myths of origin present a conflictual or at least interventionary explanation of order.

But on the biblical reading, God creates not through violence or intervention but through a nonviolent act of speech. God thinks, wills, and speaks the world into existence. Therefore, it seems as though nonviolence is metaphysically basic. Moreover, since God speaks the world in its entirety into existence, his knowledge of things is not passive and derivative, but rather active and creative. Things don't exist and subsequently God knows them; rather, God knows them and therefore they exist. Another crucial implication of this teaching is that all of creation, in every detail, is marked by intelligibility. Nothing in the universe is dumbly there; rather, everything is marked, at least to some degree, by harmony, order, reasonability. And this theological idea was indeed one of the necessary conditions for the emergence of the modern physical sciences. Unless a scientist has the mystical conviction that the world is intelligible, she will not go out to meet it with confidence. Further, it would be impossible to prove on scientific grounds that this is the case, since the very scientific method depends upon the assumption of it. In the language of Joseph Ratzinger, objective intelligibility is grounded in a more primordial subjective Intelligence.[10]

In the Genesis account, all created things come forth from the Creator in a kind of stately procession, one major aspect of creation following another and according to a definite temporal rhythm: "And there was evening and there was morning, the first day" (Gen. 1:5). We are meant to sense here a sort of liturgical rite, a procession of ministers. As is customary, the final character in a liturgical procession is the one who will lead the praise, and so we find human beings taking the final place in the procession of created things, for their role will be to lead all of creation in a chorus of praise to their Maker. Correlative to this point is the

10. Joseph Ratzinger, *Introduction to Christianity*, 2nd ed., trans. J.R. Foster (San Francisco: Ignatius, 2004), 151–158.

subtle dethroning of false claimants to divinity that is implicit in this great poem. For practically everything mentioned in the creation account—the earth itself, mountains, animals, the sun and stars, etc.—was at some time in the ancient world worshipped as a divinity. By insisting that these are all creatures, the biblical author is holding off any form of idolatry: these are not to be worshiped; rather, they are to be worshipers in a great chorus of praise. St. Augustine commented that the very essence of sin is turning from the Creator to creatures, by which he means the rendering of some finite, conditioned thing as unconditioned.[11] From its first lines, the Bible is trying to hold off this tendency. In many ways, the entire scriptural story centers around this theme of right versus errant worship.

How wonderful that God finds everything he has created good, and the ensemble of creatures very good. Any form of matter/ spirit dualism is thereby being held at bay. Though Gnostics and other dualists are compelled to see the Creator God of Genesis as a lesser or fallen divinity, the biblical author could not be clearer that the one who makes even the lowly things that creep and crawl upon the earth is the true God. This furthermore places the entire history of salvation within a properly cosmic context. The whole of creation is meant to praise God, and the whole of creation is involved in the falling away from right praise, and hence the whole of creation is the object of God's salvific action. The new heavens and new earth, dreamed of by the author of the Second Letter of Peter (2 Pet. 3:13), are the culmination of the process that commences with the creation of the material realm.

On the seventh day, after the work of creation, God rested. This hasn't a thing to do, obviously, with divine fatigue on the part of the omnipotent Creator. Rather, it expresses God's savoring of what he has made. Aquinas says that the two basic moves of the will are to seek the absent good and to rest in the possessed

---

11. Augustine, *Confessions* 1.20.

good.[12] The sabbath day is an example of the second function of the will and hence serves as an exemplar to human beings. They will indeed seek any number of absent goods, but the entire purpose of their existence is to taste and to savor the good, to rest in what they have. The sabbath is, accordingly, not a day of work but a day of play, in accord with the Aristotelian sense that the highest values are those that are sought for their own sake.[13] This is why it is entirely appropriate that the liturgy is a sabbath day activity, for liturgy is the highest form of play[14]: "So God blessed the seventh day and hallowed it, because on it God rested from all the work that he had done in creation" (Gen. 2:3).

ADAM AND EVE

There is an interesting feature in the description of the garden in which God places the first human beings: a river flows out from Eden and then divides into four branches, including the Tigris and the Euphrates. What should draw our attention is the fact that Eden must be an elevated place, a kind of mountain, if the rivers flow out from it. This is the first mention of the great biblical symbol of the mountain, a place of encounter between God and human beings. Mt. Ararat, Mt. Sinai, Mt. Tabor, Mt. Calvary, and most especially, Mt. Zion, the place of the temple, are all locales where divinity, as it were, comes down, and humanity goes up. The presence of the mountain within Eden is an anticipation of the temple mount, which, precisely as the place of right praise, was meant to hearken back to the time before the fall. God gives to Adam the command to "till" the soil of Eden (Gen. 2:15), and the verb used here is the same one later used to describe the care of the temple by the Jerusalem priests.[15]

---

12. Aquinas, *Summa theologiae* 1-2.3.4.

13. Aristotle, *Nichomachean Ethics* 1094a.

14. Romano Guardini, *The Spirit of the Liturgy*, trans. Ada Lane (New York: Crossroad, 1998), 41–44.

15. John Bergsma and Brant Pitre, *A Catholic Introduction to the Bible*, vol. 1, *The Old Testament* (San Francisco: Ignatius, 2018), 102–103.

So far, we have been describing the "priestly" function of Adam, but we might also speak of his "kingly" task. According to some of the earliest biblical commentators, Adam was given the responsibility to expand the borders of Eden, bringing the good order that comes from right praise to the wider world.

What follows the description of Eden is what I would characterize as the great permission. So much stress has been placed over the centuries on the single prohibition that God gives to Adam that we practically forget the extraordinarily rangy permission that the Lord gives to our first parent: "You may freely eat of every tree of the garden" (Gen. 2:16). The Church Fathers took the luxuriant foliage of the garden and its fruit as representative of all forms of human flourishing: the arts, the sciences, politics, friendship, etc. God, who is in possession of all the perfection of being, cannot possibly benefit from creation, and hence he has no interest, in the manner of the Greek and Roman gods, in keeping humanity at bay or limiting its joy. Rather, as St. Irenaeus has it, "the glory of God is a human being fully alive."[16] God wants us to have life and life to the full, and this extravagant divine desire is expressed in the capaciousness of God's permission.

But then, we do indeed hear of the single prohibition: "But of the tree of the knowledge of good and evil you shall not eat, for in the day that you eat of it you shall die" (Gen. 2:17). These are among the most studied words in the literature of the world, and they have given rise to a variety of interpretations. I'd like to explore only two of them. The first, associated with Irenaeus and Hegel and coming to expression in the thought of Paul Tillich in the twentieth century, places a stress on the transition from a sort of dreaming innocence to something like mature self-possession.[17] On this reading, our first parents were more like adolescents than

16. Irenaeus, *Against Heresies* 4.20.7, in *Catechism of the Catholic Church* 294.

17. Paul Tillich, *Systematic Theology*, vol. 1 (Chicago: University of Chicago Press, 1973), 259–260. See also Irenaeus, *Against Heresies* 3.22.4, 3.23.5; Georg Wilhelm Friedrich Hegel, *Lectures on the Philosophy of Religion*, trans. and ed. E.B. Speirs (London: Kegan Paul, Trench, Trübner & Co., 1895), 276–278.

fully constituted adults, living in a state of naïve and inexperienced innocence. Utterly under the heteronomous tutelage of God, they had not yet come to mature freedom and responsibility. At the prompting of the serpent, they do indeed fall away from God, but at least they fall toward something resembling freedom and self-possession. Like every teenager ever after, they tumble awkwardly into adulthood, recklessly choosing sheer autonomy over heteronomy. The answer—and it emerges in the long history of salvation—is theonomy, whereby they find their own freedom and integrity precisely in relation to the God who is not a rival to them. At the terminus of this interpretive trajectory, we find Jesus' words to his Apostles: "I do not call you servants any longer . . . I have called you friends" (John 15:15).

A second reading, articulated beautifully by St. John Paul II in his "theology of the body" talks on the book of Genesis, appreciates the eating of the fruit of the tree of good and evil as entirely wicked.[18] Here, the knowledge of good and evil is not so much a sign of intellectual and moral maturity, but rather a prerogative that belongs uniquely to God.[19] The being of God alone is the determining criterion in regard to moral rectitude and error. It is not a matter of cultural convention or popular consensus and most certainly not the result of an arbitrary and aggressive free choice. Therefore, the seizure of the fruit of that very particular tree evokes the tragic arrogating to oneself of what belongs uniquely to God, and hence it adumbrates the collapse of the moral project.

Both interpretations can accommodate the serpent's statement to Eve: "You will not die; for God knows that when you eat of it your eyes will be opened, and you will be like God, knowing good and evil" (Gen. 3:4–5). On the first reading, the serpent is telling a half-truth, since coming to greater maturity will indeed

18. John Paul II, "General Audience: The Boundary between Original Innocence and Redemption," September 26, 1979, vatican.va; see also Carl Anderson and Jose Granados, *Called to Love: Approaching John Paul II's Theology of the Body* (New York: Doubleday, 2009), 104–105.

19. See *Catechism of the Catholic Church* 396–398.

make the dreaming innocents more like God, but he is concealing from them the dark side of their choice of autonomy. On the second interpretation, he is simply deceiving them, for they will not in fact be like God; they will be pathetic simulacra of God, in fact losing their likeness unto the Creator. In either case, they have lost both their priestly and kingly competence. No longer connected to God, they tend to fall apart within (disintegrating) and to foster disintegration around them. The harmony within them has become a cacophony. And having succumbed to the wiles of the serpent, they lose their capacity to go on the march, extending the borders of Eden outward. We will interpret much of the Old Testament as God's patient attempt to restore the priestly and kingly identities of human beings.

On both readings, they move from innocence to guilt, and hence the knowledge of their nakedness as something shameful naturally follows. That the original sin is closely allied to sexual choice should not be surprising, since this most powerful of urges, in a way, forces the existential question. Under the pressure of that overwhelming desire, a decision at the fundamental level has to be taken. Having made fig leaves to cover their nakedness, they hide themselves in the underbrush of Eden. This provides a balance to their initial errant move of trying to grasp at divinity. When that attempt fails, they go to the other extreme and attempt to hide from God. But God, of course, finds them immediately. The one who is the sheer act of to-be itself cannot be either grasped or avoided, for he is, simultaneously, *superior summo meo et interior intimo meo*, as St. Augustine put it.[20] That is to say, he is greater than any finite being could ever understand or control, and he is closer to a creature than the creature is to itself. A supreme existent could be, in principle, understood according to conventional categories and hidden from somewhere on the metaphysical grid

20. Augustine, *Confessions* 3.6.11 (PL 32:688). For an English translation, see Augustine, *Confessions*, trans. F.J. Sheed, ed. Michael P. Foley (Park Ridge, IL: Word on Fire Classics, 2017), 50: "Yet all the time you were more inward than the most inward place of my heart and loftier than the highest."

that he has in common with other finite things. But with regard to the unconditioned reality, neither strategy is possible. This is why both the grasping at the fruit of the forbidden tree *and* the attempt to hide are pointless. We will see this theme reiterated over and again in the narratives, in the prophets, and in the poems.

The curse that God pronounces over the serpent and over Adam and Eve should not be read as an instance of divine pique. The God of the Bible is not like the easily offended gods of the classical world, who stand in a relationship of psychological and even physical need vis-à-vis human beings. God's punishments are not expressions of personal vengeance; they are best read as the consequences that follow naturally from sin. Since all things and all people are connected to one another through their common participation in God, a spiritual alienation from the Creator will result in a disintegration of creation, humans falling into disharmony with one another and with the realm of nature. We can sense the latter in God's words to the serpent: "I will put enmity between you and the woman, and between your offspring and hers; he will strike your head, and you will strike his heel" (Gen. 3:15), as well as in God's observation to Adam: "Cursed is the ground because of you; in toil you shall eat of it all the days of your life; thorns and thistles it shall bring forth for you. . . . By the sweat of your face you shall eat bread until you return to the ground, for out of it you were taken" (Gen. 3:17–19). The compromising of the man-woman rapport can be sensed in the childish blame game that breaks out in the presence of the divine judge: "The man said, 'The woman whom you gave to be with me, she gave me fruit from the tree, and I ate" (Gen. 3:12). In God, all things hold together; apart from God, they disintegrate. When Adam and Eve walked in easy fellowship with the Lord in the Garden, they were in the attitude of right praise, for they were moving with the Lord, listening to his voice. Expelled from Eden, they fall out of the stance of orthodoxy (*ortho doxa*, "right praise") and hence enter, spiritually speaking, into a desert.

The Council of Trent sees the effects of original sin as the loss of "holiness" and "justice."[21] Holiness, which is related to wholeness or integrity, is compromised through incorrect worship. When something other than the Creator is placed at the center of one's concerns, the elements that make up one's personality split apart from one another. Justice has to do with right ordering, rendering to each his due. What is peculiarly due to God is praise. When this is undermined, fundamental justice is lost, and from that loss follows the rupturing of right relationship with nature and with one's fellows.

THE EFFECTS OF THE FALL

So far, we have covered, more or less, the key themes in the first three chapters of Genesis. Chapters 4 through 11 lay out, in a beautifully encapsulated manner, the consequences of the original sin, the basic permutations and combinations of human dysfunction. Chapter 4 tells the story of Cain and Abel, the sons of Adam and Eve, and we see in this narrative so much of the psychology and patterns of behavior that mark those in rebellion against God: rivalry, jealousy, resentment, anger at God, and ultimately murderous violence. Abel is a keeper of sheep, and he brings as a burnt offering to God the first fruits of his flock; Cain is a tiller of the soil, and he brings "an offering of the fruit of the ground" before the Lord (Gen. 4:3). God, we are told, preferred Abel's sacrifice to Cain's, but we are not told why. Various scholars and commentators over the centuries have speculated that perhaps Abel's bringing the first fruits made a difference or perhaps that Abel's offering is an anticipation of the animal sacrifices in the Jerusalem temple, which were more highly valued than grain offerings, but the bottom line is that we just don't know why God preferred one over the other, and in some ways, that is the point. Frequently, in the biblical stories, God acts in anomalous

21. Council of Trent, *Decree Concerning Original Sin*, in *Compendium of Creeds*, ed. Denzinger et al., no. 1511. See also *Catechism of the Catholic Church* 375–376, 399–400.

and unpredictable ways, showing preference or favor in a manner that can seem arbitrary. But so it must, to some degree, always seem to finite minds. It would be arrogant in the extreme to presume that we could comprehend the divine purpose in every circumstance, and therefore the proper attitude is one of hope and receptivity. In point of fact, God addresses Cain when he sees his creature crestfallen and reminds him that, if he does well, he will be accepted. In other words, the choice that God makes is not, finally, of one over the other, but as we shall see throughout the biblical narrative, of one for the sake of the other. Cain's original sin, which gives rise to his murderous violence, is a failure to appreciate this dynamic.

What follows, of course, is the brutal and cold-blooded killing of his brother Abel. Resentment and jealousy lead to murder, and this pattern will repeat itself up and down the ages. But the God who cannot be hidden from asks, "Where is your brother Abel?" Lying, Cain claims he doesn't know, and then famously adds, "Am I my brother's keeper?" (Gen. 4:9). The implied answer is yes, since he is both a blood brother to Abel and, as a fellow creature of God, an ontological sibling as well. As if to hammer home the point, Cain is made, as a punishment, to wander the earth—which is to say, disconnected from family, community, common worship. Then, in a supreme irony, Cain, the wanderer and fratricide, becomes the founder of the first city.

To be sure, there is, throughout the Bible and especially in the book of Genesis, a kind of polemic against urban life, and we will return to this theme later, but for the moment, it is fascinating to remark the extraordinary perceptiveness of the author of Genesis in seeing that what can look like a just and flourishing society is so often predicated upon a primordial act of violence or some deeply dysfunctional attitude. In the twentieth century, René Girard speculated that all fallen forms of human organization are grounded in the scapegoating mechanism[22]—which is to say, the exclusion and victimization of some group characterized as other. Long before Girard, St. Augustine remarked the parallel between the founding of Rome in an act of fratricide (Romulus killing his twin Remus) and the biblical assertion that a brother-killer is the founder of all cities.[23]

The key difference, which Augustine took to be significant, is that in the case of Rome, the original fratricide is seen as positive, whereas in the case of the biblical city, it is decidedly negative. Very much in line with this instinct, the Gospel of Matthew presents the devil as showing Jesus all of the kingdoms of the world in a single glance and declaring that he, the devil, would give them as a gift if Jesus but bowed down in worship before him. Jesus refuses, of course, but for our purposes at the moment, it is worth noting that the devil can offer every city in the world only in the measure that they all belong to him (Matt. 4:8–10). We recall that, in the New Testament, the two privileged names for the dark power are *ho diabolos* and *ho Satanas*—which is to say, the scatterer and the accuser. Both impulses are present in the founder of cities. Both will be undone by the founder of the kingdom of God.

What commenced with the murder of Abel in chapter 4 has become, by chapter 6, a generalized moral and spiritual collapse. The Bible is keenly sensitive to the interdependence of all things, especially as this manifests itself among human beings. Sin tends to spread like a disease, passing from one to another and from generation to generation. So we hear in Genesis 6:11: "Now the earth was corrupt in God's sight, and the earth was filled with violence." The original creation, which God found very good, has now devolved into chaos, and just as nonviolence is the principal quality of God's creative act, so violence has become *the* mark of the sinful human tribe.

22. See René Girard, *The Scapegoat*, trans. Yvonne Freccero (Baltimore, MD: Johns Hopkins University Press, 1986); René Girard, *Things Hidden Since the Foundation of the World*, trans. Stephen Bann and Michael Metteer (Stanford, CA: Stanford University Press, 1987).

23. Augustine, *The City of God* 15.5.

What follows, however, is one of the most important tropes in the Scriptures—namely, the singling out of a particular righteous man and his family in order to effect, in time, the re-creation of the fallen race. Nowhere is this clearer than in the choice of Abraham, but the theme is adumbrated here. God hates sin, but he is never satisfied simply with allowing the effects of sin to run their course. Rather, he concocts a sort of rescue operation, precisely through Noah and his family. The ark that the Lord commands Noah to build is designed to house a microcosm of God's good creation, even as the fallen world is swallowed up by the return of the watery chaos, the flood that hearkens back to the *tohu wabohu*. Taking representatives of all of the animals aboard links us to the creation narrative, and this signals, once again, that the salvation of human beings is inextricably linked to the salvation of the entire cosmos.

Eden, as we saw, is a kind of mountain and hence an evocation of Mt. Zion; in a similar way, the ark of Noah is an anticipation of the temple, the place where all of creation, under the headship of human beings, offers praise to God. The careful description of the building of the ark and the delineation of its proportions point forward to similar accounts of the construction of the tabernacle in the desert during the Exodus and of the Jerusalem temple. It is absolutely no accident that the great cathedrals of the Christian era were constructed with Noah's ark in mind, for they too were meant to be sanctuaries for a remnant of creation in the midst of the *tohu wabohu* of the sinful world. As was the case with the Jerusalem temple, the Gothic cathedrals were covered, inside and out, with symbols of the created order: stars, moon, sun, animals, plants, etc. In his *City of God*, St. Augustine reads the history of salvation, from biblical times through the era of the Church, as a tale of Noah's ark—the little ship, filled with a holy remnant, bouncing on the waves of the stormy sea.[24]

---

24. Augustine, *The City of God* 15.26.

After one hundred and fifty days, God causes the storm to subside, and the ark comes to rest on Mt. Ararat. Once he knows that the waters have sufficiently receded, Noah opens the doors of the ship and lets the life out. Though the temple is of central significance as the place of right praise, Israel is not meant to stay permanently in the temple; rather, they are invited to go out into the world. The Ark has been a place of safety, but the life that was preserved there was not meant to stay confined on a boat, but rather to reinvigorate the world. This represents a rhythm of withdrawal and advance that obtains throughout the history of Israel and of the Church. At times, Israel and the Church have to hunker down, carefully cultivating a form of life that is threatened. But hunkering down is not the default position—on the contrary. Adam was meant to go forth from the garden to Edenize the rest of creation; so Noah is meant to exit the ark, becoming a kind of new Adam. The command that the Lord gives to the new Adam, "Be fruitful and multiply, and fill the earth" (Gen. 9:1), is one that will be repeated whenever God makes a covenant with his people throughout salvation history. Fertility, fecundity, life to the full will always be the marks of God's favor and presence.

It is of supreme importance that the first move that Noah makes upon exiting the ship is to offer sacrifice to the Lord: "Then Noah built an altar to the LORD, and took of every clean animal and of every clean bird, and offered burnt offerings on the altar" (Gen. 8:20). Once again, orthodoxy, right praise, is the key to everything else. The new order that Noah hopes to establish on the purified earth must be grounded in the worship of God, or it will founder.

The downward trajectory of God's people toward idolatry and dissolution is foreshadowed in the curious story with which the Noah narrative ends—namely, that of the drunkenness of Noah. The great patriarch is identified as the first vintner, and we hear that he drank of the fruit of the vine and became drunk. Lying naked and senseless in his tent, he represents the compromising of the mind and will that conduce inevitably toward sin. Noah's son Ham comes into the tent and sees his father in this disgraceful state, and the patriarch's other sons cover up their father. The shameful nudity of Noah is meant, of course, to call to mind the shame that Adam and Eve experienced regarding their own nakedness after their rebellion. On one of the Sistine Chapel ceiling frescoes, Michelangelo beautifully expresses this moral and spiritual declension, depicting the drunk and naked Noah in a pose pathetically reminiscent of the noble posture of Adam at the moment of creation. The message is clear: even after the flood, trouble will come.

In chapter 11, we see another form that this trouble typically takes. We are told that all of the human race spoke one language and that a particular group, having migrated from the east, resolved to "build [themselves] a city, and a tower with its top in the heavens," so that they could "make a name" for themselves (Gen. 11:4). Even at this early stage of the narrative, the attentive biblical reader should be on guard, for a particularly vivid red flag is being waved: through their own heroic effort, human beings will attempt to scale the heavens, moving into the space of God, taking to themselves divine prerogatives. God wants humans to be fully alive, but the divine life cannot, even in principle, be seized; it can only be received as a gift. Therefore, Promethean projects, designed to grasp at divinity and inflate the ego, are spiritually poisonous. God's coming down and confusing the language of the builders of the tower should not be construed as an arbitrary punishment or an act of cruelty; rather, it should be seen as a salutary gesture—God undermining a dysfunctional, imperialistic type of unity. The right sort of unity is on display, much later in the story of salvation, when, on the morning of Pentecost, those from all over the Roman world hear the one message of Jesus in their own various languages (Acts 2:6).

After the glorious opening of Genesis, we have followed an almost completely negative path, the original sin propagating itself until the entire world became corrupt, and then, even after a thorough cleansing and restart, the human race has fallen, once again, into pride and dissolution. A basic biblical pessimism in regard to the human project is unmistakably on display and will continue to be insisted upon throughout the Scriptures. There is no sense of perfectibility in the Bible, no conviction that, given enough political, economic, or cultural reform, or given the influence of a sufficient number of heroic figures, things will straighten out. If the fundamental problem is in the mind and will of human beings, no amount of thinking or willing will address it. A power must come from outside. Evolution from within is not the solution, but rather invasion from without. No merely human voice or collectivity of human voices will articulate the path forward; only a Voice transcendent to the human project will direct the rescue operation.

ABRAHAM

And this is precisely what we find as chapter 12 of Genesis commences. From chapters 12 through 25, we find a narrative account of four generations of a family, which functions as the kernel, the seed, of a great people, formed according to the mind and heart of God. The mission of that people, on the scriptural reading, is to become, eventually, a beacon to the rest of sinful humanity, the vehicle by which the word of the true God goes out to all the nations. The story commences with Abram from Ur of the Chaldeans.

The first word from the Lord to Abram is that he has to move: "Go from your country and your kindred and your father's house to the land that I will show you" (Gen. 12:1). The tendency of the sinful ego is to rest in itself, a condition Paul Tillich calls "*in sich ruhenden Endlichkeit*" (self-complacent finitude).[25] The self-obsessed ego wants the path of least resistance; it wants to rest in its own

25. Paul Tillich, *Die religiöse Deutung der Gegenwart; Schriften zur Zeitkritik* (Stuttgart: Evangelisches Verlagswerk, 1968).

world. The voice of God will thus sound to the sinner as a voice from without, summoning him to adventure. It is no accident that most hero's stories—from Jason and the Argonauts to Bilbo and Frodo—commence with a call to leave the comforts of home and to venture into the unknown. So Abram must leave everything he knows and go to a country he knows nothing about. That he listens to this voice is the key to everything good that happens to his people throughout salvation history. The entire narrative of the people Israel turns on this question: Do they listen or not? God assures Abram that, if he follows the voice, the Lord will make of him a great nation: "I will bless you, and make your name great, so that you will be a blessing. I will bless those who bless you, and the one who curses you I will curse; and in you all the families of the earth shall be blessed" (Gen. 12:2–3). This last observation is what links the remainder of the story of Israel with the opening eleven chapters of Genesis, for Abram is indeed singled out, and his people will indeed be called the specially chosen people, but he is singled out and they are chosen not for themselves but for the world. The first eleven chapters did not deal with Israel, but rather with humanity as a whole, and it is *for* humanity as a whole, indeed for the cosmos in its entirety, that Abram is called.

The summons and journey of Abram culminate in the gift of a place. When he and his family come to Canaan, the Lord appears to Abram and says, "To your offspring I will give this land" (Gen. 12:7). Throughout the history of Israel, this particular plot of earth, east of the Mediterranean, west of the Jordan, from Dan in the north to Beer-sheba in the south, would be of crucial importance. Whether they were loving it, longing for it, fighting over it, defending it, planting it with cities, counting its people, mourning its loss, or singing of its beauty, the Promised Land would be a unique obsession of the descendants of Abram. This, of course, is because it was much more than a piece of real estate; it functioned as a symbol of the divine favor, the land flowing with milk and honey, the base of operations for the announcement of God to all the nations, and ultimately, an anticipation of the ultimate homeland of heaven.

Though convinced of the Lord's gift of land, Abram worried that he had no physical heir. But God's word came to him: "Look toward heaven and count the stars, if you are able to count them. . . . So shall your descendants be" (Gen. 15:5). More important even than the land would be the family born of Abram's flesh and of his faith. They would be, in time, as numerous as the living things that came forth from the hand of the Creator God, and they would fill not only the Promised Land itself, but rather the whole earth. To seal this extraordinary promise, God led Abram through an elaborate ritual involving the severing in half of a goat and a ram and the offering of a turtledove and a young pigeon. Abram passed between the pieces and then, as night fell, "a smoking fire pot," evocative of the divine presence, passed between them (Gen. 15:17). This was a gesture that in the ancient near east typically accompanied the making of a covenant, implying, "May this same thing happen to me should I break the agreement that we have made."[26] Not so much an exchange of goods and services, in the manner of a contract, a covenant was much more an exchange of hearts, a pledge of mutual loyalty: in the phrase repeated frequently throughout the Bible, "I will take you as my people, and I will be your God."

This covenant was reiterated in even more extravagant language when Abram turned ninety-nine. On the assumption that Abram remains "blameless," God promises that he will raise up from him and for him a people "exceedingly numerous," and because of this fecundity, the patriarch will now be known as Abraham, which carries the sense of "father of many" (Gen. 17:1–2, 5–6). As a sign of the covenant, God asks that every male in the family of Abraham be circumcised, establishing thereby, in their flesh, a connection between the divine promise and the perpetuation

26. Robert Alter, *The Hebrew Bible: A Translation with Commentary*, vol. 1, *The Five Books of Moses* (New York: W.W. Norton, 2019), 49n8.

of their clan. Land, people, promise, circumcision, ritual, moral demand—the essential features of Israelite life—are already in place. Now we might easily be tempted to say that this covenant language reflects simply the extravagant wish-fulfilling fantasy of a minor ancient Middle Eastern tribe, but we are brought up short when we take into account the undeniable fact that Abraham's family—through Judaism, Islam, and Christianity—has indeed spread throughout the world in the most astonishing way.

In time, Sarah, the wife of Abraham, gives birth to their son, Isaac, though both parents, we are told, are in their upper nineties. The theme of unlikely conception, and birth against all natural expectation, is an extremely common one in the Bible, signaling the primacy of grace and the indispensability of trust in divine providence. The boy is called Isaac, from the Hebrew term designating laughter, partly because his mother had laughed at the implausibility of it when the child's birth was predicted and partly because, as Sarah puts it, "God has brought laughter for me" (Gen. 21:6).

Son of his extreme old age, a gift beyond his wildest hope, and the bearer of the sacred promise, Isaac was everything to Abraham—which is why it is surpassingly strange, and of signal theological moment, when God demands that Abraham sacrifice his son as a burnt offering. Because the narrative style of the biblical author is so austere and understated, and because he remains, for the most part, uninterested in exploring what we would call psychological motivations and feelings, it is perhaps easy to miss the sheer awfulness of this story. Surely Kierkegaard was right to state that the only proper response to it is fear and trembling,[27] and surely generations of believers have found their convictions about God shaken by it. Not to sense all of this is proof that one has simply not been paying attention.

27. See Søren Kierkegaard, *Fear and Trembling*, in *Fear and Trembling / Repetition*, ed. and trans. Howard V. Hong and Edna H. Hong (Princeton, NJ: Princeton University Press, 1983), 1–124.

For three days, Abraham journeyed with Isaac to the land of Moriah, where the sacrifice is to take place. One cannot begin to imagine the depth of the patriarch's agony as this trip unfolds: walking side by side with Isaac, conversing with him, watching him as he laughs and plays, heedless of his fate. On the final stage of their itinerary, Abraham walks with his son alone up the mountain, the former carrying the knife and the latter carrying the wood for the offering. When Isaac says to his father, "The fire and the wood are here, but where is the lamb for a burnt offering?" (Gen. 22:7), Abraham's heart must have shattered from grief and guilt. When they get to the place of sacrifice, Abraham binds Isaac to the altar (hence the Hebrew name for this event, the *Akedah* [binding]) and raises his hand to slay the boy. Only at the last moment does an angel of the Lord intervene to stop the killing: "Abraham, Abraham! . . . Do not lay your hand on the boy or do anything to him; for now I know that you fear God, since you have not withheld your son, your only son, from me" (Gen. 22: 11–12). In the wake of this breathtaking event/non-event, Abraham is once again reassured that the Lord will make him father of a great nation, indeed a blessing to all the nations of the world.

Even though the narrative has a "happy" ending, we might be forgiven for posing more than a few questions. What God would ever put a human being through such a dreadful ordeal? What man would have abided by such a morally objectionable command? What sort of religion would place such an offensive tale in its most sacred book? Before one even thinks of providing an interpretation of this story, she should allow those questions to weigh on her, to puzzle and confound her. For something indeed has to break in us, something has to give way, before we can take in what this narrative is conveying. Abraham loves Isaac as much as anything or anyone in this world *can* be loved. Among the finite things of the world, the boy is Abraham's supreme value. He would have sacrificed everything for him: wealth, pleasure, honor, power, status, even his wife and extended family. Yet Isaac, like every other creaturely good, belongs to God, and his value is inferior to God's surpassing value. Therefore, even he must be "sacrificed" to God and God's purposes; even his worth has to be situated in the context of God's greater worth. Isaac belongs to God, not God to Isaac. None of this would be hard to see if we had never fallen; but having fallen, we need to be wrenched out of a sinful stance of hyperattachment to creaturely goods, which is precisely why the language and practice of sacrifice is called for. Walking in rhythm with God and appreciating all things from the standpoint of God was easy in the Garden of Eden, but on the desert ground of the fallen world, there is no proper communion with God without sacrifice. This truth has been enacted already in Noah's ritual sacrifice as well as in Abraham's, but it came to clearest and most awful expression in the *Akedah*, the binding of Isaac.

But that is only part of the story, spiritually speaking. The lower goods of the world have to be sacrificed to God in the measure that they have come to take the place of God. But precisely because God is not the supreme being, not one competitive reality among others, whatever is sacrificed to him does not accrue to him as a sort of benefit, becoming an advantage in a zero-sum game. Rather, it breaks, as it were, against the rock of the divine simplicity and self-sufficiency and comes back to the benefit of the one who made the sacrifice. And this is what is symbolized in the interruptive move of the angel, who gives back to Abraham what he had endeavored to sacrifice. When seen within this properly theological perspective, all objections along forensic or psychological lines simply fall away. God is not cruelly manipulating Abraham or compelling his hapless creature to commit a crime. What we have in this admittedly strange scene is a sort of icon representing certain key dynamics in the spiritual order, which have to be interpreted with spiritual eyes. A relatively superficial fear and trembling gives way once we grasp this, permitting the emergence of a more authentic fear and trembling before the living God, whose glory is that we be fully alive.

As we mentioned, Genesis 12–50 basically tells the story of four generations of the same family: Abraham to Isaac to Jacob to Joseph, with myriad subnarratives and scenes. Of the four principal figures, Isaac, the son of Abraham, is the least developed. From the moment of the *Akedah*, where he appears as a largely passive and youthful figure, until he reaches old age, practically all we hear of Isaac, aside from a few incidental tales, is that he married Rebekah, and the story of his betrothal and marriage centers much more around her than him. One feature of that tale is worth dwelling upon—namely, the manner in which she was discovered. We hear that Abraham had sent a trusted servant to return to Abraham's home country to find a bride for Isaac. The man found his way to the city of Nahor, and while waiting by the well, made a kind of bargain with God: "O Lord, God of my master Abraham, please grant me success today. . . . Let the girl to whom I shall say, 'Please offer your jar that I may drink,' and who shall say, 'Drink, and I will water your camels'—let her be the one whom you have appointed for your servant Isaac" (Gen. 24:12–14). After the beautiful Rebekah presented herself at the well and responded exactly as the servant had envisioned, he knew he had found Isaac's wife. What makes this more than simply a charming story of divine providence is that it sets the tone for a number of similar encounters throughout salvation history: Jacob finds his wife by a well (Gen. 29:1–14), as does Moses (Exod. 2:15–22), as, in a curious manner, does Jesus, who makes a kind of spiritual marriage with the Samaritan woman whom he meets by Jacob's well (John 4:1–42). It is no accident, of course, that marriage, the vehicle by which Israel propagates itself and thus fulfills the promise, is proposed precisely at a spot that desert people would associate with life.

JACOB

The biblical parsimony in regard to Isaac is not duplicated in regard to his son Jacob. With Jacob, we find an entire arc of life, comparable to those of Joseph, Moses, and David, and with a similar psychological perceptiveness and theological richness. We first discover Jacob grasping at the heel of his twin brother as the two exit the womb of their mother, Rebekah. From this infant grappling, we learn that Jacob will be something of a wrestler and that a conflict with his older brother will be the hinge on which his life will turn. Right away, the archetypal difference between the twins is highlighted: "Esau was a skillful hunter, a man of the field, while Jacob was a quiet man, living in tents," and while Isaac loved Esau, Rebekah preferred Jacob (Gen. 25:27–28). This clear differentiation, rife with symbolic overtones, has made the brothers fascinating to psychologists, but it is meant primarily to communicate something about the chosen people. Throughout their history, they will be marked by internecine conflict, brothers, as it were, grappling with one another, culminating in the centuries-long battle between Israel and Judah, the northern and southern tribes. This proved not only politically compromising but, more importantly, spiritually disastrous, for a divided nation would be unable to fulfill its mission as a unifying force for the tribes of the world.

From the story of Cain and Abel, we already know that the book of Genesis tends to favor the younger child over the older, but the theme emerges with particular clarity in the twenty-fifth chapter. Coming in from the field, Esau smells a savory dish that his brother is preparing. Displaying a rather crude grasp of culinary finery, Esau says, "Let me eat some of that red stuff, for I am famished!" Sensing an opportunity, the ambitious and far cleverer brother replies, "First sell me your birthright." Unfazed, the elder twin readily agreed to surrender his most precious spiritual possession for some "red stuff" (Gen. 25:30–32). To be fair, neither brother comes out of this episode looking particularly good: Esau is appallingly immature and superficial, while Jacob is disturbingly avaricious for power and ruthlessly manipulative. Though he will indeed inherit the promise and come to spiritual leadership, Jacob, like his son Joseph after him, will require a lengthy preparation.

The sale of his birthright at a comically low price is but a preparation for the famous scene in which Esau finds himself duped out
of the formal blessing of his father through the machinations of
Jacob and their mother. Covering his smooth skin with animal fur
that bore the scent of the field, Jacob managed to fool his nearly
blind father into thinking that he, Jacob, was Esau and to procure
the sought-after and irrevocable blessing. When the subterfuge
is made clear, Isaac remains powerless to retract his benediction,
and Esau can do nothing but cry out in anguish. Thus Jacob, the
younger son, does indeed come to bear the promise, but we shall
see, in accord with a sort of biblical law of karma, that he must pay
dearly for what he has received. Fearful for Jacob's life, Rebekah
urges him to go to her brother, Laban, and seek refuge.

While on his way, Jacob is graced by one of the most profound and seminal encounters with the sacred in the entire Old
Testament tradition. Near Beer-sheba, Jacob takes a stone as an
improbable pillow and lies down for the night. He dreams of "a
ladder set up on the earth, the top of it reaching to heaven; and
the angels of God were ascending and descending on it." And in
the dream, the Lord spoke to him, saying, "I am the LORD, the
God of Abraham your father and the God of Isaac; the land on
which you lie I will give to you and to your offspring; and your
offspring shall be like the dust of the earth, and you shall spread
abroad to the west and to the east and to the north and to the
south; and all the families of the earth shall be blessed in you and
in your offspring" (Gen. 28:12–14). The "ladder," which Robert
Alter renders as a "ramp" (Gen. 28:17),[28] is probably something
akin to a ziggurat, a stepped incline, and the ascent and descent of
the angels is a signal that this ladder is a conduit, a link between
the realm of contingent reality and the unconditioned realm of
God. As Jacob will recognize after awaking from the dream, this
means that the very place where he slumbered is specially charged

28. Robert Alter, *The Hebrew Bible*, 1:100.

with the presence of God, that it has a sort of sacramental quality. But more broadly, it entails that Israel itself, God's specially chosen people, will function as a place of connection between heaven and earth. From Israel, the longing and prayers of the human race will go up to God, and through Israel, the grace of God shall descend. Mind you, I am insisting that this connectivity has to do with the whole of God's family, and not simply Israel. As God's own speech makes clear, "all the families of the earth shall be blessed" in the family that comes forth from Jacob. We have in this ladder, therefore, a kind of master metaphor for the whole of Israelite life: covenant, prophecy, temple, liturgy, sacrifice—all of it will function as a conduit between God and the world he is endeavoring to save.

From a Christian point of view, it is crucially important to note Jesus' own reference to this scene in the first chapter of the Gospel of John. Addressing Nathaniel, who had been flabbergasted by Jesus' knowledge of him from a distance, the Lord says, "'Do you believe because I told you that I saw you under the fig tree? You will see greater things than these.' And he said to him, 'Very truly, I tell you, you will see heaven opened and the angels of God ascending and descending upon the Son of Man'" (John 1:50–51). In this extraordinary observation, Jesus gathers all of the institutions of Israel under his aegis, implying that he himself is the fulfillment of temple, prophecy, liturgy, etc. He himself is the definitive ladder between heaven and earth, that toward which the whole of Israelite history was looking and tending.

Waking from his dream, Jacob exclaims, "Surely the LORD is in this place—and I did not know it!" He then takes the stone upon which he had rested his head, sets it up as a sacred marker, anoints it with oil, and declares, "This stone, which I have set up for a pillar, shall be God's house" (Gen. 28:16, 22). What the patriarch is anticipating, obviously, is the Jerusalem temple, which will come to be recognized as the place of encounter *par excellence*, the locale that God will uniquely choose as his dwelling place.

After his life-defining meeting with the Lord, Jacob, still following his mother's advice, comes to the land of Laban, his uncle. Sitting down by a well, he meets Laban's beautiful daughter Rachel and, exhibiting almost superhuman strength, he single-handedly removes the stone covering to the well and waters Rachel's flock. This pattern is, of course, familiar to us, since it unfolded in a practically identical way in regard to the finding of Rebekah as a wife for Isaac, and it will be repeated, much later, with respect to Moses' discovery of Zipporah, daughter of Jethro, as his wife. Since the promise made to Abraham, Isaac, and Jacob had to do with progeny, it is no surprise that the finding of wives and the procreation of children is of prime importance to the biblical author.

Laban, we discover, has two daughters, Rachel and Leah, and Jacob is enamored of the former. He makes an agreement with Laban that he will work for his uncle for seven years in exchange for Rachel's hand in marriage, and since he loves her so, the years "seemed to him but a few days" (Gen. 29:20). At the close of the seven years, arrangements are made for the union, but on the night of the wedding, Leah is swapped for Rachel, though Jacob doesn't realize it. Enraged upon discovering the subterfuge, Jacob complains, and Laban offers the rather lame excuse that, in his country, the youngest daughter is never given in marriage before the older and then he extracts from Jacob the promise to work another seven years to obtain Rachel. The trickster has been tricked. The one who gained the blessing through deception is now deprived of his love through deception. Though it is decidedly more a book of grace than of rough justice, something like a law of karma often obtains within the Bible: as Jesus would put it, "the measure you give will be the measure you get" (Matt. 7:2). At the same time, this is never simply a matter of tit for tat, for God presides over the entire scenario in love, achieving his providential design. Though Jacob was undoubtedly frustrated and angry, his long apprenticeship and unexpected association with Leah, as well as his marriage to Rachel, will result in the sons that God wants as the progenitors of the twelve tribes of Israel.

All told, Leah would bear Jacob six sons and a daughter, one of Leah's maids would bear him two more, one of Rachel's maids another two, and finally Rachel herself would give birth to two sons, Joseph and Benjamin. What Jacob originally wanted was marriage and children with Rachel, and he was compelled to wait and work fourteen years to achieve the marriage—and many more years to father the children. But the entire time, when the patriarch was almost certainly cursing his fate, God was accomplishing his own purpose, as it were, behind Jacob's back, eventually giving Jacob more than he could have imagined. We find this theme of the noncompetitive and noninterruptive quality of God's causality everywhere in the Bible. The one who is the Creator of all, the unconditioned existent, does not have to manipulate or work around the beings that he has created, even those creatures of his who have free will. Rather, divine and human agency can cooperate, each acting within its proper scope. The prophet Isaiah will express the notion with admirable understatement: "O Lord . . . it is you who have accomplished all we have done" (Isa. 26:12 NAB).

Finally, having fathered many children and having amassed an impressive fortune, Jacob resolves to return home and make peace with the brother whom he had, long ago, duped out of his rightful inheritance. He sends out messengers and receives the unnerving response that Esau is indeed coming to meet him, but with a small army of four hundred men. Jacob can only imagine that his brother, who had become a local potentate, is seeking revenge. It is on the eve of the confrontation with Esau that Jacob, in accord with his identity as a grappler, engages in arguably the most famous wrestling match in human history. We are told that Jacob, having sent his family ahead of him, is left alone. Then, "a man wrestled with him until daybreak" (Gen. 32:24). Who was this figure? We are not directly told, though at the close of their fight, his opponent gives Jacob a new name, Israel, and explains,

"You shall no longer be called Jacob, but Israel, for you have striven with God and with humans, and have prevailed" (Gen. 32:28). It is certainly true that Jacob has been a fighter all his life. Coming out of the womb, he contended with Esau, and then he battled his brother for the inheritance. For seven years, he fought Laban for the right to have Rachel, and then he was compelled to fight him for seven more. And it is also true that he usually came out the winner in these contests. But what is fascinating in his opponent's account is the insistence that he has also, in the process, wrestled with God.

In many mysticisms, philosophies, and religions, both ancient and contemporary, God is presented as an impersonal force, which can be approached by us but which remains fundamentally indifferent to us. This is true, for example, of Aristotle's prime mover, Spinoza's absolute, or Schleiermacher's infinite;[29] but none of these has a thing to do with the biblical conception of God, who is emphatically a person, passionately and actively involved in the world that he has made, especially in the lives of human beings who bear his own image and likeness. We are searching for God of course, but the God of the Bible is searching for us with an even greater intensity. For a thousand reasons, we wrestle with God, seeking to understand his purpose, his activity, his seeming inactivity; but for ten thousand reasons, God wrestles with us—luring us, cajoling us, threatening us, promising us great things. As a theologian, I have spent most of my life grappling with God, and at times, I have been sorely tempted to let go, but God has not let me go. Moreover, like Jacob, I have been wounded in the fight, permanently affected, marked: "When the man saw that he did not prevail against Jacob, he struck him on the hip socket; and Jacob's hip was put out of joint" (Gen. 32:25). At the same time, I have never come away from a battle with God without

29. Aristotle, *Metaphysics* 12.1071b; Baruch Spinoza, *Ethics*, in *The Collected Works of Spinoza*, trans. Edwin Curley, vol. 1 (Princeton: Princeton University Press, 1985), 408–446; Friedrich Schleiermacher, *On Religion: Speeches to Its Cultured Despisers*, trans. John Oman (London: Kegan Paul, Trench, Trübner & Co., 1893), 36, 39, 101.

being blessed in some way. Keeping a distance from God or merely seeking him on one's own terms yields no blessing. But getting in close contact with him, wrestling with him, even when such an engagement seems fruitless, always produces a benediction.

That Jacob receives the name Israel, which in turn becomes the name of the people that comes forth from him, is of tremendous moment. Just as Israel as a collectivity across many centuries functions as a Jacob's ladder, connecting God and humanity, so Israel as a family has the privilege of wrestling with God on behalf of the world. In a way, every people seeks after God; but Israel wrestles with God, and that has made all the difference. The Bible itself, which has blessed countless individuals across space and time, is the product of this peculiarly Israelite identity.

In a sense, after this hyperdramatic and mystical account, the meeting between Jacob and Esau is something of an anticlimax. Yet how wonderful that, despite Jacob's fears, his brother meets him with consummate graciousness. After bowing to the ground seven times as a signal of his obeisance and repentance, Jacob looks up to see Esau racing toward him, not in aggression, but in eagerness to embrace: "Esau ran to meet him, and embraced him, and fell on his neck and kissed him, and they wept" (Gen. 33:4). The reconciliation of the brothers—Jacob's penitence and Esau's forgiveness—is a beautiful icon of what a reconciled Israel could become for the rest of the world. It anticipates the gathering of all the tribes under the headship of David, the unity of the nation under Solomon, the return of the exiles from Babylon, and eventually, the coming together of the Mystical Body of Christ.

JOSEPH AND HIS BROTHERS

After describing Jacob's confrontation with the angel and his reconciliation with Esau, the author of Genesis moves into what amounts to a novella focusing on Jacob's next-to-youngest son, Joseph. It is no exaggeration to say that the story of Joseph is one of the most beautifully told, psychologically profound, and theologically illuminating narratives that has come down to us from the ancient world. It easily ranks with the story of David in 1 and 2 Samuel, and though it is, of course, much briefer, it compares in literary quality with the *Iliad* and the *Odyssey*. That Thomas Mann, one of the most sublime writers of the twentieth century, could compose a novel of nearly fifteen hundred pages on the basis of a narrative that takes up about fifteen pages in most Bibles witnesses to the extraordinary power of the stories regarding Joseph.

As the thirty-seventh chapter of Genesis opens, we hear of Joseph at the age of seventeen. He is described as a shepherd, which, given the typical biblical association, anticipates Joseph's role as leader. But as is so often the case, this future shepherd of Israel has to endure a long and painful apprenticeship before he will be ready to lead. Since he was the child of his father's old age, Joseph was the particular favorite of Jacob, who gifted the boy with a lovely long-sleeved robe, probably hinting at something like royal status. Naturally, his brothers hated him. Making matters worse, Joseph was a dreamer who never hesitated to share his dreams with his family. And making matters worse still, no Freudian feats of dream interpretation were required to understand that these nighttime fantasies served to aggrandize Joseph's ego. In one, he and his brothers were binding sheaves, when suddenly Joseph's stood upright and those of his brothers bowed down in homage; in another, the sun, moon, and stars—the cosmic elements themselves—paid homage to Joseph. When the boy lays out the second dream, even his adoring father upbraids him for arrogance: "What kind of dream is this that you have had? Shall we indeed come, I and your mother and your brothers, and bow to the ground before you?" (Gen. 37:10). That Joseph was a man of physical attractiveness, extraordinary intelligence, self-determination, and practical skill becomes eminently clear in the course of the narrative, but as a seventeen-year-old, he quite obviously was not ready to channel those gifts in a positive direction. Though the dreams proved perfectly prophetic—his brothers would indeed bow down to him one day—their fulfillment would be a long time coming.

At his father's prompting, Joseph goes to visit his brothers, who are tending the flock. When they see him coming, they conspire to slay him: "Here comes this dreamer. Come now, let us kill him and throw him into one of the pits; then we shall say that a wild animal has devoured him" (Gen. 37:19–20). So they strip him of his special coat and throw him into a pit. At Judah's suggestion, they don't murder the boy, but rather arrange for his sale to a passing caravan of Ishmaelite traders on their way to Egypt. Icarus-like, Joseph, who had certainly been flying too high, is now cast down—down into the pit and then "down" into Egypt. This is the humiliation of the self-elevating ego, which is always a necessary propaedeutic to real transformation: one must go down in order, properly, to rise high.

Though he is passing through a time of enormous trial, and though things will get even worse for him, Joseph, we are told, is under the special providence of God: "The LORD was with Joseph" (Gen. 39:2). He is sold into the service of Potiphar, a high official in the government of Egypt and special confidant of the Pharaoh, and in short order, he is entrusted with the running of Potiphar's household. As is true throughout his life, his physical attractiveness and his obvious gifts serve him well. However, also very much in accord with a biblical pattern, Joseph's beauty is a source of enormous trouble as well. We are told that Potiphar's wife, finding the young slave enticing, tries to seduce him: "Lie with me." Citing his loyalty to his master as well as the commands of his God, Joseph refuses her importuning. She persists day after day, and finally, when she finds herself alone with Joseph, she again orders, "Lie with me," but this time, she catches hold of Joseph's garment, and when the young man escapes, he leaves the vestment in her hand, giving her ample evidence with which to frame him (Gen. 39:7–15).

And so, Joseph's downward journey continues. Potiphar in his rage sends Joseph to prison, where he is compelled to spend several years. Given what we found out regarding Joseph's self-absorption and indifference to the feelings of his brothers, we ought not to be surprised that his chastening humiliation takes considerable time. The way out of the pit comes through dreams. When he very successfully interprets the prophetic dreams of two of his fellow prisoners, his skill comes to the attention of Pharaoh himself, who is endeavoring to understand two of his own confounding dreams. A fascination with dreams has certainly persisted across cultures and across the centuries, and various methods of divination have been practiced. What is crucially important in regard to Joseph is that he claims no specialized skill or mystical method. Rather, as he plainly says to one of his fellow prisoners, "Do not interpretations [of dreams] belong to God?" (Gen. 40:8). The point is that, from his earliest days, Joseph remains open to the direction of God and that he continues, even in his darkest moments, to attend to what God is telling him through his own dreams and those of others.

Pharaoh had dreamt of seven healthy cattle devoured by seven emaciated cattle and of seven plump ears of grain devoured by seven blighted ears. With blithe confidence, Joseph interprets these as both indicating that Egypt would experience seven years of agricultural plenty followed immediately by seven years of drought and famine, and that, if steps are not taken, the famine will be so severe that "all the plenty will be forgotten" (Gen. 41:30). Therefore, he concludes, Pharaoh must appoint someone immediately to preside over the fields and granaries of Egypt so as to prepare, even now, for the disaster to come. So impressed is the king with this reading of dreams and this canny assessment of the practical situation that he immediately appoints Joseph as a sort of prime minister with plenipotentiary power over the entire realm. In one fell swoop, the slave, languishing hopelessly in prison, is lifted to a position of almost limitless authority, and the shepherding role, foreseen for Joseph from his youth, is now, in the most unexpected way, realized.

From the moment of his ascent, Joseph's gifts of mind, will, and imagination are focused on bringing succor to the people of Egypt. If he had come to power when he was a boy of seventeen, bragging to his brothers about his dreams of glory, he undoubtedly would have used his position and authority to aggrandize himself or punish his enemies or satisfy his various lusts. It was precisely the long period of confinement, rejection, and deep suffering that worked an alchemy in his soul and prepared him for the task at hand. Power is spiritually valid only when it remains tied to truth and to love; untethered from those, it wreaks havoc. In the New Testament account of Jesus before Pilate, we see the latter state of affairs. When Jesus tells the Roman governor that he has come to testify to the truth, Pilate responds, either with contempt or weary cynicism, "What is truth?" and then he sends a man he knows to be innocent to his death. In the Crucifixion of Jesus, we see the result of Pilate's indifference to both truth and love.

Another key biblical theme is signaled in Joseph's rise to power, one that we see in the stories of Moses, Esther, and Daniel—namely, the infiltration of a child of Israel into the leadership of a foreign nation. Though it will remain mostly only seminal and surreptitious in the Old Testament, the meaning of this motif will emerge with clarity in the New Testament. As we have seen, Israel is meant not for itself but for the world. Finally, the chosen people are destined to bring the God of Israel to all the nations. We see this benign invasion for the first time in the rise of a Hebrew slave to the summit of Egyptian society. And we see a further signal of Israel's universal attractiveness in the streaming of the people toward the Egyptian granaries during the famine that Joseph predicted. When the Egyptians themselves cry out, the Pharaoh says, simply enough, "Go to Joseph; what he says to you, do," and in time the surrounding nations were compelled to follow the same advice: "Moreover, all the world came to Joseph in

Egypt to buy grain, because the famine became severe throughout the world" (Gen. 41:55, 57). So, in the Christian dispensation, all the nations would come to Jesus, the King of Israel, for their spiritual sustenance.

As Joseph foresaw, Egypt and the surrounding countries, after seven years of plenty, fall victim to a devastating drought. Deeply affected are Jacob and his remaining eleven sons. And so, the old patriarch directs his children to journey to Egypt and procure provisions, which in turn leads to one of the most poignantly ironic scenes in the Bible. As was foreshadowed in his teenage dreams, the brothers of Joseph do indeed bow down to him in homage, though they have no idea that it is Joseph, covered as he is in the finery, makeup, and headgear of an Egyptian potentate.

What ensues is a carefully orchestrated drama in which Joseph, fully controlling the situation, compels his brothers to answer for what they did to him many years before. In a way, Joseph acts out the role of the God of justice vis-à-vis his errant brothers. At the same time, in typically biblical fashion, we also see, it is fair to say, some of Joseph's own limitations on display, for there is more than a little cruelty in what he does to his brothers and, indirectly, to their father. After hearing their appeal, he baldly tells them, "You are spies; you have come to see the nakedness of the land!" (Gen. 42:9). When they strenuously object, Joseph tells them that, to prove their veracity, they must produce their youngest brother, who remains with their father in Canaan. Knowing full well that this request will break their father's heart but realizing that they have no choice, they acquiesce. When Jacob hears the news, he is, indeed, devastated: "If harm should come to him on the journey that you are to make, you would bring down my gray hairs with sorrow to Sheol" (Gen. 42:38). The brothers undoubtedly know that they are being punished for their cruelty to Joseph, and Jacob undoubtedly fears that he might be placing his youngest son in the questionable hands of those who, he suspects, had something to do with Joseph's death.

When they present themselves once more before Joseph to petition for more grain, all seems to go well, but then the vizier of Egypt plants a silver cup in the traveling bag of Benjamin. When the brothers set out for home, they are stopped by one of Joseph's assistants, who accuses them of theft. Upon examining their baggage, he finds the cup with Benjamin, and the group returns, terrified, to Joseph. At this point, Judah makes a speech, one of the longest and most affecting in the entire Old Testament. He lays out the entire scenario to Joseph, once again emphasizing that the loss of Benjamin would be beyond devastating for their father, and then offers himself in place of the young man: "Now therefore, please let your servant remain as a slave to my lord in place of the boy; and let the boy go back with his brothers" (Gen. 44:33). With these words, the price has been paid, the imbalance redressed. For a brother who had abandoned Joseph, his own flesh and blood, to slavery is now willing to become a slave in order to liberate Benjamin. Moved by Judah's offer and satisfied that justice has been done, Joseph, through tears, reveals his identity: "I am Joseph. Is my father still alive?" When his brothers, stupefied, huddle around him, he continues, "I am your brother, Joseph, whom you sold into Egypt. And now do not be distressed, or angry with yourselves, because you sold me here; for God sent me before you to preserve life" (Gen. 45:3–5).

Two observations are in order here. First, having expressed the divine judgment, which is never arbitrary or cruel but rather curative, Joseph now gives voice to the divine mercy and forgiveness. His embrace of his brothers, who had grievously sinned against him, is a foreshadowing of the father's embrace of the prodigal son (Luke 15:20) and Jesus' forgiveness of the disciples who had denied, betrayed, and abandoned him. Even after they had performed a kind of satisfaction, they still received far more than they deserved. So it goes with the divine grace. The second point has to do with the problem of evil, and this is one of the first and most pointed biblical references to it. The story of Joseph and his brothers is, quite frankly, filled with terrors: fierce jealousy, cruelty, indifference to one's own family, manipulation, false accusation, the buying and selling of human beings, unjust imprisonment, forced exile, humiliation, starvation, and existential anxiety. What, we might be permitted to ask, is the point of all this? How does this rather awful story make spiritual sense? Joseph says, "For God sent me before you to preserve life" (Gen. 45:5). At the climax of this narrative, Joseph is the man who is effectively feeding the world, but what made that state of affairs possible is the entire train of events that the author of Genesis has traced. We will see this point made again and again in the Bible, most emphatically in the book of Job: God permits evils within his creation in order to make possible certain goods that could not have come about in any other way. To be sure, while Joseph was languishing in prison, unjustly condemned, and while his brothers were contemplating the prospect of summary execution at the hands of the Egyptian vizier, their lives seemed unrelievedly bleak. But the Bible consistently takes the long view and urges patience with the working out of a divine purpose that typically remains opaque to us.

And in point of fact, we must keep this great scriptural principle in mind as the narrative moves from climax to denouement. The brothers return to Canaan and tell their father the impossibly good news about Joseph. Subsequently, at the invitation of the Pharaoh himself, the entire extended family makes their way to Egypt to take up residence on prime real estate in the land of Goshen. In a scene of almost unbearable poignancy, Joseph rides out on a chariot to meet his aged father, and when the two of them meet, they embrace, and Joseph, we are told, "wept on his [father's] neck a good while" (Gen. 46:29). We might be tempted to say, at this point, all's well that ends well. But keeping that biblical long view in mind, we must acknowledge that the transplantation of Jacob's family to Egyptian soil, effectively abandoning the land promised to him and his forebears, leads by a fairly short route to the centuries-long enslavement of Israel. The "Egyptianizing" of

Israel is given special emphasis in the very last words of the book of Genesis, when we learn that Joseph himself, upon his death, was embalmed in the distinctively Egyptian manner and placed "in a coffin in Egypt" (Gen. 50:26). From that small seed would grow the Israelite presence, but on alien soil.

To be sure, from this tragedy would come the liberation, which stands, to this day, at the heart of Jewish consciousness and as, for Christians, a correlate to Christ's liberation of humanity from the slavery of sin. God's providence, as we will discover in the book of Wisdom, "reaches mightily from one end of the earth to the other, and . . . orders all things well" (Wis. 8:1), various goods emerging but often only after and because of deep suffering.

Exodus

THE EXODUS AS SPIRITUAL DELIVERANCE
How wonderful that at the very heart of the story of Israel is an act of liberation from slavery. It is impossible not to see the massive influence this narrative has had on the development of the political consciousness of the world. In his most characteristic act, the God of Israel delivers his people from bondage and brings them to a place of freedom. Practically every movement for liberation, at least in the West, owes a great deal of its power to this archetypal account.

At the same time, we must appreciate that the political liberation of Israel from literal slavery has also been seen, from the beginning, as a metaphor for spiritual deliverance, liberation from sin and death. In Origen's magnificent reading, the Israelites stand for all that is in accord with the will of the Creator, and the Egyptians for those forces that stand athwart God's purposes.[1] Thus, the story being told concerns the perennial struggle in us and in our communities between grace and sin. It is crucial to keep both of these interpretations in view as we read this pivotal text.

Another principal preoccupation of the author of Exodus is the delineation of those practices and beliefs by which the people Israel defines itself, or better, is defined by the God who liberates them. Law, covenant, right worship, sacrifice, ritual, sacred meal, etc. are all explored in the course of the narrative. Precisely because

---

1. See, for example, Origen, *Homilies on Exodus* 1.5, 2.1, 5.4.

Jesus is seen as the fulfillment of all of these, Exodus remains of prime importance for Christian readers.

MOSES AND THE BURNING BUSH

As Exodus commences, we hear that the clan that came to Egypt with Jacob—seventy strong—has grown to be a mighty band, "so that the land was filled with them" (Exod. 1:7). We are meant to hear the overtones of the creation account and of the promise made to Abraham, but we also cannot help but see that this multiplication of Israel is happening on foreign soil and hence will become a source of conflict. Indeed, a king comes to Egypt who "did not know Joseph," who had no memory of what that great Israelite had accomplished for Egypt and for the world (Exod. 1:8). This man turns on fast-growing Israel and commences to persecute them, eventually reducing them to slavery. With Origen's hermeneutic in mind, we might see this as the inevitable war between the forces of God and the forces of the enemy within the human heart. When the energies congruent with God's purpose grow, the darker powers never fail to notice and seldom fail to counterattack. In the spiritual order, it often happens that the best in us—mind, will, imagination, passion—comes to serve the worst in us.

So dire does the situation become that Pharaoh orders the immediate execution of every male child born to Israel. When a boy is born to a man and woman from the house of Levi, his mother ignores the order and places the child in a basket, which she releases onto the surface of the Nile. The Hebrew word used to describe the basket, *tevah*, is the same word employed to describe the ark of Noah, and the theological sense is much the same.[2] This child, Moses, is the remnant of God's good creation in the midst of chaos, the small seed from which the tree of Israel will sprout again. As Noah's ark floated on the open ocean of the floodwaters, so Moses' little barque floats on the Nile. And in accord with God's

2. Robert Alter, *The Hebrew Bible: A Translation with Commentary*, vol. 1, *The Five Books of Moses* (New York: W.W. Norton, 2019), 216n3.

providence, the *tevah* is discovered by Pharaoh's daughter, who, moved with pity at the plight of the crying boy, takes him into her home and raises him as her son. Very much in the manner of Joseph, an Israelite has found his way into the heart of the Egyptian establishment, against which, in time, he will lead a rebellion.

The Bible passes over the entirety of Moses' development, for we next encounter him as a grown man going out to see the suffering of his people. Though we know nothing of his education and formation, the author gives us, in a few deft strokes, a sense of Moses' personality. Seeing an Egyptian beating a Hebrew, Moses kills the aggressor and quickly buries him in the sand. A few days later, he attempts to intervene in an argument between two Hebrews and is sharply rebuked: "Who made you a ruler and judge over us? Do you mean to kill me as you killed the Egyptian?" (Exod. 2:14). Understanding that his murder has become widely known, he immediately flees the country. So what do we know of Moses? He is clearly a man of moral principle but also more than a little imperious, self-important, judgmental, rash, and violent. In time, he will become the liberator of his people, but at this point in the narrative, he is like the young Joseph: full of potential, but also full of himself, and not ready for the kind of leadership that God wants him to exercise. A time of trial and testing will be required, and as is so often the case in the Bible, this will take place in the desert.

Arriving in the land of Midian, Moses comes to a well, and in accord with the biblical pattern already on display in the stories of Rebekah and Rachel, he finds his wife there, in this case, Zipporah, daughter of Reuel (also called Jethro). She bore a son, whom Moses named Gershom, which carries the sense of being a stranger in a foreign land. Many years pass, and we are meant to appreciate the extraordinary transition that Moses undergoes from Egyptian prince to simple shepherd, which signals the de-Egyptianizing of Israel—in spiritual terms, the purification from the influence of negative impulses and motivations. Only after this desert time is Moses ready for the encounter with the God of his fathers.

It takes place on Mt. Horeb, deep in the Sinai wilderness, when Moses was acting as shepherd to the flock of Jethro. We hear that "the angel of the LORD appeared to him in a flame of fire out of a bush" (Exod. 3:2). Moses noticed the extraordinary fact that the bush, though on fire, was not being consumed. As interpreted by the theological tradition, this apparition signals the absolutely unique manner in which the Creator God relates to his creation—which is to say, nonviolently and noncompetitively. Precisely because he is not a being operating within a shared metaphysical framework with other beings, God can come close to a creature, indeed in the most intimate way, without undermining the integrity of the creature. In point of fact, the closer God comes, the more beautiful and luminous the creature becomes. Nowhere is this principle on more perfect display than in the Incarnation, which involves the coming together of a divine and human nature without mixing, mingling, or confusion—that is to say, without any compromising of either divine or creaturely integrity.[3] And this is why the Virgin Mary, in whose womb this Incarnation was realized, is often compared by the Church Fathers to the burning bush.[4]

Curious to know and eager to grasp the meaning of this event, Moses says, "I must turn aside and look at this great sight, and see why the bush is not burned up." But immediately he is repulsed. The Lord says to him, "Moses, Moses! . . . Come no closer! Remove the sandals from your feet, for the place on which you are standing is holy ground" (Exod. 3:3–5). The unconditioned source of existence itself can never be known through an aggressive move of the intellect nor corralled in the categories that apply to finite things. Moses was approaching the mystery of the burning bush with the intellectual attitude of the analytical scientist, but this

---

3. Council of Chalcedon, "Definition of the Two Natures of Christ," in Heinrich Denzinger et al., *Compendium of Creeds, Definitions, and Declarations on Matters of Faith and Morals*, 43rd ed. (San Francisco: Ignatius, 2012), no. 302.

4. See, for example, John of Damascus, *On Divine Images* 2.20; see also Gregory of Nyssa, *On the Birth of Christ* (PG 46, 1133 D–1136 B) and Severus of Antioch, *Homily* 67 (PO 8, 349–350) in Luigi Gambero, *Mary and the Fathers of the Church: The Blessed Virgin Mary in Patristic Thought*, trans. Thomas Buffer (San Francisco: Ignatius, 1999), 155, 312.

is never appropriate when dealing with the Creator, for the very ground of being can never be directly grasped. In a way, the entire tradition of apophaticism in theology is anticipated in the warning to Moses to take off his sandals. Especially on rocky and uneven ground, sandals give the one who wears them a certain confidence and insouciance, but that kind of self-assurance is never correct when one stands in the presence of God.

Having kept Moses at an appropriate distance, God then speaks his heart in an extraordinarily direct and intimate manner: "I am the God of your father, the God of Abraham, the God of Isaac, and the God of Jacob" (Exod. 3:6). Though unapproachable, though unconditioned, though so holy that he can never be grasped or manipulated, God is no distant, impersonal force. Rather, he knows Moses and his people by name—Moses, who is a humble shepherd, and his people, who are lowly slaves in Egypt. The God of the burning bush cannot be grasped, but by the same token, he cannot be avoided. And this paradox is altogether reasonable when we consider that the Creator of the universe is not a particular being, but rather the sheer act of being. Were he a thing, however ontologically impressive, one could, through the requisite effort, both grasp and avoid him. But the true God always keeps those who would come to know him off-balance.

The strangeness and unconditionality of God's manner of existence is given classic expression in the name that he reveals to Moses. When the discalced shepherd inquires after the name of the one who has been addressing him from the burning bush, he receives this famously mysterious answer: "I Am Who I Am" (Exod. 3:14). Of course, oceans of ink have been spilled in the attempt to explain this title, *Ehyeh-Asher-Ehyeh*. It is perhaps most literally rendered from the Hebrew as "I will be who I will be,"[5] but the Septuagint translates it into Greek as *ego eimi ho*

---

5. Robert Alter, *The Hebrew Bible*, 1:222–223.

on (I am the one who is).[6] Since *Asher* could have an impersonal referent, Robert Alter insists that the traditional "I am that I am" cannot be excluded as a valid translation of the Hebrew.[7] In any case, what the enigmatic name seems to convey is the qualitative difference between the divine manner of existing and that which characterizes anything other than God. In a certain sense, of course, the name does not define God, but in another sense, it signals what sets him apart. Translating this passage into more properly metaphysical language, Thomas Aquinas, as we saw, says that what God is coincides with the fact of God's existence, so that God's very nature is to be.[8] Now, that which simply is must necessarily transcend the realm of ordinary experience utterly, since that order is made up exclusively of particular existents; at the same time, that which simply is must be available in and present to every aspect of ordinary experience, since it (he) creatively grounds whatever is found within that order.

Thus, *Ehyeh-Asher-Ehyeh* is indeed, simultaneously, ungraspable and unavoidable. The Psalmist expresses God's unavoidability in beautiful poetic language: "Where can I go from your spirit? Or where can I flee from your presence? If I ascend to heaven, you are there; if I make my bed in Sheol, you are there. If I take the wings of the morning and settle at the farthest limits of the sea, even there your hand shall lead me, and your right hand shall hold me fast" (Ps. 139:7–10). And the prophet Isaiah expresses God's ungraspability in equally evocative terms: "For as the heavens are higher than the earth, so are my ways higher than your ways and my thoughts than your thoughts" (Isa. 55:9). To hold these affirmations in tension, both intellectually and behaviorally, is crucial for the one who wants to be in right relation to God. Typically, we sinners, like Adam and Eve before us, try some version of the two

6. Randall K. Tan, David A. deSilva, and Isaiah Hoogendyk, eds., *The Lexham Greek-English Interlinear Septuagint: H.B. Swete Edition* (Bellingham, WA: Lexham, 2012), Exod. 3:14.

7. Robert Alter, *The Hebrew Bible*, 1:222n14.

8. Thomas Aquinas, *Summa theologiae* 1.2.3, 1.3.4.

basic strategies of control or avoidance: we attempt to manipulate God or to run from him. Presumably, Moses required the long discipline of the desert in order to be rid of both of these errant tendencies and to be ready to hear the voice of the One Who Is.

And when *Ehyeh-Asher-Ehyeh* speaks, he utters a word of liberation: "The cry of the Israelites has now come to me; I have also seen how the Egyptians oppress them. So come, I will send you to Pharaoh to bring my people, the Israelites, out of Egypt" (Exod. 3:9–10). If we follow the Origenist line of interpretation sketched above, we might see that deliverance from Egypt is, symbolically speaking, freedom from false worship and from a faulty relationship with ultimate reality. How significant that the first request that Moses will make of Pharaoh is that Israel be delivered "so that they may celebrate a festival" to God in the wilderness (Exod. 5:1). Right praise is the first step toward spiritual freedom.

OUT OF EGYPT

When Moses presents this demand of the king of Egypt, Pharaoh responds with scorn: "Who is the LORD, that I should heed him and let Israel go? I do not know the LORD, and I will not let Israel go" (Exod. 5:2). Like a refrain throughout this first section of Exodus, we hear that "the LORD hardened the heart of Pharaoh" (Exod. 9:12; 10:20, 27; 11:10; 14:8), and searching out the puzzle of why the all-good God would "harden" the heart of anyone, confirming him in his resistance, has been a major preoccupation of Christian theologians in the West for centuries. To follow the sinuous lines of that debate would take us too far afield, and I would suggest that we might cut the Gordian knot and observe simply that this "hardening" primarily is meant to convey the resistance to healing and liberation that is inevitably present in any individual or society that is being called out of sin. Once a person (or community) has settled into a dysfunctional way of operating, it is exceedingly difficult to get him (or them) to think and act in a new way. Indeed, those enmeshed in the ways of sin don't "know" the Lord and won't, willingly, do his bidding. The stubbornly irrational resistance of Pharaoh is symbolically congruent with the personal experience of every sinner who has been summoned to a new manner of thinking and acting.

In point of fact, Pharaoh, upon hearing the request of Moses and Aaron, becomes even more difficult and tyrannical, requiring the Hebrew slaves to produce their usual quota of bricks and yet refusing to provide them straw. This in turn prompts the slaves to complain against their would-be liberators: "The LORD look upon you and judge! You have brought us into bad odor with Pharaoh and his officials, and have put a sword in their hand to kill us" (Exod. 5:21). In the early stages of any process of authentic religious conversion, things usually become more difficult for the one undergoing the change. At least he had found a *modus vivendi* in the old order. While the old is being thrown off but before the new has fully arrived, he suffers so much that the conversion itself is jeopardized, and the one encouraging the change is demonized.

At the prompting of the Lord, Moses and Aaron return to Pharaoh and demand, once again, that he set the Israelites free. During this visit, we get a clearer sense of the properly theological context for the conversation between oppressor and oppressed. Aaron throws his staff at Pharaoh's feet and it turns into a serpent, likely a Nile river cobra, but the king of Egypt summons his sorcerers, who similarly transform staffs into snakes. However, Aaron's serpent devours the others. What is of signal importance here is that the serpent, a depiction of which was present on the headdress of the Pharaoh, represented the authority of the Egyptian king, and since Pharaoh was considered godlike, the swallowing of the sorcerers' snakes is a frontal assault not only on his political power but also on the religion of Egypt.

What follows this display of the power of the God of Israel are the ten plagues by which God will, eventually, compel Pharaoh to acquiesce. Much of the language used to describe these terrible

wonders hearkens back to the beginning of Genesis and the account
of creation, implying that the God who liberates is also the God
who has lordship over every aspect of nature, which he can bend
to his purpose. The first plague, turning the Nile and its canals
and tributaries into blood, is not only a great display of power but
also a dethroning of a particularly potent Egyptian god, for the
Nile was seen as having divine qualities. The next plague, that of
frogs that pullulate throughout the land, calls to mind the Creator
God's giving rise to all those things that creep and crawl upon
the earth and hence signals that God's authority over creation
is universal. When God produces gnats in suffocating numbers,
the sorcerers of Egypt try to duplicate the feat but are unable,
prompting them to admit that they are fighting against a power
greater than themselves. Still, Pharaoh's heart remains hardened.
Flies come and torment the Egyptians, and their livestock are struck
with disease; then, they are plagued with boils and by hail and by
swarms of locusts. But each time, when the trial passes, Pharaoh
refuses to budge. Signaling a reversion to the *tohu wabohu* before the
creation of light, God plunges Egypt into "a darkness that can be
felt," though the children of Israel remain in the light (Exod. 10:21).
Once again, the Origen reading of Exodus comes to mind: Egypt
stands for what Karl Barth called *das Nichtige*, "the nothingness,"[9]
opposed to what comes to light through God's creative action, while
Israel represents God's creative purpose in the world.

When even this horrific plague does not convince Pharaoh,
God resolves to visit one more unsurpassably devastating affliction
upon Egypt: the killing of the firstborn. Just as all the earth belongs
to the Lord—as is evident in his manipulation of beasts and elements during the preceding plagues—so all human life belongs
to him. He has given it, and he can take it for his purposes. In
advance of their liberation, the Israelites are to eat a sacred meal,
at the center of which is an unblemished lamb, whose blood they

9. Karl Barth, "God and Nothingness," in *Church Dogmatics*, ed. G.W. Bromiley and T.F.
Torrance, vol. 3.3, *The Doctrine of Creation, Sections 50–51* (London: T&T Clark, 2010), 1–78.

are to smear on the doorposts and lintels of their homes so that the angel of death might see and pass over their domicile. Just as trouble began with a bad meal—Adam and Eve eating of the fruit of the tree of the knowledge of good and evil—so redemption is tied to a rightly ordered meal, commanded by God and serving to bring the families of Israel together. This Passover meal, which calls to mind God's act of liberation, becomes, of course, the defining ritual of the Israelite nation. All of its particular details are meant to call to mind the One Who Is and his characteristic act of granting freedom, both political and spiritual, to his people. As God describes what he is going to do the night of Passover, he adds, almost as an aside, "On all the gods of Egypt I will execute judgments" (Exod. 12:12). This *obiter dictum* names, in point of fact, what God is primarily about in this first part of the book of Exodus: delegitimizing the false gods, the worship of whom introduces spiritual poverty and enslavement. The people and leadership of Egypt are indeed under judgment, but behind their dysfunction is the nonbeing of the Egyptian deities, which are, accordingly, principally under judgment.

An odd detail, which is mentioned twice in the book of Exodus (Exod. 3:22; 12:33–36), is that, as the Israelites quit the country of their enslavement, they take extensive amounts of jewelry of silver and gold from their former taskmasters, for "the LORD had given the people favor in the sight of the Egyptians" (Exod. 12:36). The Church Fathers read this curious episode as an anticipation of the manner in which the Christian tradition will draw to itself all that is precious in the cultures that it evangelizes. Thus, the silver and gold of Egypt might be construed as representing, for example, the philosophy and art of Greece, the legal structure of Rome, and the mathematical speculation of Islam. Through God's grace, cultures once alien or even hostile to Christianity end up offering their treasures to the Church.

We hear that when the Lord leads the companies of Israel out of Egypt, he takes them not by the most direct way, but rather by a roundabout route along the Red Sea. For he fears that they might be seized by a longing to return, and this would be facilitated if they went by the expected path. We encounter here for the first time a theme that will resound throughout this section of Exodus: the difficulty of the journey and the temptation to return even to a condition of enslavement. So wrenching is the process of conversion that reversion to sin seems preferable in comparison.

In fact, the power of the old form of life is given beautiful symbolic expression in Pharaoh and his army, now roused to attention by the stark fact of the exodus of their slaves: "What have we done, letting Israel leave our service?" (Exod. 14:5). Can we hear this as the voice of sin, crying out for those spiritual powers of mind and will that it has allowed to slip out of its control? So the king and his mighty army set out to chase down defenseless Israel, and they trap the wandering former slaves on the verge of the Red Sea, forcing them to cry out to Moses, "What have you done to us, bringing us out of Egypt? . . . For it would have been better for us to serve the Egyptians than to die in the wilderness" (Exod. 14:11–12). So ingrained are the ways of sin that abandoning them appears to us sinners as a type of death. At this terrible juncture, Israel is compelled entirely to trust in the divine power. No strategy of theirs, no move either military or diplomatic, could possibly extricate them from their bind. And so Moses, at the prompting of the Lord, stretches his hand over the sea and causes the waters to be divided. We are indeed commanded to cooperate with grace, for God positively invites the engagement of our powers in the process of salvation. But grace always has first place. Just as an addict, upon entering the twelve-step process, must surrender his life to a higher power, so the sinner, effectively addicted to her own ego and attachments, must let go and permit God to act.

Even as the Israelites, through the power of God, pass through the sea on dry land, the Egyptians do not relent, but come after them. Can anyone doubt the Bible's seriousness in regard to the stubbornness of the old way of life? We hear that the wheels of the

Egyptians' chariots become clogged in the mud, and when Moses stretches his hand back over the sea from the safety of the far shore, the waters come crashing down upon Pharaoh's soldiers, wiping out everyone. Even in the face of divine opposition, it comes on; even knowing that it will destroy itself in the very act of asserting its prerogatives, it presses forward. What matters most, theologically speaking, in this absolutely pivotal narrative is that the God of Abraham, Isaac, Jacob, and Moses is primarily known as a God who *saves* his people. Though the Bible does indeed sometimes indirectly speak of God in a more musing, philosophical manner, its far more typical mood and style is to praise God for his salvific power: "Then Moses and the Israelites sang this song to the LORD: 'I will sing to the LORD, for he has triumphed gloriously; horse and rider he has thrown into the sea. The LORD is my strength and my might, and he has become my salvation'" (Exod. 15:1–2). And so, in the Christian dispensation, Jesus' very name, *Yeshua*, means "God saves." Even in the high Christological debates of the early centuries of the Christian era, wherein theologians used achingly high abstract language to clarify the relationship between Jesus' divinity and humanity, the focus was always on exploring the conditions for the possibility of the Lord's *saving* power. In a way, soteriology has always been the driving interest behind even the most philosophically articulated Christology.

DESERT WANDERING AND THE GIFT OF THE LAW
After the account of the dramatic escape from Egyptian bondage, the author of Exodus describes the desert wandering of the Israelites, which culminates in the encounter with God at Mt. Sinai and the gift of the Law. Like Abraham, their distant forebear, the Israelites are a pilgrim people, on the move, pressing forward at the prompting of God, and like the great patriarch, they will enter into a specialized covenant with the Lord by which their identity will be established. The people of Abraham, Isaac, and Jacob will become a people under the tutelage of the Law.

After the initial thrill of liberation, Israel feels, once again, the tug back to Egypt and the at least familiar way of life they knew. Plagued by hunger, they complain to Moses: "If only we had died by the hand of the LORD in the land of Egypt, when we sat by the fleshpots and ate our fill of bread; for you have brought us out into this wilderness to kill this whole assembly with hunger" (Exod. 16:3). In answer, the Lord rains a mysterious "bread" from heaven, which is termed "manna," since the people wondered just what it was: *"Man'hu"* (What is it?). In this strange substance, we sense something of signal importance—namely, that even as God sustains his people physically, his ultimate purpose is to sustain them spiritually. Coming "from heaven," the manna is an evocation of the higher, supernatural life to which he is summoning his people. Jesus, of course, makes explicit reference to the manna in the Eucharistic discourse from the sixth chapter of John's Gospel: "Your ancestors ate the manna in the wilderness, and they died. This is the bread that comes down from heaven, so that one may eat of it and not die. I am the living bread that came down from heaven" (John 6:49–51). The Eucharistic bread and wine are the supernatural, immortalizing sustenance that the people of God need as they make their way through the wilderness of this mortal life.

The Eucharistic overtone is heard even more clearly when we learn that the Israelites ate the manna for forty years—which is to say, the entire period of their wandering in the wilderness before entering into the Promised Land. So, too, with the sacramental food of the Eucharist, which is taken up to the moment when full communion with the risen Christ is attained, after a long exile, in the heavenly place.

As they continue their sojourn in the desert wasteland, the people become thirsty and, once again, complain to Moses: "Why did you bring us out of Egypt, to kill us and our children and livestock with thirst?" (Exod. 17:3). When Moses carries, with some frustration, this complaint to the Lord, God tells him to strike a rock with the staff used to strike the Nile, and out gushes water for the entire community. One of the most abiding symbols in the biblical literature for the soul's longing for God is thirst: "My soul thirsts for you; my flesh faints for you, as in a dry and weary land where there is no water" (Ps. 63:1); and "Everyone who thirsts, come to the waters" (Isa. 55:1). And Jesus himself picks up on this theme, saying, "Let anyone who is thirsty come to me, and let the one who believes in me drink" (John 7:37–38). The need for God is not superficial; it is not one requirement among many. It is a matter of life and death. Therefore, the condition for the possibility of living a true spiritual life is to awaken to this visceral and abiding need for God. The water that gushes from the rock at Meribah and satisfies the entire Israelite community and its livestock is evocative of the inexhaustible grace of God's own life. When he addresses the woman at the well in John's Gospel account, Jesus says, "Those who drink of the water that I will give them will never be thirsty. The water that I will give will become in them a spring of water gushing up to eternal life" (John 4:14). Under Moses' leadership, Israel is learning to direct its hunger and thirst to the only source that can satisfy those longings. The manna in the desert and the water from the rock at Meribah are visible signs of the invisible grace of the unconditioned reality.

Just after the narrative concerning the waters of Meribah, we find the curious account of Israel's battle with the Amalekites. Though on the surface it is the story of a skirmish between ancient Middle Eastern tribes, it carries an extraordinary spiritual significance and in many ways sets the tone for the numerous similar stories of battles between Israel and its foes throughout the Bible. Following the Origenistic hermeneutic, we ought to read Amalek as, like the Egyptians, a symbol of those forces opposed to God's creative intentions. While the battle rages, Moses stands atop a hill stretching forth his miraculous staff. As long as his arms are strong, the fight goes well for Israel, but when he tires and lowers the staff, the momentum shifts to the Amalekites.

Eventually, Aaron and Hur come to support the arms of their leader, and Moses remains steady until sunset. As a result, Israel cuts down Amalek with the sword. What spiritual insight do we gain from this pithy and rather brutal narrative? The Origenistic interpretive approach is confirmed by the fact that the victory is won not so much through military prowess as through prayer. We will see much the same thing, of course, in the story of the conquest of Jericho. What sustains the forces of Israel as they battle their spiritual enemies is a steady connection to God. When they become untethered from the Creator or when they blithely presume upon their relationship to him (when the arms of Moses are allowed to come down), they falter; and we shall see this dynamic up and down the texts of the Old Testament. This story of the Israelite army, Moses, Aaron, and Hur also functions as a striking icon of the Church in its variegated work. There are some who are directly involved in the active engagement of the culture, others who are primarily dedicated to the life of prayer, and still others who, financially and institutionally, support those who pray. Together, they do the work of defeating Amalek. If I might draw attention to a final confirmation of the Origenistic hermeneutic in this regard, the author of Exodus, as a conclusion to the account of the battle, adds, "The LORD will have war with Amalek from generation to generation" (Exod. 17:16). To be sure, Israel will, from time to time, struggle with the tribe of the Amalekites, but the sweeping nature of this conclusion points much more in the direction of an open-ended, ongoing battle with the forces of sin and death across time.

Having dealt with Amalek, Israel comes, at last, to the area around Mt. Sinai, the elevated place where Moses had heard the voice coming from the burning bush. We saw that the Garden of Eden itself is imagined as a height; we saw that Abraham's test took place on Mt. Moriah; now we deal with the most important mountain described in the Torah. Mountains, where humanity goes up and divinity, as it were, comes down, are privileged points of encounter. They represent the mystical conversation between God and his people. Later, of course, David will establish his capital city, and his son Solomon will construct the holy temple on Mt. Zion, "true pole of the earth," in the language of the Psalmist (Ps. 48:2 Grail). Thus, it is altogether appropriate that the definitive law and covenant with Israel will be sealed on the sacred height of Sinai: "Now therefore, if you obey my voice and keep my covenant, you shall be my treasured possession out of all the peoples. Indeed, the whole earth is mine, but you shall be for me a priestly kingdom and a holy nation" (Exod. 19:5–6).

This divine introduction to the events surrounding the giving of the Law is one of the most pivotal texts in the Old Testament, for it specifies what had been implicit since the call of Abram— namely, that Israel is chosen for the sake of the world. To state it more precisely, they have been called to offer right praise, the very orthodoxy that was lost in the Garden of Eden, and thus to become a "holy" nation. To be sure, this designates a separation, but always a setting apart for the sake of the whole. This is why it is crucially important to note God's insistence that "the whole earth" is his. Even as he chooses Israel, he is not for a moment forgetting his moral and ontological connection to all the nations, indeed to all of creation. Whatever holiness Israel exhibits and whatever priestly functions they accomplish will be on behalf of everyone else. This theme will emerge with special clarity in the writings of the prophets, particularly Isaiah, but it will positively explode in the texts of the New Testament, where Jesus is celebrated as the fulfillment of the priestly vocation of Israel.

What follows in the rest of the book of Exodus—and indeed in much of the remaining books of the Torah—is a description of the moral and liturgical laws by which Israel becomes a people set apart. It is worth noting, once again, that none of these prescriptions are for God's sake, as though God requires for his perfection or happiness the performance of certain human acts moral and liturgical. The God who is the sheer act of existence and who brought the universe into being in its entirety couldn't possibly need anything from his creation. Rather, all of these commands are for the sake of Israel and, through Israel, for the rest of humanity. God will indeed be pleased when Israel follows them, not because he derives some benefit from the performance, but rather because his glory is that his human creation be fully alive, if I might borrow the language of St. Irenaeus.[10]

As a propaedeutic to Moses' ascent of Mt. Sinai for his conversation with God, the Lord warns that no one of the Israelites should even touch the side of the mountain until the trumpet sounds and that, even after the permission is given, they may not go up the mountain unless they had consecrated themselves and washed their clothes. God's presence on the mountain, furthermore, is accompanied by thick smoke, which wraps around the summit of Sinai, and even the priests are commanded not to "break through" to the Lord on their own initiative (Exod. 19:21). Once more, we should not construe all of this distantiation and obfuscation as a sign of God's insecurity and need to be honored, but rather as an unambiguous reminder to Israel of the Lord's otherness—the fact, therefore, that he cannot, even in principle, be grasped. The smoke, the trumpet, and the warnings are attempts to hold off the tendency to grasp at the fruit of the tree of the knowledge of good and evil.

In chapter 20 of the book of Exodus, we come to grips with one of the most important texts in the biblical tradition, for here are laid out the Ten Commandments, the formal moral laws by which Israel is to be governed. Both the Jewish and Christian theologians of the Middle Ages tended to read these as basically identical to the first principles of the natural law—which is to say, the building blocks of any and all moral reasoning. Their perdurance across space and time and in a variety of cultural forms supports this interpretation. We should certainly avoid the

10. Irenaeus, *Against Heresies* 4.20.7, in *Irenaeus on the Christian Faith: A Condensation of Against Heresies*, trans. and ed. James R. Payton Jr. (Eugene, OR: Pickwick, 2011), 116.

temptation to read these commandments as arbitrary expressions of the divine will. On that interpretation, the various acts that the commandments prohibit would be wrong precisely because God has so declared. By the same token, we ought not to see them as conforming to some moral normativity extrinsic to God, so that God would command them because he recognizes them as good. Rather, these laws should be understood as expressions of God's own moral nature, thus dissolving the dilemma made famous by Socrates in the *Euthyphro*: Are acts good because the gods love them or do the gods love them because they are good?[11] We might conclude that certain acts are good in the measure that they participate in the supreme goodness of God himself.

The first and most important commandment is this: "I am the LORD your God, who brought you out of the land of Egypt, out of the house of slavery; you shall have no other gods before me" (Exod. 20:2–3). As we see in the third chapter of Genesis, the essence of sin is false worship, turning something less than God into God, confusing creature and Creator, accepting the conditioned as the unconditioned. Every other form of moral and spiritual dysfunction follows from this most fundamental distortion. Hence, the necessarily first move in the ethical transformation of Israel is the dethronement of false gods. Practically without exception, the failures of Israel throughout the rest of the biblical revelation are a function of disobeying this commandment. The rider on the first commandment—namely, the prohibition against making idols in the form of anything in heaven or earth or in the sea—parallels the move made in the opening verses of Genesis in which all of the elements that make up the universe are identified as the creatures of a higher power and hence de-divinized.

The next commandment, "You shall not make wrongful use of the name of the LORD your God" (Exod. 20:7), classically rendered as "You shall not take the name of the Lord your God in vain,"

---

11. Plato, *Euthyphro* 10a.

probably has less to do with what we would call "swearing" and more to do with the use of God's name in conjuration. To employ the holy name of God in order to bring about some desired state of affairs would be to engage in a superstitious manipulation of God. Hence, it is still another example of grasping at divinity.

The third commandment, "Remember the sabbath day, and keep it holy" (Exod. 20:8), is amply elaborated, which is certainly a sign of its centrality in the Israelite religious imagination. The author of Exodus reminds us that this injunction follows upon God's own resting after the work of creation and that it extends widely to "your son or your daughter, your male or female slave, your livestock, or the alien resident in your towns" (Exod. 20:10). In short, it is a moral requirement with a binding force over the whole of the society. It is a sanctification not of space but of time, and it has to do with the act of savoring. Thomas Aquinas says that the two great moves of the will are to seek the absent good and to rest in the good possessed.[12] We human beings spend the majority of our time exercising the first move of the will, and we are quite poor at the second. The sabbath is the time when we are prevented by divine law from achieving and compelled to savor, to taste, to rest. Though God is indeed in all things in the most intimate way, typically we do not aver to him. The seventh day forces us to look and to see ultimate reality.

The remaining commandments have to do with the ethical implications of the exclusive worship of God in regard to our dealings with one another. Jesus, of course, makes this connection as explicitly as possible when he comments that there are two commandments—namely, to love the Lord our God with all of our mind, soul, and strength, and a second, like the first, to love our neighbor as ourselves (Matt. 22:37; Mark 12:30; Luke 10:27). The link between the two is not arbitrary or ungrounded, and I might state the connection first metaphysically and then more

---

12. Thomas Aquinas, *Summa theologiae* 1-2.3.4.

ethically. Since God is the unconditioned reality, that which exists by reason of itself, every creature—which is to say, every conditioned existent—is intimately bound to God. Were God to withdraw his sustaining causality, even for an instant, a creature would revert to nonexistence. Hence, it is simply impossible to love the Lord without loving that which he, in the most complete sense, causes to be. Relatedly, as Thomas Aquinas specified, in loving God we are obligated to love what God loves,[13] and God must love every creature in the measure that he wills them the good of existence.[14] These are the ties, both ontological and moral, that bind the first "table" of the law to the second.

We might say that the commands of the second table are designed to bring Israel into conformity not so much with an abstract moral norm, but rather with the God whom they have been enjoined to worship. Under the rubric that one tends to become what one worships, the worshipers of the one who is just and compassionate must become conformed to his justice and compassion. All the remaining commandments serve this end.

The fourth commandment enjoins Israel to "honor your father and your mother, so that your days may be long in the land that the LORD your God is giving you" (Exod. 20:12). It should not be surprising that, as the Law turns our attention to our fellow human beings, it should commence with those closest to us. But there is also something rather more particularly Jewish here, for we also see the absolutely central role that family plays in the moral life of Israel. God consistently describes himself in the Scriptures as the God of a clan or a family, and his constantly repeated promise is that, if Israel is faithful, he will make them fruitful. And if we broaden our perspective, we can appreciate the honoring of father and mother as a sort of code for the honoring of the tradition from which one has come and by which one has been unavoidably shaped. Whatever freedom accomplishes always takes place within

13. Thomas Aquinas, 2-2.23.1 ad 2.
14. Thomas Aquinas, 1.20.2.

the context of what Paul Tillich called "destiny."[15] Honoring that which is always already given is the condition for the possibility of authentic individual freedom. However, it is instructive to note that even this intense devotion to parents and to the received tradition cannot supersede the demands of the first table of the Law. This is made eminently clear in Jesus' rather blunt words to the man who sought leave to bury his father before embarking on a career of following Jesus: "Let the dead bury their own dead" (Matt. 8:22; Luke 9:60).

The fifth commandment, "You shall not murder" (Exod. 20:13), hinges upon a principle defended throughout the Bible—namely, God's sovereign lordship over life. God gives life to all living things, and it remains his prerogative to take it away. Even the prohibition of eating meat with blood, repeated frequently throughout the Scriptures, is contingent upon the conviction that blood is life and life belongs to God. Robert Alter and others have reminded us that the familiar King James rendering of this injunction as "Thou shalt not kill" is somewhat misleading, since the Hebrew clearly indicates not simply the taking of life but something much closer to the criminal or unjust taking of life.[16] Hence, the translation "You shall not murder" catches the spirit of the Hebrew more accurately. The classical Christian moral tradition has respected this difference in distinguishing between, for example, the direct killing of the innocent, which is intrinsically evil, and, say, the killing of a combatant in the course of a just war or the killing of an aggressor who is attacking one's life.

Now, if the prohibition against murder has to do with the most egregious violation of the overall command to love and to act justly, then the remaining injunctions have to do with related but less intense failures in that regard. It is no accident that the legislation moves immediately from murder to adultery, for as even the

15. Paul Tillich, *Systematic Theology*, vol. 1 (Chicago: University of Chicago Press, 1973), 182–186.

16. Robert Alter, *The Hebrew Bible*, 1:297n13.

most cursory survey of history, literature, and experience reveals, violations in the arena of sexuality are particularly destructive of human well-being, at both the individual and communal level. That the Bible is not puritanical or Gnostic with respect to sex is blazingly evident. As we have seen already with some frequency, the surest sign of God's covenantal favor is that his people multiply fruitfully. And from the very opening pages of Genesis, we gather that God loves the multifarious bodies that he has made. Therefore, we must resist the suggestion, offered regrettably up and down Christian history and especially prevalent today, that the command not to violate sexual norms has anything to do with dualism or a despising of the pleasures of sex. Yet at the same time, the biblical authors are intensely aware of how destructive and counter-indicated are the violations of the marriage vow. When we transgress the most solemn commitment we have made to another human being, the deepest center of the self is massively affected. And the negative impact that this sin has against one's spouse and the wider community is hard to measure. The spiritual and moral tradition has, of course, widened the scope of this prohibition against the violation of the marriage vow to include any and all misuse of sexuality. Biblically minded people have debated for centuries just how widely inclusive this should be, but no one shaped by the scriptural mindset could doubt, under the rubric of *corruptio optimi pessima* (the corruption of the best is the worst), that the exercise of sexuality in a self-centered, manipulative, or violent way is particularly repugnant to the purposes of God.

What follows is the seventh commandment—namely, the prohibition against stealing. To be sure, the moral tradition has refined this command so that the taking of another's property so as to respond to an extreme need can be countenanced—for example, the taking of bread so as to feed one's starving family. However, the general prohibition against robbing another's belongings remains a fundamental building block of the moral life, for it amounts to a respect for the dignity of one's neighbor. Some commentators have helpfully observed that this commandment has to do not only with the taking of a neighbor's physical property but also of more intangible values such as his good name and reputation. And this observation segues neatly into the eighth commandment, which deals with the bearing of false witness. Since God makes the entire universe through a great act of speech, our speech is of signal importance. It is meant, to state it simply, to serve both truth and love. Once again, the tradition of moral theology has made fine distinctions that would permit the withholding of the truth under certain circumstances, but the general concern that speech should be ordered to the truth remains altogether valid. In the Letter of James, we find the splendid observation that though the tongue is a very small organ, it is powerful indeed, somewhat in the manner of the tiny rudder that steers the entire ship (James 3:1–5). False speech, amounting to deception or calumny or both, can massively undermine both individuals and communities—and evidence of this is overwhelming up and down the centuries.

The final two commandments both inveigh against "coveting"—in the first case, one's neighbor's house, and in the second case, one's neighbor's wife. Whereas the previous five commands prohibit certain forms of action or behavior, the last two warn against attitudes of the mind and longings of the will. Christians might sense here an anticipation of Jesus' strict regulations in the Sermon on the Mount against even lusting after a woman in one's heart (Matt. 5:27–28). In the light of René Girard's theorizing, we might remark here a warning in regard to mimetic or imitative desire—which is to say, wanting something precisely because someone else wants it.[17] This is to be sharply distinguished from desiring, for example, a car similar to the one that a friend has. Mimetic desire covets what the neighbor has *because* the neighbor desires it. On Girard's reading, it is just this kind of desire that tends to lead by a short route to conflicts that

17. René Girard, *Things Hidden Since the Foundation of the World*, trans. Stephen Bann and Michael Metteer (Stanford, CA: Stanford University Press, 1987), 283–298.

can be resolved only through the scapegoating mechanism. One wonders whether the biblical author, without subscribing, *avant la lettre*, to every detail of the Girardian theory, nevertheless grasped its fundamental dynamics.

Before transitioning to a consideration of the liturgical laws that ought to govern Israel, the author of Exodus spends time, in chapters 21 through 24, exploring some casuistic applications of the general moral law articulated in the Ten Commandments. Some speculate that this section of Exodus, which does indeed have similarities with the Code of Hammurabi and other ancient legal documents, represents a particularly ancient strand of the biblical tradition. I will focus on just a few items in this section.

We first remark that chapter 21 commences with a discussion of the proper treatment of slaves—a theme that has, at least in the last two hundred and fifty years, deeply bothered many biblically formed people. How could the sacred Word of God speak so blithely of this horrific practice, calmly laying out certain restrictions and caveats while seeming to overlook that slavery is in itself a moral outrage? And to be sure, "positive" or at least morally bland references to slavery can be found throughout the Bible, both Old Testament and New, a fact often averred to by defenders of the practice as late as the mid-nineteenth century. A distinction made by the contemporary theologian William Placher is useful here—namely, between what is in the Bible and what the Bible teaches.[18] There is no question that approbation of slavery is "in the Bible," but what so many of those opponents of slavery throughout history, who drew inspiration precisely from the Scriptures, clearly show is that the practice is not necessarily "what the Bible teaches." To determine this latter truth, we must attend not simply to individual passages, but rather to the overarching themes, patterns, and trajectories of the entire Bible. With that

18. William C. Placher, "Contemporary Confession and Biblical Authority," in *To Confess the Faith Today*, ed. Jack L. Stotts and Jane Dempsey Douglass (Louisville, KY: Westminster / John Knox, 1990), 66.

principle in mind, one might remark that the Scripture's clear insistence upon the dignity of the individual, the command to love even our enemies, the injunction to care for the most vulnerable, the universality of the offer of salvation, and many other related motifs besides, and conclude, along with many fervently Christian abolitionists of the eighteenth and nineteenth centuries, that the Bible does not in fact teach the moral legitimacy of slavery.

A second theme from this section that I should like to consider is the so-called *lex talionis*, which is formulated in Exodus 21:23–25: "If any harm follows, then you shall give life for life, eye for eye, tooth for tooth, hand for hand, foot for foot, burn for burn, wound for wound, stripe for stripe." On the face of it, this prescription seems brutal indeed, but we must consider it within the cultural framework of the time and in light of the natural tendencies of aggrieved human beings. First, a consensus of commentators from both antiquity and the medieval period is that the intention of the author is to provide a rational basis for a monetary compensation for an offense.[19] Knowing full well that it would be next to impossible to apply this law literally in regard to partial injuries, the biblical lawmakers were providing a template for at least relatively accurate monetary settlements. A second observation is that, if anything, the *lex talionis* sets a severe limit to brutality. In the heat of anger and filled with resentment, most wounded parties would seek revenge in a completely disproportionate manner—say, killing a man for robbery. By setting offense and retribution in such tight correlation, this famous law constrains the furies rather than unleashing them.

Having glanced at these particular applications of the moral law, we turn to the crucially important twenty-fourth chapter of Exodus, wherein the renewed covenant between God and his people is sealed, and Moses and a handful of his colleagues are

19. See, for example, *Bava Kamma* 83b, in *Koren Talmud Bavli: Noé Edition*, vol. 23, *Bava Kamma Part 1*, ed. Adin Even-Israel Steinsaltz (Jerusalem: Koren, 2016); Moses Maimonides, "The Laws of Injury and Damages," in *Mishneh Torah: Sefer Neziki (The Book of Damages)*, trans. Eliyahu Touger (Brooklyn, NY: Moznaim, 1997).

given an intimate experience of the Lord. Both of these serve as a propaedeutic to the lengthy discussion, in the remainder of Exodus, of the liturgical life of Israel, its worshipful intimacy with the God who created and liberated them. In a manner meant to evoke the various sections of the tabernacle and eventually the Jerusalem temple, the author tells us how the vast multitude of the people stay at a distance, at the foot of Mt. Sinai, while Aaron, Nadab, and Abihu, along with seventy elders, climb the height with Moses. But they then remain at a certain remove, and Moses alone goes to the summit to commune with the Lord. The mystical tradition has read this passage as evocative of the various stages that one must pass through in order to attain intimacy with God. And it construes the climbing of the mountain as symbolic of the arduous effort required to come to a vision of the Lord, even as it sees the invitation offered to Moses alone as an indication that real closeness with the Creator of the world is possible only through the free gift of grace.[20]

Having seen and spoken with God, Moses then comes back down the mountain to tell the people what he had heard, and they respond, "Everything that the LORD has spoken we will do" (Exod. 19:8). In light of the troubled story that will follow, this confident affirmation can only strike us as sadly ironic. Subsequently, Moses constructs an altar, a place of worship, at the foot of Sinai and erects twelve pillars to evoke the tribes of Israel. Then, in one of the most striking gestures recorded in the Old Testament, he takes the blood of sacrificed oxen into bowls and splashes some on the altar and some, astonishingly, on the people themselves, sealing the covenant between God and Israel. Both the covenant of Noah and the covenant of Abraham involved the slaughter of animals, but in neither case were human beings literally covered in the blood of those animals. Since blood symbolizes life, the gesture indicates that, in exchange for their moral and liturgical

20. See, for example, Gregory of Nyssa, *The Life of Moses* 1.43–46; John of the Cross, *The Ascent of Mount Carmel* 1.5.6–7.

rectitude, God would give Israel his very life. Of course, Christians see in this an anticipation of the unsurpassably sacred moment when, at the climax of his life, Jesus takes a cup of Passover wine and declares it the chalice of his Blood, the Blood of the new and everlasting covenant, and then invites his disciples to drink it, taking his lifeblood into themselves. And they cannot help but see the blood of Jesus staining the altar of the cross as a fulfillment of Moses' splashing of blood on the altar at the foot of Sinai.

What follows is one of the most beautiful and mysterious passages in the Old Testament. After the covenant has been ratified, Moses and his three intimate colleagues, Aaron, Nadab, and Abihu, along with the seventy elders, go to the top of the mountain, and they see the God of Israel. Since the great tradition both biblical and theological has identified the seeing of God as the culmination of the spiritual life, we must attend to this scene with special care. God is presented in a straightforwardly anthropomorphic way, as is typically the case in the first two books of the Bible. We are even told that he has feet, for "under his feet there was something like a pavement of sapphire stone," and that he has a hand, which he refrained from laying on the heads of his visitors (Exod. 24:10–11). We should not literalize this language, for how could the Creator of the universe in its every detail be simply identified with an ordinary creature within the universe? As the biblical revelation unfolds, the implications of this theology of the Creator become ever clearer, and God is more typically characterized as a transcendent spirit. However, the literal language does serve the purpose of highlighting the intimacy of the encounter with God, along the lines of friends coming together. Sounding a theme that is heard up and down the Bible, the author of Exodus tells us that "they ate and drank" with the Lord (Exod. 24:11). From the meal laid out in the Garden of Eden ("You may freely eat of every tree of the garden" [Gen. 2:16]), through the Passover supper and Jesus' open table-fellowship, to the heavenly banquet promised in Isaiah (Isa. 25:6–10), we find that the consummation of the divine-human relationship is likened to the sharing of food and drink. This master metaphor of festivity and interactivity serves to balance the perhaps too static and passive simile of seeing.

We are indeed told that the men saw God, but the author draws our attention away from God to the "pavement of sapphire stone, like the very heaven for clearness" that lay under the deity's feet (Exod. 24:10). The point is that even as they see God, they don't see him; even as they come into God's presence, their eyes are drawn to the floor. The spiritual and theological tradition will develop this insight in remarkable ways, suggesting that even in heaven, even as the blessed enjoy the vision of God, they remain still hungry and thirsty for more. As Thomas Aquinas puts it, what the saints see for the first time in heaven is just *how incomprehensible* God is.[21] Mind you, this is not meant to be a discouraging proposal, but a hopeful one: the more the blessed drink, the more they want; the more they know, the more they want to know. Heaven, on this reading, is endless exploration into the mystery of God.

After the sacred supper, God invites Moses to come with him alone and to receive the Law inscribed by the Lord on tables of stone. The stability of the stone symbolically evokes, of course, the permanence and reliability of the moral law, but it is also worth noting that the prophet Jeremiah will predict the day when God writes the Law not on stone but on the heart (Jer. 31:33). The Law inscribed on the tablets of Sinai is still, to a degree, a heteronomous imposition, a rule coming from outside as a limit on Israel's sinful inclinations. But the ultimate goal is to make the transition from heteronomy to theonomy, the Law becoming second nature to Israel, carved into the hearts and minds of God's people.

As chapter 24 comes to a close, we hear of still another meeting between God and Moses, each detail of which carries

21. Thomas Aquinas, *Summa theologiae* Suppl. 3.92.3.

important symbolic significance. As Moses goes, once more, up the mountain, he finds Sinai covered in smoke. We have been told of seeing God, but that seeing is always a sort of non-seeing, precisely because the unconditioned reality cannot become, in any ordinary sense, an object for a finite sensorium or consciousness. Even as we construct metaphors and conceptual analogies for God, we recall the words of the Fourth Lateran Council: *in tanta similitudine maior dissimilitudo* (in however great a similarity, a greater dissimilarity).[22] Nevertheless, we are told of the "glory" of the Lord settling on Sinai. The Hebrew word at play here is *kabod*, which can carry the sense of "weight" and also "splendor." Both meanings are probably intended, for by "weight" we understand the supreme importance of God, the simple fact that communion with him outweighs any other consideration, and by "splendor" we understand his unsurpassable beauty and attractiveness. God's truth appeals to the mind and his goodness to the will, but his beauty calls forth a value response from what we might term the "heart," the seat of affectivity. "Glory" in this latter sense has to involve visibility, and hence it serves to balance the obscurity implied in the image of the cloud.

We hear that the glorious cloud covered Sinai for six days and that on the seventh, God called to Moses out of the splendid obscurity. The play of six and seven calls to mind the work of creation and the sabbath that follows, insinuating that the most intense communion with the Creator takes place on the day of rest when Israel sets down its practical tasks and worships the Lord. Once again, the priestly quality of the holy people is stressed, as well as the enduring significance of right praise in the life of Israel. Before bringing this astonishing chapter to a close, the author of Exodus shares one last image. In a rather cinematic manner, he

---

22. This maxim paraphrases the Latin text of the Fourth Lateran Council, which reads: "*Quia inter creatorem et creaturam non potest tanta similitudo notari, quin inter eos maior sit dissimilitudo notanda.*" (For between Creator and creature no similitude can be expressed without implying a greater dissimilitude.) *Compendium of Creeds*, ed. Denzinger et al., no. 806, 269.

moves us from Moses' point of view to that of the people gathered in wonder at the foot of the mountain. From their perspective, the glorious cloud looks like "a devouring fire." To be sure, God's appearance and activity are often compared to fire in the biblical texts. Fire rains down in judgment on Sodom and Gomorrah (Gen. 19:24); fire comes from heaven to consume the sacrifice of Elijah on Mt. Carmel (1 Kings 18:38); Jesus says that he has come to light a fire upon the earth (Luke 12:49); the Holy Spirit appears to the Apostles at Pentecost as tongues of fire (Acts 2:3); the author of the Letter to the Hebrews compares God to a "consuming fire" (Heb. 12:29). Is there any natural element that is, at the same time, as dangerous and as compelling as fire? We rightly are frightened at the prospect of the pain and devastation that fire can cause, and yet most of us are drawn irresistibly to witness the beauty of fire. So it goes with God, who is, as Rudolf Otto famously described him, *tremendum et fascinans* (both terrifying and fascinating).[23]

TABERNACLE, WORSHIP, AND SACRIFICE

Immanuel Kant gave voice to a perspective that is, today, the default position for the majority of people in the West—namely, that religion has fundamentally to do with ethics. In his widely influential text *Religion Within the Limits of Reason Alone*, Kant argued that most of the beliefs and practices that we associate with religion—sacraments, prayer, liturgy, ritual, doctrine, creeds, etc.—are finally about making us ethically upright. When we focus on those secondary matters for their own sake, we are alienated from the true purpose of religion. The Kantian perspective would be expressed by many today along these lines: "As long as you are a decent person, it doesn't really matter what you believe or how you worship." Say what you will about Kant's account, the author of the book of Exodus would rather emphatically take issue with it. For almost all of the final fifteen chapters of Exodus

23. Rudolf Otto, *The Idea of the Holy*, 2nd ed., trans. John W. Harvey (Oxford: Oxford University Press, 1958), 12–24, 31–40.

69

are dedicated to priesthood, sacrifice, ritual, and liturgy, and no indication whatsoever is given that these matters are somehow less important than the moral law discussed so thoroughly in the preceding five chapters. In point of fact, given that Exodus is followed by the twenty-seven chapters of the book of Leviticus, almost entirely dedicated to a discussion of matters liturgical and ritual, we might be forgiven for thinking just the opposite.

Just after the intense encounter in the luminous cloud, God tells Moses to instruct the people to gather up a variety of precious things: "gold, silver, and bronze, blue, purple, and crimson yarns and fine linen, goats' hair, tanned rams' skins, fine leather, acacia wood, oil for the lamps, spices for the anointing oil and for the fragrant incense, onyx stones and gems to be set in the ephod and for the breastpiece" (Exod. 25:3–7). All of this will be for the purpose of constructing a sanctuary or a tabernacle in the wilderness as a dwelling place for God. Since the people is on the move, this cannot be a permanent structure, but rather something like an elaborate tent, which the people could strike and pitch as needed. That said, it seems rather clear that what is being described is in fact a fairly close approximation of the Jerusalem temple, already destroyed and rebuilt at the time when the book of Exodus was being finally edited. The tabernacle will be, in any case, the successor of the mount of Eden, Mt. Moriah, Jacob's stone, and Mt. Sinai—which is to say, a place of prayerful encounter between the liberating God and his people. The Lord tells Moses to make this structure "in accordance with all that I show you concerning the pattern of the tabernacle and of all its furniture" (Exod. 25:9). In a way at least vaguely evocative of Plato's demiurgos making the world according to the pattern of the preexisting forms,[24] God will determine the production of the tabernacle as a sort of earthly representation of the heavenly temple. The implication, made fully explicit in the final book of the Bible, is that the worship offered

24. Plato, *Timaeus* 29a.

by God's people below points to the perfect worship offered by the saints and angels in the heavenly tabernacle.

We learn that the tabernacle is to be divided into three major sections: a large public court and then a smaller section, the place of worship proper, divided into the Holy Place and the Holy of Holies where the ark of the covenant was to be reserved. The theme of division and separation is an important one in the Scriptures since the very notion of holiness involves the state of being set apart. Israel will be a holy people in the measure that they are other than the peoples who surround them, just as God is other than the world he has made. We might think in this context of the walls of Jerusalem that were considered so crucial for the maintenance of the integrity of the people Israel. Thus, the tabernacle as such is separated from the general environment, but then, within the overall structure, further separations are maintained, until we come to the small space of the Holy of Holies.

The construction of the Ark is described in intimate detail: "They shall make an ark of acacia wood; it shall be two and a half cubits long, a cubit and a half wide, and a cubit and a half high. You shall overlay it with pure gold, inside and out you shall overlay it. . . . You shall make two cherubim of gold; you shall make them of hammered work, at the two ends of the mercy seat . . . you shall make the cherubim at its two ends. The cherubim shall spread out their wings above. . . . They shall face one to another" (Exod. 25:10–20). Next come the instructions for the making of a gold-plated table on which plates of incense, flagons, bowls, and "the bread of the Presence" shall be placed (Exod. 25:23–30). The bread of the Presence (or perhaps of the "Face") were twelve loaves, evocative of the tribes of Israel, which were offered symbolically to the Lord on a weekly basis and which only the priests were permitted to eat. Finally, we learn how an elaborate menorah of pure gold is to be constructed: "The base and the shaft of the lampstand shall be made of hammered work; its cups, its calyxes, and its petals shall be of one piece with it; and there shall be six branches going out of its sides" (Exod. 25:31–32). The menorah, which had the practical value of lighting up the Holy Place, probably had a complex symbolic meaning as well. It has been suggested that it was meant to evoke the light that was the first of God's creatures, the six days of creation, and the identity of Israel as the light of the nations.

We also find numerous verses in chapters 26 and 27 dedicated to a description of the walls, decorative hangings, and curtains around and inside the tabernacle. Here is just a small sample: "There shall be fifteen cubits of hangings on the other side, with three pillars and three bases. For the gate of the court there shall be a screen twenty cubits long, of blue, purple, and crimson yarns, and of fine twisted linen, embroidered with needlework" (Exod. 27:15–16). The variety of colors probably served to symbolize the variety of elements that make up the cosmos, since the tabernacle of Israel, the place where the God of all creation is rightly praised, has a properly cosmic purpose.

Chapters 28, 29, and 30 are dedicated to the choosing, clothing, and ordaining of priests for the tabernacle. Once more, since the overall identity of Israel is that of a "priestly" people, or a nation who gives God right praise, the author of Exodus is massively interested in this small caste within Israel—the sons of Aaron and, more generally, the tribe of Levi—who, in a formal sense, will perform the rituals of sacrifice, prayer, and praise. Again, I might offer just a small sample of these instructions: "These are the vestments that they shall make: a breastpiece, an ephod, a robe, a chequered tunic, a turban, and a sash. When they make these sacred vestments for your brother Aaron and his sons to serve me as priests, they shall use gold, blue, purple, and crimson yarns, and fine linen" (Exod. 28:4–5). The ceremony of anointing comes in for special attention: "For Aaron's sons you shall make tunics and sashes and headdresses. . . . You shall put them on your brother Aaron, and on his sons with him, and shall anoint them and ordain them and consecrate them, so that they may serve me as priests" (Exod. 28:40–41). Set apart by their lineage, by their distinctive vestments, and by their sacred ordination, the priests will offer sacrifice on behalf of the people and will be permitted to operate within the sanctuary. The sacrificial dimension of their priestly work is given special emphasis in the striking description of the ordination ritual: "Now this is what you shall do to them to consecrate them, so that they may serve me as priests. Take one young bull and two rams without blemish, and unleavened bread, unleavened cakes mixed with oil, and unleavened wafers spread with oil. . . . You shall bring the bull in front of the tent of meeting. Aaron and his sons shall lay their hands on the head of the bull, and you shall slaughter the bull before the LORD" (Exod. 29:1–2, 10–11). Like Noah, Abraham, Jacob, and Moses before them, these ordained priests of the tabernacle (and later the temple) will bring the people close to God precisely through this symbolic gesture of returning to God what God has already given, establishing a loop of grace, gift returned in thanksgiving for gift given.

Having surveyed these extraordinary and lengthy treatments of the decoration, furnishings, and activities of the tabernacle, we are perhaps permitted to wonder what precisely was the point of all of it. Once again, as post-Kantians, we are comfortable with the notion that right moral behavior ought to accompany one's belief in God, but is so much liturgical fussing really necessary? Thomas Aquinas, whose treatments of what he calls the ceremonial precepts of the Old Law are among the most extensive in the *Summa theologiae*, would answer yes. It is instructive to see how the medieval *magister sacrae paginae* (master of the sacred page) deals with the standard objection to what is being laid out in this section of the book of Exodus. In question 102 of the *prima secundae* of the *Summa*, Thomas considers this issue. To the objector who would maintain that there is no sufficient reason for these ceremonial laws, Thomas explains that there are two foci to divine worship—namely, the God who is adored and the human beings who offer the adoration. In regard to God himself, there is absolutely no need for any of this liturgical display or for a particular place of worship since the immaterial God is "confined to no bodily space."[25] It is not the case that the tabernacle is literally God's unique habitation, which Thomas further demonstrates through appeal to 1 Kings: "But will God indeed dwell on the earth? Even heaven and the highest heaven cannot contain you, much less this house that I have built!" (1 Kings 8:27). On the other hand, in regard to the people Israel, "there was need for a special tabernacle or temple to be set up for the worship of God," since human beings possess bodies and a sensorium.[26] Once again, in accord with the consistent biblical principle, *we* need right praise in order to find spiritual and moral equilibrium, and we require that that praise be expressed in a bodily manner lest it devolve into an abstraction. Thomas makes another intriguing observation in this context. Insisting once again that the purely immaterial God cannot be confined in an earthly structure, he nevertheless asserts that the tabernacle is the place where the *name* of God is specially reverenced. Thomas again quotes Solomon, who calls the temple the place of which God said, "My name shall be there" (1 Kings 8:29), concluding, "From this it is evident that the house of the sanctuary was set up, not in order to contain God, as abiding therein locally, but that God might be made known there by means of things done and said there."[27]

Thomas makes a further clarification, grounded in the revelation of Christ as the true temple or place of right worship (John 2:13–22). Once we understand that Jesus is himself the right ordering of divinity and humanity, we can appreciate all of the practices, accoutrements, decorations, and sacrifices of the tabernacle as prefigurements of Christ's own beautiful and enduring sacrifice of praise offered on the cross. And indeed, light, bread, altar, blood, priesthood, sacrifice, temple veil, etc. are all referenced in the Gospel accounts of Jesus' death.

25. Thomas Aquinas, *Summa theologiae* 1-2.102.4 ad 1.
26. Thomas Aquinas, 1-2.102.4 ad 1.
27. Thomas Aquinas, 1-2.102.4 ad 1.

The book of Exodus ends with a mention of the cloud of God's glory that covers the tent of meeting. We will find the same visual motif in 1 Kings, when, upon the dedication of the great temple, God's presence is signaled by a thick smoke that fills the place (1 Kings 8:10–11). Once again, the true God, though immanent, even palpably so, can never be seen with our eagle eyes or controlled by our categorizing minds. The incense used at Catholic and Orthodox liturgies to this day makes much the same point.

And when the cloud goes up from the temple, it is the signal to Israel that it is time to move. We are dealing, after all, not with a fixed edifice but with a tent, ready to be struck. So Israel wanders until it finds its true home, thus evoking the spiritual unmooredness that is typical of those who seek after God in this world. Following the cloud, Israel is finding its way in relation to its right worship of God, spelled out so clearly in the final chapters of Exodus.

Leviticus

Both Genesis and Exodus contain puzzlements and passages both dry and deeply strange, but both books are also filled with some of the most affecting and theologically powerful stories ever recorded. It would be easy enough for any reader to recognize them as "spiritual" texts. It is not quite as effortless to say the same thing in regard to the next book of the Torah, the (at least to the contemporary reader) almost thoroughly enigmatic book of Leviticus. As the title suggests, it is a text of special interest to priests, the sons of Levi, whose vocation it is to give God right praise and to regulate the liturgical and ritual behavior of the Israelite people.

Hence, we find in this shortest of the books of the Pentateuch myriad prescriptions dealing with sacrifice, the proper slaughtering of animals, distinguishing between clean and unclean food, the recognition and treatment of skin diseases and genital discharges, the correct preparation of the altar, the proper vesture of priests, etc. Much of it can seem to the contemporary reader odd, irrelevant, or even offensive, and it would appear, consequently, that she is unlikely to draw any inspiration from this ancient book. But the more one stares at it, and the more one allows oneself to be drawn into its rhythm and world, the more the incantatory quality of Leviticus emerges. And the more closely the Christian pays attention to it, the more she realizes how crucial it is as an interpretive key for the priestly and sacrificial work of Jesus.

One might say that the central theme of Leviticus is separation. We hear how the parts of lambs and birds should be separated in preparation for sacrifice; we learn that clean animals should be sharply distinguished from unclean ones; we come to understand how the priestly caste is to be set apart from ordinary worshipers; etc. All of this is in service of determining how the people Israel should be defined over and against every other nation on the earth, which is simply another way of stating that Israel is and ought to be a specially "holy" people. Now, in accord with the general biblical principle already articulated, this otherness is finally in service of the world, the very distinctiveness of Israel serving as the means by which all the nations, in time, are to be rendered holy. But before it can become a missionary force, Israel has to have a clearly demarcated identity, and nowhere in the Bible are the details of this process of identification more obviously laid out than in the book of Leviticus.

SACRIFICES AND OFFERINGS

It all commences with a call to sacrifice: "The LORD summoned Moses and spoke to him from the tent of meeting, saying: Speak to the people of Israel and say to them: When any of you bring an offering of livestock to the LORD . . ." (Lev. 1:1–2). We first notice that God is inside the tabernacle and Moses is outside of that holy place, signaling that Israel is not fully ready to come into the sacred presence of God. The entire book of Leviticus, therefore, is an extended meditation on how the chosen people, through ritual and moral action, readies itself for this encounter. Just as God called Moses from the burning bush to liberate his people, so now he calls the leader of Israel to form the newly freed slaves into a holy people, and this will take place, first and foremost, through sacrifice. We have already sketched the principal lines of a theology of sacrifice, and we need not repeat the principles we articulated. The act of slaughtering, cutting up, and burning an animal as a presentation to God sums up, in a primordial sense, the identity of Israel as a people who live not for themselves but for the Lord. They are not to gather the goods of the world primarily for their own benefit and pleasure, but they are to see the whole of creation as a gift of God's grace and hence as something to be returned to God as a gift.

The first of the sacrifices described in Leviticus is the holocaust or burnt offering, which is appreciated as an act of atonement for sin. We must not interpret this as a pessimistic and neurotic preoccupation with sin, but rather, with John Henry Newman, as an indication that natural religion has "almost invariably worn its dark side outward."[1] Newman teaches that, through conscience, human beings readily discern two truths, one positive and the other negative—namely, that God exists and that we are alienated from him. Due to this coming together of insights, men and women, from the beginning, have tended to articulate their religious beliefs and practices along sacrificial lines. In a word, they know that something must be done in order to set right a relationship to ultimate reality that sin has rendered off-kilter. All of the details that the author of Leviticus lays out regarding the preparation of the animal for sacrifice—"the bull shall be slaughtered before the LORD"; "the burnt offering shall be flayed and cut up into its parts"; "[the male sheep or goat] shall be slaughtered on the north side of the altar before the LORD, and Aaron's sons the priests shall dash its blood against all sides of the altar" (Lev. 1:5–6, 11)—are meant to express the psychological and spiritual attitude of the one who makes the sacrifice: what is happening to this animal by rights should be happening to me. The cutting, bleeding, and slaughtering are expressive of what the classical moral tradition calls "contrition" or crushing.[2] Once again, God doesn't "need" any of this in either a psychological or metaphysical sense, but

---

1. John Henry Newman, *An Essay in Aid of a Grammar of Assent*, ed. I.T. Ker (Oxford: Clarendon, 1985), 252–253.

2. See, for example, Augustine, *Expositions on the Psalms* 51.21, in *Saint Augustine: Expositions on the Book of Psalms*, ed. Philip Schaff, trans. A. Cleveland Coxe, vol. 8, A Select Library of the Nicene and Post-Nicene Fathers of the Christian Church, First Series (New York: Christian Literature Company, 1888), 196; Gregory the Great, as cited in Thomas Aquinas, *Summa theologiae* Suppl. 3.1.1.

the sinner needs it in order to come, rightly ordered, into the presence of God.

In chapter 2, we hear of "grain offerings" to the Lord, which were probably substitutes for those who did not have the means to procure an animal for sacrifice. We are told that, having poured oil on it and added frankincense, the sacrificer turns "this token portion into smoke on the altar, an offering by fire of pleasing odor to the LORD" (Lev. 2:2). What pleases the Lord is the attitude of contrition and self-immolation of the offerer implied in the outward sign. Then, in chapter 3, the author describes "a sacrifice of well-being," called in other translations "a peace offering" or "a communion sacrifice" (Lev. 3:1). Whereas in the cases of the first two types of offering, the stress is laid upon atonement for sin, here the emphasis lies on the reconciling power of the sacrifice. Returning a portion of God's creation to God as a sign of love, repentance, and thanksgiving sets things right in the one who makes the return. It produces peace in a troubled soul.

Having laid out these three fundamental types of sacrifice, the author of Leviticus goes on to prescribe the sort of sacrifices required to atone for "unintentional" sins of the people, both of the priests and of ordinary Israelites (Lev. 4:2). We need not descend into the details of these rituals, but it is worth pondering the emphasis that the author places on the unintentional quality of certain offenses. Displaying a perhaps surprising insight for someone from the ancient world, he realizes that alienation from God is not exclusively the result of deliberate and conscious choice, but rather can be the function of ignorance, inherited assumptions, bad habits, and other systemic influences. In fact, that Leviticus mentions these unintentional offenses before ever getting to those born of deliberate choice suggests an at least inchoate grasp of what the Christian Church understands by original sin and its enduring effects. We are, whether we know it or not, sinners before we ever actually sin on our own.

THE LEVITICAL PRIESTHOOD

After this delineation of the sacrificial enterprise, the author turns toward the indispensably important question of who would offer sacrifice on behalf of the people. We have already seen a good deal of this in the book of Exodus, but Leviticus gives us a finely detailed account of the ordination/consecration of Aaron and his sons as the first priests. It commences, once again, with a divine summons: "The LORD spoke to Moses, saying: Take Aaron and his sons with him, the vestments, the anointing oil, the bull of sin offering, the two rams, and the basket of unleavened bread; and assemble the whole congregation at the entrance of the tent of meeting" (Lev. 8:1–3). That the entire people are present for the ritual impresses upon the reader that what is going to unfold has an implication for the knitting together of Israel and, through Israel, the world. Priests—which is to say, those who stand as mediators between God and humanity—are the bridge-builders between immanence and transcendence and the repairers of broken relationships, both among human beings and between human beings and God.

We are then treated to an elaborate description of the vestments peculiar to the priesthood, including tunic, sash, robe, ephod, breastpiece, turban, and, on the turban, a gold ornament. It is probably impossible for contemporary Christians on the far side of the Reformation divide not to read this in terms of the distinction between the Catholic priesthood, with its equally elaborate ritual vestments, and the far more austere Protestant ministerial and liturgical style. Suffice it to say, ancient Israel certainly felt that it was important to present the priest not only as a teacher of the word but as a symbolically charged figure, whose ordination set him apart as a sacramental sign. In his famous homilies on Leviticus, Origen, probably the greatest scriptural commentator in the patristic tradition, offers us wonderful allegorical readings of the various priestly vestments, appreciating them as evocative of various virtues that a priestly people should possess.[3] Though rich and suggestive, Origen's interpretations need not be taken as the final word. Indeed, we might be forgiven for seeing some of them as a tad arbitrary and extravagant. Perhaps the suggestion of St. Ambrose is more useful—namely, that the colors and textures of the priestly vesture and ornamentation were intended to signify the myriad elements of the cosmos, united in and through the sacrifices of Israel's priesthood.[4]

What is perhaps most intriguing in this section of Leviticus, considering the rather spectacularly checkered history of Israel's worship, is that, of all people, Aaron should be designated as the first high priest and his sons as the first priests. Aaron, after all, was the one who, due to the long absence of Moses on the mountain, encouraged the people to create the golden calf and then led them in worship (Exod. 32). In a word, he is the archetype of the idolater. And just after their installation as priests, the two sons, Nadab and Abihu, present "unholy fire before the LORD, such as he had not commanded them." As a result, "fire came out from the presence of the LORD and consumed them, and they died before the LORD" (Lev. 10:1–2). Anticipating the story in 2 Samuel of Uzzah touching the tottering ark of the covenant as David was bringing it into Jerusalem (2 Sam. 6:1–11), this narrative certainly highlights the awfulness of God and the utter spiritual seriousness involved in coming into his presence. But more than this, it draws attention to the long history of idolatrous, irreverent, and corrupt worship among the Israelite people. Priests are a glorious manifestation of the holiness of Israel, and in line with the adage *corruptio optimi pessima*, they are, far too often, the source of dissension and scandal—a situation not unknown to us in our time.

And thus we see that, though the priestly offerings in both tabernacle and temple would continue for over a thousand years of Israelite history, the conviction of the people, especially their

3. Origen, *Homilies on Leviticus* 6.
4. Ambrose, *Exposition on the Christian Faith* 2, Intro., 12–13.

prophets and teachers, would be that none of these sacrifices finally effected the reconciliation and atonement that Israel longed for. Again, this was due either to the corruption of the temple and its officers or to the insincerity and impurity of those who offered sacrifice—or to some combination of the two. But in the prophets and Psalms, one can discern a longing that the temple would one day be made clean and that the perfect sacrifice would at last be presented.

It was precisely with this yearning in mind that many of the first Christians endeavored to interpret the death of Jesus, seeing it not simply as a brutal Roman execution or the devastating conclusion to a once-promising religious career, but rather as the culmination, the recapitulation of all of the sacrifices called for in the book of Leviticus, the unsurpassably solemn act by which God and his faithful people were at last reconciled. Anticipating Jesus' mission, John the Baptist declared, "Here is the Lamb of God who takes away the sin of the world!" (John 1:29). In the Gospel of Mark, Jesus himself announces, "For the Son of Man came not to be served but to serve, and to give his life a ransom for many" (Mark 10:45). In his Letter to the Romans, St. Paul characterizes Jesus as the one "whom God put forward as a sacrifice of atonement by his blood" (Rom. 3:25). In his greeting to the seven churches at the beginning of the book of Revelation, John writes, "Grace to you and peace from him who is . . . and from Jesus Christ, the faithful witness, the firstborn of the dead . . . who loves us and freed us from our sins by his blood" (Rev. 1:4–5). In his Letter to the Ephesians, Paul urges his readers to be imitators of Christ who "loved us and gave himself up for us, a fragrant offering and sacrifice to God" (Eph. 5:2). In the tenth chapter of the Letter to the Hebrews, we hear that "it is by God's will that we have been sanctified through the offering of the body of Jesus Christ once for all" (Heb. 10:10). And in that same evocative tenth chapter of Hebrews, we find the verse that can function as the hermeneutical key to the Christian understanding of Jesus' sacrifice in relation to the sacrifices of ancient Israel: "Consequently, when Christ came into the world, he said, 'Sacrifices and offerings you have not desired, but a body you have prepared for me; in burnt offerings and sin offerings you have taken no pleasure. Then I said, "See, God, I have come to do your will, O God"'" (Heb. 10:5–7).

What the first followers of Jesus saw, in a word, is that the sacrifices, first described in Exodus and Leviticus and later enacted in the Jerusalem temple, had been vivid anticipations of the final and definitive sacrifice offered by Jesus on the cross. Another way to state this is to say that the sacred offerings of the Old Covenant had been recapitulated, fulfilled, brought to a new pitch in the sacrifice of Jesus. Just as the people of ancient Israel saw themselves in the slaughtered bulls and lambs, appreciating the suffering of those animals as symbolic manifestations of their own contrition, so the first Christians saw themselves, and indeed all of humanity, in the crushed and broken body of the Lord Jesus. As St. Paul would put it with characteristic pith and energy, "For our sake he made him to be sin who knew no sin, so that in him we might become the righteousness of God" (2 Cor. 5:21). Paul goes so far as to speak of the Father's wrath being poured out on the Son, signaling God's hatred not of his Son but of the sin that his Son willingly bore. If I might adapt the language of Leviticus a bit, the Father's wrath burned up the sin that his Son had become, and that holocaust proved a pleasing odor unto God. And because this offering was made by the divine Son on our behalf and accepted by the divine Father, it became the perfect and unrepeatable sacrifice, the final reconciliation between God and his people.

CLEAN AND UNCLEAN ANIMALS

Commencing in chapter 11, the author of Leviticus offers a finely detailed account of animals both clean and unclean—which is to say, those that Israel is allowed to consume and those she is prohibited from consuming. At first glance, this seems to be the

THE GREAT STORY OF ISRAEL

part of a generally arcane text least applicable to our time and to those seriously seeking to live the spiritual life. To give just a handful of examples, we are told that "any animal that has divided hoofs and is cleft-footed and chews the cud—such you may eat," but that animals that do not fulfill these two conditions—for example, the "rock badger," "the hare," and "the pig"—are not to be eaten (Lev. 11:3–8). Moreover, we are instructed that fish that have fins and scales are clean, while those denizens of the waters which have neither fins nor scales are "detestable." Further, we hear that "all winged insects that walk upon all fours are detestable to you. But among the winged insects that walk on all fours you may eat those that have jointed legs above their feet," including locusts, crickets, and grasshoppers (Lev. 11:10, 20–21). The distinctions appear, at best, comically arbitrary. And did not Jesus himself, as simply and directly as possible, declare all foods clean (Mark 7:19)? So what precisely is the point in dwelling on these fussy, even neurotic, preoccupations with the edible and the inedible? To be sure, many contemporary commentators with an interest in the social psychology of ancient peoples might find these texts fascinating. But once again, why would the spiritually minded reader take them seriously?

I would like to suggest that, in our attempt to understand the spiritual significance of this section of Leviticus, we first look back to a relatively obscure passage from the book of Genesis. The first reference in the Bible to clean and unclean animals is not in Leviticus but in the story of Noah and the ark: "Then the LORD said to Noah, 'Go into the ark. . . . Take with you seven pairs of all clean animals, the male and its mate; and a pair of the animals that are not clean, the male and its mate'" (Gen. 7:1–2). Now, since we heard at the very beginning of Genesis that everything that God has made, including those things that creep upon the ground, is good, and that the ensemble of them is very good, this "uncleanness" can have nothing to do with some inherent ontological imperfection. Nothing in Genesis has a Gnostic or Manichean implication. But perhaps the first mention of the distinction between clean and unclean taking place within a narrative about the general sinfulness of the earth gives us a clue. Might the unclean animals be those who are functioning as symbolically evocative of the moral and spiritual degradation associated with sin? That this interpretation carries weight is indicated in the next mention of the distinction in the Noah story. When the floodwaters recede, and Noah lets the life out, his first move is a liturgical one: "Then Noah built an altar to the LORD, and took of every clean animal and of every clean bird, and offered burnt offerings on the altar. And when the LORD smelled the pleasing odor, the LORD said in his heart, 'I will never again curse the ground because of humankind'" (Gen. 8:20–21). In a word, the "clean" animals are those who are sacrificed for the sake of their "unclean" counterparts. It is not the case that the former are ontologically pure and the latter impure, but rather that, in the economy of salvation, the former have the privileged role of offering themselves for the latter. And might we apply this insight to the relationship between the faithful and the unfaithful within Israel, and also to the rapport between Israel, the specially chosen nation, and the other nations of the world? It is not so much a Manichaean game of good and evil but of the sacrificial love of the "clean" for the "unclean."

This manner of reading finds added support when we turn to a pivotally important New Testament text for Jews formed by the Law articulated in the book of Leviticus. In the tenth chapter of the Acts of the Apostles, we find the story of the vision that Simon Peter had on a roof in the seaside town of Joppa. While waiting for lunch to be prepared, the hungry Apostle falls into a trance and sees "the heaven opened and something like a large sheet coming down, being lowered to the ground by its four corners." Contained in this sheet are "all kinds of four-footed creatures and reptiles and birds of the air." Having surveyed this menagerie, Peter hears a voice saying, "Get up, Peter; kill and eat." But thoroughly formed in the etiquette of Leviticus, Peter protests, "By no means,

Lord; for I have never eaten anything that is profane or unclean."
The voice speaks a second time: "What God has made clean,
you must not call profane." Three times the voice reiterates the
command, and then the sheet is drawn up to heaven. At that
moment, representatives of a Roman centurion called Cornelius,
whom an angel had directed to seek out Peter in Joppa, arrive. At
their prompting, Peter undertakes a journey to Caesarea to the
home of Cornelius, and upon seeing the Roman and his family,
the pious Jew comments: "You yourselves know that it is unlawful
for a Jew to associate with or to visit a Gentile; but God has shown
me that I should not call anyone profane or unclean." Therefore,
he reaches out to embrace Cornelius and to initiate him into the
Church: "I truly understand that God shows no partiality, but
in every nation anyone who fears him and does what is right is
acceptable to him. You know the message he sent to the people of
Israel, preaching peace by Jesus Christ—he is Lord of all." While
Peter was still delivering this speech, we are told, "the Holy Spirit
fell upon all who heard the word," and the Apostle gave permission
for Cornelius and his entourage to be baptized (Acts 10).

All of the interpretive pieces are now in place. The tight
association between the vision at Joppa and the visit to Cornelius
demonstrates that the acceptance of both clean and unclean animals
is correlated to the acceptance of both Jews and Gentiles into
the kingdom of Christ. Indeed, the entire role of Israel in the
course of many centuries was to be a sacrifice on behalf of all the
nations, Israel functioning as the means by which the Gentiles
would be drawn to God. This happened, to be sure, through the
laws and rituals of ancient Israel—including the dietary laws of
Leviticus—but it is brought to fulfillment in that perfect Israelite,
the glory of his people Israel, Jesus of Nazareth (see Luke 2:32). In
his sacrificial life and death, in his Body offered in the Eucharist
and on the cross, the "unclean" are brought close to God. Doesn't
Paul make much the same point in many of his writings? "There is
no longer Jew or Greek, there is no longer slave or free, there is no

longer male and female; for all of you are one in Christ Jesus. And if you belong to Christ, then you are Abraham's offspring, heirs according to the promise" (Gal. 3:28–29). And most pointedly, in the Letter to the Ephesians, "He has abolished the law with its commandments and ordinances, that he might create in himself one new humanity in place of the two, thus making peace, and might reconcile both groups to God in one body through the cross" (Eph. 2:15–16). The clean having been sacrificed on the cross for the unclean, all are brought together as one body in the crucified Christ.

THE DAY OF ATONEMENT

With chapter 16, we come to the heart of the book of Leviticus, for this chapter is an exploration of the priestly activities on the Day of Atonement, the holiest day of the liturgical calendar. To this point, we have been following a detailed description of sacrifice and priesthood, but now we come to the moment when both sacrifice and priesthood reach their fullest expression. We are told that the Lord commences to provide these instructions "after the death of the two sons of Aaron, when they drew near before the LORD and died" (Lev. 16:1). It is as though we readers must be reminded of the dangers of approaching God unworthily before we ourselves enter into the holy place. "Tell your brother Aaron not to come just at any time into the sanctuary inside the curtain before the mercy seat that is upon the ark, or he will die" (Lev. 16:2). The reference here is to the holy day when, once a year, the high priest may enter into the most sacred part of the tabernacle/temple and commune intimately with the God of Israel. That smoke or "a cloud" covers the presence of the Lord is congruent with the imagery of the pillar of smoke that we have seen throughout the story of the Exodus, but, more generally, it is an indication of the otherness and inescapable mysteriousness of the Creator God.

Aaron is to come into the Lord's presence, first and foremost, with a bull and a ram, sacrificing the latter as a burnt offering and the former for his own purification. No priest of Israel can ever forget his own wickedness and profound unworthiness to perform the task that is his. Moreover, he must be clothed in the distinctively priestly vestments that we have already considered. Origen observes that all of the clothing—tunic, undergarments, sash, and turban—are made of linen; which is to say, they are made of plant fibers that come from the earth. On Origen's reading, this will have a Christological implication—namely, that Jesus the high priest is wrapped in the earthly garment of his humanity—but we might also suggest that it signals, in the Old Testament context, the cosmological significance of what the high priest does. Literally wrapped in the earth, his act of atonement will have implications not just for the people Israel but for creation itself. Along with the bull for his own cleansing, Aaron is instructed to take two goats from the people to be used as a sin offering. Placing them at the entrance of the tabernacle, Aaron casts lots, determining which one is "for the LORD" and which "for Azazel" (or for "a scapegoat") (Lev. 16:8). The first he brings into the Holy of Holies and presents to God as reparation for the people's sin.

There is no question that Aaron the high priest represents the people Israel before God, but we must also remember that, precisely as priest, or bridge-builder between divinity and humanity, he also represents the God of Israel himself. We saw earlier in the book of Exodus that the miter or turban worn by the high priest was to be emblazoned with a gold sign bearing the name of the Lord: "You shall make a rosette of pure gold, and engrave on it, like the engraving of a signet, 'Holy to the LORD'" (Exod. 28:36). Enacting his sacred role, he was indeed both penitent Israel and a symbolic representation of the God who forgives. We see this coming together of identities in the central ritual act of the high priest on the Day of Atonement. Entering into the Holy of Holies, he sprinkles blood of both the goat and the bull upon the mercy seat, the very dwelling place of the Lord; then he goes out, passing to the other side of the veil, and puts some of the blood on the four horns or corners of the altar and then sprinkles it generally over the surface of the altar. Going into the Holy of Holies, he is sinful Israel seeking forgiveness; coming out again, he is the Lord God offering his lifeblood for the healing of his people and, by extension, his creation.

Having performed these indispensably important rituals, Aaron finally lays his hands on the scapegoat, symbolically imposing upon it the sins of the nation. Subsequently, he sends the animal into the wilderness, the place of barrenness where the dark spiritual powers hold sway. As the goat is driven out into the desert, the tradition specifies, he is beaten and whipped by the penitent crowd, in accord with the symbolic logic we explored above. Whereas the first goat could be brought into the sacred presence, since it embodies the sorrowful repentance of the people, this second goat cannot, since it symbolizes the pure negativity of sin, that which stands simply in opposition to God, the *tohu wabohu* of moral dysfunction. God loves sinners and forgives them, but he hates sin. Repentant sinners can indeed stand in his presence, but sin is simply cast out.

With these clarifications in place, we can turn to the extraordinary text from the Letter to the Hebrews, which uses precisely this crucially important liturgy of the Day of Atonement to understand the meaning of Jesus' sacrifice on the cross. The author, almost certainly a former temple priest or at the very least someone well acquainted with the rituals and practices of the temple, rehearses for his readers many of the details that we have just studied: "For a tent was constructed . . . in which were the lampstand, the table, and the bread of the Presence; this is called the Holy Place. Behind the second curtain was a tent called the Holy of Holies. . . . Such preparations having been made, the priests go continually into the first tent to carry out their ritual duties; but only the high priest goes into the second, and he but once a year, and not without taking the blood that he offers for himself and for the sins committed unintentionally by the people" (Heb. 9:2–3, 6–7). In a word, he knows the liturgical tradition that has endured from the tabernacle in the desert, through the Jerusalem temple, to his own day. But he is convinced that these acts, as beautiful and necessary as they have been, have not fully accomplished what they were meant to accomplish. They have not functioned with complete adequacy as the bridge between divinity and humanity. In saying this, of course, he was only echoing what many of the prophets of Israel had already said.

But in the dying and rising of Jesus, he sees that the old sacrifices have been fulfilled, that they function, therefore, as a template for understanding the meaning of the death of the Lord. What would have struck practically any first-century person as simply dumb suffering and the tragic end of a promising life is now appreciated as the culmination of the history of Israel and the sign of the restoration of creation. Here is his thesis statement: "But when Christ came as a high priest of the good things that have come, then through the greater and perfect tent (not made with hands, that is, not of this creation), he entered once for all into the Holy Place, not with the blood of goats and calves, but with his own blood, thus obtaining eternal redemption" (Heb. 9:11–12). As "high priest," Jesus functions as bridge-builder, but because he is, in his very person, the coming together of divinity and humanity, his priestly work will be perfect, unsurpassed. At the very outset of the Letter to the Hebrews, we find a Christology as "high" as any in the Gospel of John: "[Jesus] is the reflection of God's glory and the exact imprint of God's very being, and he sustains all things by his powerful word" (Heb. 1:3). The one who is undoubtedly a human being is, at the same time, God, and hence he *is* the very reconciliation of heaven and earth. Priesthood, in the fullest sense of the term, is not simply his function but his ontological identity.

Hence, the action that he took at the end of his earthly life— going to the cross in the course of a Roman execution—was in fact the supreme priestly action, and the blood that he shed was the blood of the supreme sacrifice. Now, since the person under consideration was a divine person, every one of his acts, words, and gestures has an infinite range as well as an eternal significance and application. Therefore, the offering that he made to his Father was not like those made, year after year, by the Israelite high priest in the temple; rather, his was once and for all and of eternal import. It is correct then to understand his sacrifice not simply as an event that took place on a squalid hill outside Jerusalem around the year 30, but also as *taking place* in the eternal temple, what the author of the Letter to the Hebrews calls "the greater and perfect tent (not made with hands, that is, not of this creation" (Heb. 9:11). He is referring here to the heavenly prototype of the tabernacle according to which the earthly tabernacle was constructed, as the book of Exodus informs us.

THE HOLINESS CODE

With the seventeenth chapter of Leviticus, we come to what is commonly referred to as the "holiness code"—which is to say, a series of exhortations and prohibitions designed to render the entire people of Israel like unto God. The central preoccupation of chapter 17 is something that probably strikes the contemporary reader as bizarre—namely, the spilling and eating of blood. Thus, "If anyone of the house of Israel slaughters an ox or a lamb or a goat in the camp, or slaughters it outside the camp, and does not bring it to the entrance of the tent of meeting, to present it as an offering to the LORD . . . he shall be held guilty of bloodshed; he has shed blood, and he shall be cut off from the people." And, "If anyone of the house of Israel or of the aliens who reside among them eats any blood, I will set my face against that person who eats blood, and will cut that person off from the people" (Lev. 17: 3–4, 10). We can solve a bit of the puzzle when we recall that blood was seen by ancient Israel as the premier symbol and sign of life, and since life belongs to God alone, no human being may claim control over it.

God gives life and God alone can take it away, and the life of whatever lives is God's unique possession. Within our cultural framework, this seems anomalous, for we hold that everything belongs to the sovereign human will. But this is repugnant not simply to good ethics but to correct metaphysics as well. As St. Paul put it, "Whether we live or whether we die, we are the Lord's" (Rom. 14:8). One's own life and the lives of those with whom one deals are part of a much larger and more mysterious context of meaning, determined by the divine will. In a sense, everything else in the moral order flows from this fundamental perception.

Now, the reader of the New Testament should be especially interested in this chapter of Leviticus because of what Jesus says and does in the sixth chapter of the Gospel of John. After the miracle of the multiplication of the loaves, a large crowd confronts Jesus in the synagogue at Capernaum. Jesus tells them not to seek for bread that perishes, but rather for the bread that lasts unto eternal life. When they press him, he says, "Very truly, I tell you, it was not Moses who gave you the bread from heaven, but it is my Father who gives you the true bread from heaven. For the bread of God is that which comes down from heaven and gives life to the world" (John 6:32–33). Pressed further, he specifies, "The bread that I will give for the life of the world is my flesh" (John 6:51). At this, they balk, "How can this man give us his flesh to eat?" (John 6:52). And then comes the devastating answer, surely repugnant to Jesus' Jewish audience shaped by the holiness code of the book of Leviticus: "Very truly, I tell you, unless you eat the flesh of the Son of Man and drink his blood, you have no life in you" (John 6:53). If the consuming of animal flesh with the blood still in it is against the express will of God, how much more objectionable would be the eating of human flesh and blood? Given every opportunity to clarify the meaning of his shocking words, softening them perhaps in a metaphorical direction, Jesus intensifies matters: "Those who eat my flesh and drink my blood have eternal life, and I will raise them up on the last day; for my flesh is true food and my blood is true drink" (John 6:54–55). It is remarkable that the Greek term translated in this context as "eat" is not, as we would expect, *phagein*, typically used to designate the way human beings consume food, but rather *trogein*, which has the sense of gnawing or chewing in the mode of an animal. Not surprisingly, many in Jesus' Jewish audience find this too much to take: "When many of his disciples heard it, they said, 'This teaching is difficult; who can accept it?'" (John 6:60), which prompts Jesus to turn to his inner circle and ask, a bit plaintively, "Do you also wish to go away?" (John 6:67).

Now, there is much to say here in regard to the Church's teaching on the Real Presence of Jesus in the Eucharist, but I would like to emphasize for our purposes the extraordinary way in which the book of Leviticus helps to shed light on this famous exchange. The shedding and eating of blood was forbidden because it involved the usurping of God's privileged lordship over life. If Jesus were simply another prophet, merely a human agent, his words would be outrageous, and his Jewish interlocutors would be utterly justified in abandoning him. They are understandable and credible only in light of his properly divine identity. Since God is the Lord of life, and blood the symbol of life, God is indeed permitted to feed others with his blood. In other words, what Jesus says in John 6 does not represent a mere human being arrogating to himself lordship over life; rather, it is the altogether legitimate speech of the one who is in fact the Master of life.

There is a tight connection between the seventeenth chapter of Leviticus and the eighteenth, which deals largely with matters sexual. The link, to state it bluntly, is bodily fluid: blood in the first case and seminal fluid in the second. Both of these liquids are intimately connected to life and the propagation of life, and Israel is meant to be the community that bears the divine life to the world. Hence, the proper management of blood and sex becomes a matter of enormous moment both morally and spiritually. At the outset of chapter 18, God speaks to Moses, telling him to tell the people that they shall not "do as they do in the land of Egypt, where you lived" nor "as they do in the land of Canaan, to which I am bringing you" (Lev. 18:3). Again, the set-apart quality of Israel is insisted upon, and in this chapter, that holiness will have to do with the manner in which God's people engage in sexual intercourse.

We find first a number of specifications of the prohibition against incest: "None of you shall approach anyone near of kin to uncover nakedness. . . . You shall not uncover the nakedness of your father. . . . You shall not uncover the nakedness of your father's wife. . . . You shall not uncover the nakedness of your sister"; etc. (Lev. 18:6–9). Then, we have a clear condemnation of the sacrificing of children to Molech, which could involve either a dedication of children to a false god or the literal killing of children to mollify this deity. Next, we hear the prohibition of homosexuality: "You shall not lie with a male as with a woman; it is an abomination." And finally, we hear a condemnation of bestiality: "You shall not have sexual relations with any animal and defile yourself with it, nor shall any woman give herself to an animal to have sexual relations with it" (Lev. 18:22–23).

Now, libraries of books have been written on these motifs, in recent years especially on the theme of homosexuality, and I have no intention of entering into the details of these debates and discussions. I would simply mention the connection between these various prohibitions and the master command on offer from the very beginning of the Torah and accompanying every major covenant between God and Israel: "Be fruitful and multiply" (see Gen. 1:28, 9:1, 22:17). The God of life wants to spread life across the face of the earth, and the privileged vessel of that communication is the holy people Israel. Therefore, the fecundity of Israel—spiritual to be sure, but physical as well—matters enormously. The propagation of life is, on the biblical reading, perhaps the surest and purest sign of the divine grace. Consequently, we can see, clearly enough, why the various sexual practices just referenced are ruled out of court. All of them are barren, incapable of bringing forth healthy life, repugnant to the continuation through history of the chosen people.

In chapter 19, we find a series of moral commands that are strongly reminiscent of the Ten Commandments, including the injunctions to honor one's parents, to honor God through keeping holy the sabbath day, not to steal, and not to defraud. Something new that Leviticus 19 brings is the command not to reap to the very edges of one's field or to harvest every grape from one's vineyard so that "the poor and the alien" might find sustenance (Lev. 19:10). Of note is the concreteness of the injunction, which prevents concern for the poor from devolving into a pious velleity. We also find something that appeals to our contemporary sensitivity to the needs of those with disabilities: "You shall not revile the deaf or put a stumbling block before the blind." Summing much of this up, the Lord says, "You shall not hate in your heart anyone of your kin. . . . You shall not take vengeance or bear a grudge against any of your people, but you shall love your neighbor as yourself" (Lev. 19:14, 17–18). To be sure, Jesus himself, when asked to sum up the law, made reference to the *shema* prayer in Deuteronomy 6 and then to this last injunction regarding neighbor love. What emerges as unique to Jesus is the radical expansion of the meaning of "neighbor," so as to include not simply one's kin, family, or countrymen, but rather anyone of any background or nationality who is in need of love. Once more, we can see the principle that Israel represents the seed that will, in Christ, burst forth for the benefit of the world.

THE GREAT FEASTS

A final theme from the incomparably rich book of Leviticus that I should like to explore is that of the consecration of time. Commencing in chapter 23, the Lord speaks to Moses about the sabbath day and about the great feasts that ought to punctuate the year. Since we have treated the sabbath elsewhere in this book, I will focus my attention on the great feasts, the "appointed festivals" that particularly sanctify certain moments in time. The author of Leviticus first mentions the celebration that takes place on the "fourteenth day of the month"—namely, Passover—and then the two feasts that closely accompany Passover, the festival of unleavened bread and the festival of first fruits. The spiritual dynamics of Passover—protection from death, liberation from slavery, the eating of the sacrificial lamb, etc.—are well known. The related feasts call to mind, respectively, the unleavened bread that Israel ate in its haste to leave Egypt and the grain offering that it made upon entrance into the Promised Land. Therefore, all of these holy days have to do with God's great act of deliverance and the passage of Israel from bondage to freedom.

The Gospels use these holy days to explicate the meaning of Christ's redemptive work. The Last Supper—which in the synoptics is a Passover meal, and which, in John, takes place on the day when the Passover lambs are sacrificed in the temple, and which involves Jesus' identification of bread with his sacrificed body and wine with his blood poured out—is obviously and profoundly marked by Paschal themes. Moreover, the hasty escape from Egypt, symbolized by the unleavened bread, anticipates Jesus' effecting of liberation from sin, and the offering of first fruits anticipates Jesus' sacrifice on the cross. The Levitical celebrations are thus lifted up into a Christological context of meaning.

Seven weeks (or approximately fifty days) after the Passover celebration is the feast of "weeks" or what would come to be called "Pentecost," from the Greek term for fiftieth. To be sure, this was a festival related to the spring harvest, but it came in time to symbolize the gift of the Law on Mt. Sinai, since that event was seen as taking place around fifty days after the Passover escape from Egypt. Accompanied by wind and fire, the God of Israel inscribed the laws expressive of his will on tablets of stone. The Church Fathers couldn't help but see a link between this first Sinai event and the echo of it on the Sinai-recalling feast of Pentecost, when the Holy Spirit, manifesting himself through wind and fiery tongues, wrote his will directly upon the hearts of the disciples of Jesus (Acts 2:1–4).

Now, these spring festivals were complemented by three fall festivals, all taking place in the seventh month, approximately October on the modern reckoning. These were, first, a "holy convocation commemorated with trumpet blasts" (Lev. 23:24); then the great Day of Atonement, which we discussed in some detail above; and finally, the feast of tabernacles or booths, which was meant to call to mind the time when the people Israel, having fled from Egypt, lived in tents in the wilderness. Though this is not referenced in Leviticus, two customs came to be associated with the festival of booths—namely, the drawing of living water, evocative of Moses drawing water from the rock in the desert, and the lighting of lamps, symbolic of the pillar of fire that guided Israel on its journey.

There is a remarkable Christological connection to this last celebration, for Jesus' participation in the feast of booths is referenced in the Gospel of John. At the beginning of the seventh chapter of John, we read: "After this Jesus went about in Galilee. He did not wish to go about in Judea because the Jews were looking for an opportunity to kill him. Now the Jewish festival of Booths was near" (John 7:1–2). After some hesitation, we learn, Jesus goes up to Jerusalem in secret to share in the feast. In the middle of the week, presumably when the celebration was in full swing, "Jesus went up into the temple and began to teach" (John 7:14), drawing considerable attention. On the last day of the festival, making a clear reference to the customary ritual of drawing living water, Jesus cries out, "Let anyone who is thirsty come to me, and let the one who believes in me drink" (John 7:37–38). And in chapter 8, playing off the tabernacles theme of the lighting of lamps, Jesus speaks out: "I am the light of the world. Whoever follows me will never walk in darkness but will have the light of life" (John 8:12). The implication is clear: Jesus is presenting himself as the God of

Israel who gave the thirsty people to drink in the wilderness and who led the wanderers to the Promised Land, and who now gives life to those dead in sin and direction to those lost in the region of unlikeness.

Just as the rituals and sacrifices of the ancient temple are recapitulated in him—"I tell you, something greater than the temple is here" (Matt. 12:6)—so the festivals that sanctify the rhythms of time find their deepest meaning in him. Chapter 23 of the book of Leviticus anticipates the entire liturgical life of the Church, cycling rhythmically through the year as an invitation to participate in the dynamism of Jesus' life, death, and rising to new life.

Numbers

The book of Numbers, whose name is derived from the elaborate enumeration of the tribes that is described in its opening chapters and again toward the end of the book, represents the continuation of the narrative regarding Israel's journey from slavery in Egypt to the Promised Land. If Exodus told of the actual liberation and the two-month journey to Mt. Sinai, and Leviticus of the roughly year-long period spent at the foot of the mountain while the Lord gave detailed ritual and moral instruction to the nation, Numbers tells of the exceptionally protracted (forty-year) period during which Israel wandered from Sinai to the border of the Promised Land. A principal concern of the author is to detail precisely why what should have been a far briefer transit took the time that it did.

More generally speaking, if we read this narrative as a symbolic expression of the journey from the slavery of sin to redemption, the book of Numbers provides remarkably insightful instruction regarding the myriad ways that we sinners in search of grace manage to get ourselves lost. Throughout Genesis, Exodus, and Leviticus, we are told of the binding covenants that the faithful Lord made with his chosen but often unfaithful people. Numbers is perhaps the clearest showing of the faithlessness of Israel and the most uncompromising articulation of what results from the violation of God's will. As such, it provides a theological template for so much of the prophetic literature that would follow. Perhaps the most vexing question that arises from the pages of the book of Numbers is how to explain the almost immediate and almost total rebellion of a people who had not only witnessed the extraordinary interventions of God on their behalf but who had also been gifted with detailed instruction in the moral, ceremonial, and ritual behaviors that would make them pleasing to God. Why, we might ask, are the prescriptions so minutely laid out in the previous two books of the Bible seemingly so ineffectual in practice?

Numbers opens in most impressive fashion, as the Lord instructs Moses to do a census of all of the Israelite males, twenty years and older, who are "able to go to war" (Num. 1:3). While Leviticus saw Israel camped and immobile, Numbers will see them on the march and spoiling for a fight. A theme that is practically ubiquitous in the Bible is that of spiritual warfare. Precisely because Israel is operating within the theater of a fallen world, its journey with and toward God will always meet with opposition. The road to spiritual victory, as we saw, is *always* blocked, and therefore the people of God are arranged for a military purpose.

The twelve tribes, in full force, are assembled as on a parade ground, taking up their positions on the four sides of the tent of meeting: Judah, Issachar, and Zebulon to the east; Reuben, Simeon, and Gad to the south; Ephraim, Manasseh, and Benjamin to the west; and Dan, Asher, and Naphtali to the north. Like the medallions of a rose window gathered harmoniously around a central figure, the tribes of the Lord are arranged in order around the center, which is the presence of the God of Israel. When this relationship obtains, Israel will remain unified and victorious; but when they seek a center other than the Lord, their consonance, as we will see, devolves rapidly into cacophony.

Once they had been assembled and once the priestly tribe of the Levites had been given final instructions, the nation set out, led by the cloud that "covered the tabernacle, the tent of the covenant." We are told that "whenever the cloud lifted from over the tent, then the Israelites would set out; and in the place where the cloud settled down, there the Israelites would camp" (Num. 9:15–17). The period of immobility at the foot of Mt. Sinai, it is now clear, was a hiatus. Just as Peter, James, and John were not meant to stay in rapt contemplation on the mount of Transfiguration, so Israel was not meant to rest permanently at Sinai. And the Law was, evidently, not intended to be mused upon philosophically, but rather put into action while the people were on the move.

Might we read this entire episode as a reflection upon the pilgrimage-like quality of the spiritual life in this world? There is something permanently restless and incomplete about our life, for we are following the prompting of God, who is leading us somewhere else. Under the rubric of Promised Land symbolism, we are to refuse any and all this-worldly humanisms that would posit perfectibility through economic, political, or psychological reform. The way forward is always the way of obedience to the demand of the unconditioned good, and this does not always correspond to what we consider most rational. Thus, "sometimes the cloud would remain a few days over the tabernacle, and according to the command of the LORD they would remain in camp; then according to the command of the LORD they would set out. Sometimes the cloud would remain from evening until morning; and when the cloud lifted in the morning, they would set out, or if it continued for a day and a night, when the cloud lifted they would set out" (Num. 9:20–21). Why was God operating in this way? Why was there no predictable pattern to his order to stay or to march? Israel did not know. But it was called to obey. Once again, this is not tantamount to a childish acceptance of pure heteronomy; rather, it is a spiritually mature acknowledgment that the purposes and strategies of the one who commands all of space and time remain, necessarily, opaque to us.

Israel—liberated; formed through ritual, sacrifice, and moral instruction; arranged into well-organized battalions; following the prompt of the Lord—seemed ready for a successful march and invasion of the Promised Land. However—and how typical of the biblical narratives this is—they almost immediately fell. Despite all of their formation, they commenced to weep and whine: "If only we had meat to eat! We remember the fish we used to eat in Egypt for nothing, the cucumbers, the melons, the leeks, the onions, and the garlic; but now our strength is dried up, and there is nothing at all but this manna to look at" (Num. 11:4–6). One of the most potent temptations away from following the higher call of God is the attraction of sensual pleasure—the delights of food, drink, and sex. As we have seen many times, the biblical authors are not the least bit Manichean or anti-materialist in their thinking, but they are indeed insistent that the demand of the *summum bonum* (highest good) must take precedence over the attraction of lesser goods. Food and drink are indeed delightful, but if they are pulling one away from the divinely appointed mission, they must be resisted. What is, again, astonishing is how readily the Israelites give in to the desire for sensual pleasure after they have been so thoroughly immersed in the higher spiritual good.

Another form of spiritual rebellion is presented in chapter 12. We hear that Moses' own siblings, Miriam and Aaron, speak out against him because he had dared to marry a "Cushite woman." Fired by both racism and jealousy, they complain, "Has the LORD spoken only through Moses? Has he not spoken through us also?" (Num. 12:2). The nation is on the march, undertaking together a great mission under the direction of the *summum bonum*, and two of the leaders within the community, people who should be especially attuned to the missionary purpose of Israel, are worried about their personal prerogatives. How often this sort of petty rivalry, I must say, obtains within the religious world. After many years of participation in the Church, I can confidently testify that this sort of temptation does perhaps more damage to the spiritual work than any other. The solution to this problem is to look, not around at the advantages and honors of others in the community, but ahead to the cloud that signals the divine purpose.

SCOUTING THE PROMISED LAND

In chapter 13, we find a description of what is arguably the most important event in this section of the Israelite journey to the Promised Land. The Lord commands Moses to send a group of men to spy out the land to which they are traveling. So Moses chooses representatives from all twelve tribes, and this group makes their way from one end of the Promised Land to the other, reconnoitering the territory and retrieving some of the fruit of the land. Upon their return, after a forty-day mission, they report their findings to the community. It is indeed, they say, a land flowing with milk and honey, but it is also inhabited by fierce men, some of them giants. The recommendation of the majority of the spies—Caleb and Joshua the exceptions—is that Israel should not enter this land, and their fearful report inspires great anxiety among the people and, incredibly, a regret that they had ever left the place of their enslavement: "Would that we had died in the land of Egypt! . . . Why is the LORD bringing us into this land to fall by the sword? . . . Would it not be better for us to go back to Egypt?" (Num. 14:2–3).

We have already seen how the desire for sensual pleasure and the preoccupation with petty games of power can distract from the mission; here, we see how fear of the very difficulty involved in fulfilling the divinely appointed task can become debilitating. Though the Israelites had set out as a military force ready to fight, when the propitious moment arrives, they fall back in cowardice. So catastrophic is this decision that God himself is on the verge of giving up on the entire project. "How long will this people despise me? And how long will they refuse to believe in me, in spite of all the signs that I have done among them? I will strike them with pestilence and disinherit them, and I will make of you a nation greater and mightier than they" (Num. 14:11–12). It is only the abject imploring of Moses that dissuades the Lord from this resolution.

Now, though he is willing to forgive the rebels and permit them to survive, the Lord nevertheless imposes a brutal punishment: "None of the people who have seen my glory and the signs that I did in Egypt and in the wilderness, and yet have tested me these ten times and have not obeyed my voice, shall see the land that I swore to give to their ancestors; none of those who despised me shall see it" (Num. 14:22–23). As always, we should read these sentences and punishments of God not as arbitrary or driven by sheer emotion, but rather as expressive of the fundamental moral law that wickedness, spiritual cowardice, and lack of faith have real consequences. Here, we should see that the attainment of the Promised Land—which is to say, the fulfillment of our deepest longings, union with God—is irreconcilable with fear. If we shrink from the spiritual challenge because we are afraid of the opposition we will face, we will, quite simply, never get what we want. God tells Moses that the rebels will all die in the desert, for God will wait them out, preventing the arrival of Israel in the Promised Land until every last one of the complainers has passed away, matching the forty days of the reconnoitering with forty years of aimless wandering.

Lest we see this resolution as simply brutal and implacable, we might consult the formula from the First Letter of John: "Perfect love casts out fear" (1 John 4:18). For John, the opposite of love is not hate but fear, for fear is primarily what locks one into the narrow space of the *pusilla anima* (small soul). The Promised Land, the goal of all spiritual striving, is nothing other than love, for love is what God is, and God is what we all finally want. What is simply incompatible, therefore, with the entry into the arena of love is fear.

THE REVOLT OF KORAH
The episode concerning the rebellion of Korah, Dathan, and Abiram, told in chapter 16 of the book of Numbers, constitutes one of the greatest biblical presentations of the temptation toward

power and position that so often obtains among leaders of the Church. What is particularly worthy of attention is how subtly Numbers lays out the manner in which ambitious people cloak their true intentions behind high-sounding ideals. We are told that the three men, along with two hundred fifty of their followers, approach Moses and Aaron and upbraid them for their illegitimate seizure of authority: "You have gone too far! All the congregation are holy, every one of them, and the LORD is among them. So why then do you exalt yourselves above the assembly of the LORD?" (Num. 16:3). Ostensibly, this is a valid argument, for God has indeed declared the whole people Israel a holy and priestly nation. So why, this trio wonders, shouldn't a strict egalitarianism obtain? Why should Moses and Aaron place themselves above everyone else? In point of fact, it is a specious argument, designed simply to hide the naked ambition of the three. For the holiness of the entire people by no means precludes legitimate leadership or prelature among them. Just as God chose Israel as a nation, so God chooses particular Israelites for servant leadership among the people, which should be obvious to even the most casual reader of the Torah to this point.

Once again, I cannot help but be struck by how contemporary this scene seems. Especially in the wake of the Second Vatican Council, which brought to the fore the altogether valid notion of the priesthood of all believers, some in the Catholic Church maintained that priestly/episcopal leadership is no longer justified and that a strict egalitarianism ought to hold sway in the liturgical and ministerial life of the Church. They were, of course, conveniently overlooking the fact that hierarchy and formal differentiation existed in the Christian community from the very beginning, commencing with Jesus' own choice of the twelve and the seventy-two and continuing through the emergence of the arrangement of diaconate, priesthood, and episcopacy even in the Pauline churches. Though I am hesitant to overgeneralize, often those in recent times who put forward such an argument displayed themselves to be, in fact, hungry to attain their own positions of power and privilege. Like Korah, Dathan, and Abiram, they were piously using the language of equality in order to achieve their own ambitions.

In one of the most dramatic and severe punishments meted out in the Bible, the three rebels and their entire retinue are devoured by the earth: "The earth opened its mouth and swallowed them up, along with their households—everyone who belonged to Korah and all their goods. So they with all that belonged to them went down alive into Sheol; the earth closed over them, and they perished from the midst of the assembly" (Num. 16:32–33). To worry about the apparent severity and injustice of the punishment—after all, why were their entire households put to death?—is to miss the point. What the author wants us to appreciate is just how awfully destructive the sort of ambition for power expressed by this wicked trio is in the life of the community that is meant to be making its way, as a disciplined spiritual army, toward the Promised Land. External opposition to the advance of this force exists, and we shall hear more about it toward the end of Numbers, but one of the most devastating internal blocks to its progress is this sort of ambition among prospective leaders within the army. The swallowing up of Korah and his co-conspirators is the unambiguous biblical signal that God frowns darkly indeed on this sort of maneuvering.

WATER FROM THE ROCK

As we have been arguing, the book of Numbers is, to a large degree, the story of Israel's rebellion against God and resistance to his purposes. Perhaps the best-known narrative of rebellion is the one recounted in chapter 20 concerning the complaint of the people Israel at Meribah in the desert. Having come to the wilderness of Zin, south of the Dead Sea, the people quarreled with Moses about the lack of water, using a now quite familiar formula: "Would that we had died when our kindred died before the LORD! Why have you brought the assembly of the LORD into this wilderness for us and our livestock to die here? Why have you brought us up out of Egypt, to bring us to this wretched place?" (Num. 20:3–5). Once again, even the place of abjection and slavery beckons to those undergoing the necessarily arduous transition to newness of life. Water, of course, is an elemental symbol in the biblical literature for spiritual life. One thinks of the living water that Jesus promises to the woman at the well, water "gushing up to eternal life" (John 4:14). So Israel is literally thirsty but also metaphorically thirsty for union with God. As before, their complaint manifests, at the spiritual level, a lack of trust in the providence of God. That the Lord has been protecting, defending, instructing, and monitoring them from the moment of their escape from Egypt should be blazingly evident; yet they fall back into skepticism regarding God's care for them. How often, in the course of the spiritual itinerary, we reach these points of desperation, these moments when we are convinced that God has abandoned us.

Making this point clear will be the central preoccupation of the book of Job, but we can say here, at least in a preliminary way, that our incapacity to appreciate the nature of the divine providence is largely a function of the massive difference between our capacity to understand reality and God's. Whereas we have command over a tiny swath of space and time, God is concerned with all of space and time. Accordingly, we frequently find God's decisions and actions impenetrable—and thus we complain. Why has God led Israel in the precise manner that he has? Israel cannot even in principle know. Hence, the purposes of God can often seem to us hopelessly obscure.

As is typical, the faithful mediator Moses intervenes on behalf of the people, and the Lord gives the following instruction: "Take the staff, and assemble the congregation, you and your brother Aaron, and command the rock before their eyes to yield its water. . . . Thus you shall provide drink for the congregation and their livestock" (Num. 20:8). As we have often seen, God delights in using secondary causes—in this case, Moses and Aaron—but it is clear that God is the one who will be providing the sustenance to Israel. What follows is one of the more puzzling scenes in the Torah. In the presence of the whole people, Moses shouts, "Listen, you rebels, shall we bring water for you out of this rock?" Then, he strikes the rock twice with his staff, and water gushes forth for the people and their flocks. All seems to have gone well, but the Lord immediately says to the two leaders, "Because you did not trust in me, to show my holiness before the eyes of the Israelites, therefore you shall not bring this assembly into the land that I have given them" (Num. 20:10, 12). The source of the puzzlement is that the misdemeanor of Moses is not immediately clear. How did he not show trust in the Lord? Some have speculated that it was the question itself, which indicated, perhaps, a lack of complete confidence. Others have opined that it was the implication in the question that it was Moses himself and not God who would cause the water to flow. Still others hold that it was his double striking of the rock, which indicated a certain impatience or disobedience on Moses' part.

In any case, we must give God the last word and admit that Moses demonstrated a lack of trust similar to that of the Israelites as a whole. He wondered whether and how God would provide—and this want of faith, the author of Numbers is insisting, is still another crucial block to the progress of the holy people toward the Promised Land. Once again, the punishment doled out to Moses seems rather harsh, but we must continue to read these scenarios of retribution as articulations of a kind of spiritual physics. In this case, failure to acquiesce totally to the divine providence and to trust utterly in its efficaciousness is irreconcilable with entry into intimate communion with God. Perhaps we can take a certain comfort in knowing that even one of the greatest heroes of the Bible, the man who saw God face to face and talked with him as a friend (Exod. 33:11), still struggled fully to see and to accept the ways of God.

THE BRONZE SERPENT

From a Christological standpoint, the story that stands at the heart of chapter 21 of Numbers is of crucial significance. Yet again, the chosen people balk and complain: "Why have you brought us up out of Egypt to die in the wilderness? For there is no food and no water, and we detest this miserable food" (Num. 21:5)—referring presumably to the manna, which God continued miraculously to provide. And so the Lord sends "poisonous" or, in some renderings, "seraph" or "fiery" serpents to bite the people, and many of them die. No biblically minded person could miss the significance of serpents, reminiscent of the crafty creature from the Garden of Eden who lured Adam and Eve into sin. Thus, this particular punishment is another way of insisting that negativity necessarily follows from rebellion against the divine will. Chastened, the people confess their sin to Moses, and the great patriarch, once more, invokes the divine mercy. The Lord instructs him to do something rather peculiar: "Make a poisonous serpent, and set it on a pole; and everyone who is bitten shall look at it and live" (Num. 21:8).

Why should such a suggestion work? We might find analogies in both the physiological and psychological orders. Immunization is predicated upon the principle that a small dose of a disease stimulates the body to defend itself against that very illness; and much psychological therapy is predicated upon the assumption that true seeing of what has harmed one leads to freedom from neurosis and psychosis. And so looking upon the serpent defuses its venom. And if we apply the hermeneutic by which the serpent is evocative of sin, we understand that, somehow, seeing sin for what it is serves to disempower the hold it has upon us.

This interpretation, of course, takes on an extraordinary dimension of depth when we take into account the way this story was used by Jesus himself. In his conversation with the Pharisee Nicodemus, recounted in the third chapter of the Gospel of John, Jesus says, bluntly enough, "And just as Moses lifted up the serpent in the wilderness, so must the Son of Man be lifted up, that whoever believes in him may have eternal life" (John 3:14–15). From another pivotal passage in John—"And I, when I am lifted up from the earth, will draw all people to myself" (John 12:32)—we know that "lifting up" is a reference to his Crucifixion. Thus, gazing upon Jesus crucified will have the same sort of curative effect that gazing upon the bronze serpent had for stricken Israel in the desert. We recall that Paul, in his Letter to the Galatians, says, "You foolish Galatians! Who has bewitched you? It was before your eyes that Jesus Christ was publicly exhibited as crucified!" (Gal. 3:1). Whether Paul was referring to his preached presentation of the crucifix or perhaps to some artistic rendering of it is unclear, but in any case, he *showed* them the crucified Christ in order to effect their salvation.

Paul himself provides the best lens through which we can understand this dynamic when he speaks, in 2 Corinthians, of the meaning of the cross: "For our sake [God the Father] made [Christ Jesus] to be sin who knew no sin, so that in him we might become the righteousness of God" (2 Cor. 5:21). On the cross, Jesus took upon himself violence, cruelty, hatred, stupidity, institutional injustice, scapegoating of the innocent—indeed, all of the dysfunction of the fallen human race. Like a sacrificial lamb, he bore all of it, offering himself on behalf of sinners. Therefore, in him and in his abjection and suffering, we can *see* the effects of sin. However, in his great act of forgiving love on that same cross—"Father, forgive them; for they do not know what they are doing" (Luke 23:34)—he displayed the conquest of sin as well, the manner in which all human wickedness is swallowed up by a divine mercy that is more powerful than anything that is in the world. Thus, by looking at this cross, the place where sin is conquered, we are cured of the poison of sin.

BALAAM AND THE TALKING DONKEY

The story of the non-Israelite seer Balaam and his talking donkey is one of the quirkiest tales in the entire Bible, and, despite its brevity, it has certainly punched above its weight, beguiling the imaginations of preachers and artists and poets over the centuries. Part of its appeal is its oddness and the way in which it manages to evade interpretations that are all too neat. The setting for the narrative is the arrival of the nation of Israel in the plains of Moab, just across from Jericho, where it poses an immediate threat to the tribes in that territory. Balak, the king of Moab, summons Balaam, a visionary and prophet from Pethor, a rather distant city on the Euphrates, in order to formally curse the invading Israelites. That Balak went to such lengths to acquire the services of Balaam testifies to the seriousness with which the peoples of this time and place took curses and blessings. Uttered by the right person at the right time, they were thought to effect significant woe or weal. Obviously convinced that Balaam was accustomed to this sort of transaction, the elders of Moab came to the visionary "with the fees for divination in their hand" (Num. 22:7). When the prophet, at the prompting of God himself, initially refuses their request, the elders return with even more money. Still Balaam refuses, until Yahweh gives him leave, permitting him to go with them but demanding that the seer only do what God would tell him.

Thus, the next morning, Balaam sets out on his donkey with the officials from Moab. At this point, we are told, curiously, that God's anger is kindled against Balaam. Why, we might wonder, would God be irate that Balaam was doing only what God gave him permission to do? We are put in mind, in fact, of the scene in Exodus where Moses was told to return to Egypt but is then opposed by God while he was on his way (Exod. 4:24). At any rate, God sends a high angel to block Balaam's path, but it is only the apparently dumb animal who sees the heavenly figure. When the donkey balks and eventually lies down, Balaam strikes him, at which point the donkey speaks: "What have I done to you, that you have struck me these three times? . . . Am I not your donkey, which you have ridden all your life to this day? Have I been in the habit of treating you this way?" (Num. 22:28–30). Only after this literally asinine intervention does God allow Balaam to see the angel wielding a sword.

We are dealing here with some delicious mockery of the foreign visionary. This supposed high-level spiritual seer, whom prominent men are willing to pay a good deal of money for his services, can in fact see nothing of the heavenly realm. But his humble pack animal can. We learn from this detail quite a bit about the attitude required to become a conduit of God's word. Perhaps the very confusion in the story—Balaam is sent by God and then prevented by God from going—is another bit of mockery: the great prophet doesn't really know how to read the divine purposes very accurately.

When Balaam comes to Moab, King Balak meets him and escorts him to the border of the Israelite camp, where he is expected to utter his formal curse. Instead, he speaks a blessing: "How can I curse whom God has not cursed? How can I denounce whom the LORD has not denounced?" (Num. 23:8). The king remonstrates with the prophet and encourages Balaam to try again, but another blessing comes forth: "The LORD their God is with them, acclaimed as king among them. . . . Surely there is no enchantment against Jacob, no divination against Israel" (Num. 23:21, 23). Balak tries a third time, taking Balaam to a great height from which he can survey the whole of the Israelite nation, and from this promontory, the prophet utters still another, and quite beautiful blessing, constituting in fact what the Church Fathers recognized as a crucial prophecy of the Incarnation: "God, who brings [Israel] out of Egypt, is like the horns of a wild ox for him; he shall devour the nations that are his foes and break their bones. . . . A star shall come out of Jacob, and a scepter shall rise out of Israel; it shall crush the borderlands of Moab, and the territory of all the Shethites" (Num. 24:8, 17).

A number of key spiritual and theological insights can be gleaned from this tale. First, we are meant to see the absolute lordship of the God of Israel over the totality of creation. Though he has specially chosen Israel for his purposes, he remains the

God who made the heavens, the earth, and the sea and all they contain. Hence, foreign kings, pagan seers, and even lowly animals can serve his purpose. Balaam's donkey might be appreciated as a distant relative, theologically speaking, of Jonah's whale. A second insight is one that we have often emphasized—namely, that Israel is chosen not for itself but for the world. Though God undoubtedly speaks in the clearest and least ambiguous way to the prophets and patriarchs of Israel, nothing prevents him from speaking, if he so chooses, through wisdom figures from other traditions, even one as compromised and confused as Balaam. In this regard, we might follow some of the Church Fathers in appreciating Balaam as a distant forerunner of the Magi, seers from a non-Israelite tradition who nevertheless grasp something of the purposes of Israel's God (Matt. 2:1–12).[1] Thirdly, in the odd stopping and starting of Balaam's itinerary, we can discern the inscrutability of God's providential designs. Because he is directing affairs in all of space and across all of time, God's ways, almost necessarily, seem puzzling, even contradictory, to us. The point is that, even in the midst of the confusion, we are summoned to obey, to listen to a higher voice.

---

1. Origen, *Homilies on Numbers* 13.7.4; Leo the Great, *Sermons* 34.2; Caesarius of Arles, *Sermons* 113.2.

Deuteronomy

Practically the entire book of Deuteronomy is presented as a series of extended orations of Moses to the people Israel as they are poised to enter the Promised Land after their long years of wandering. A sort of last will and testament of the great prophet, these speeches constitute the marching orders of the people as they embark upon their sojourn in the Promised Land. That they will be honored largely in the breach—a fact attested to by Moses himself—is one of the sad leitmotifs of the remainder of the Old Testament.

As the book opens, Moses and the tribes have just dealt with Sihon, king of the Amorites, and Og, the king of Bashan, two local potentates who had stood between them and their goal. Og is presented as a quasi-mythological figure, a giant who slept in a mammoth bed made of iron (Deut. 3:11). While the Bible is eminently clear in regard to the internal and properly spiritual obstacles that hinder the advance of Israel, the battles against Sihon and Og, like those against the Amalekites and later against the Philistines and many other enemies, indicate that external, even explicitly military, opposition also rises up against the purposes of God.

Moses commences his first speech with a summarizing rehearsal of many of the mighty deeds that God had performed for Israel during the Exodus and the desert sojourn. How crucially important memory is to Israelite religion, grounded as it is not so much in abstract philosophical speculation as in historical events, prodigious works of God. Moses sets the tone, at the beginning of

Deuteronomy, for Israel as a storytelling people, a nation shaped by narrative, vividly remembered.

As Israel is about to enter the land flowing with milk and honey, Moses asks the Lord, a bit plaintively, whether he will be able to lead them. We have already been given strong indications that Moses' hesitation or presumption at Meribah in the desert precludes his entry (Num. 20:12), but as Deuteronomy gets under-way, we hear another justification for God's punishment—namely, that Moses authorized the spying out of the land, which resulted in the general rebellion. Whatever the reason, God is surprisingly harsh with Moses: "Enough from you! Never speak to me of this matter again!" Then the Lord tells Moses, with what seems a touch of cruelty, to mount to the "top of Pisgah" and look all around—west, north, south, and east—that he might see the land that he will not be permitted to inhabit (Deut. 3:26–27). What is of particular moment here—and it is absolutely central to the Bible as well as unique among the religious traditions of the world—is the frank relativizing of the importance of the spiritual leaders of Israel. In the Old Testament, there simply is no personage greater than Moses. As the only child of Israel who is permitted to speak to God face to face, he is set apart even from Joshua, Samuel, David, Solomon, Isaiah, Jeremiah, Josiah, or Ezekiel. And yet even this exalted man is punished and set aside when God sees fit. It is always the God who speaks that finally matters and not the merely human vehicle chosen to convey the divine speech.

LISTENING TO THE VOICE OF THE LORD

Chapter 4 of Deuteronomy contains passages of crucial import for Israel's understanding of itself and of the God who has summoned it. Moses tells the people that if they follow the dictates of the Lord, the surrounding nations (always a preoccupation of the biblical authors) will say, "Surely this great nation is a wise and discerning people! For what other great nation has a god so near to it as the LORD our God is whenever we call to him? And what other great nation has statutes and ordinances as just as this entire law that I am setting before you today?" (Deut. 4:6–8). We remark that the greatness of Israel is not a function of its military prowess (though it certainly demonstrates such prowess from time to time), nor of its political importance (though under David and Solomon it will, briefly, attain a level of some significance), nor of its cultural attainments (though its writings will indeed be of fine literary quality and its sacred architecture will be widely admired), but rather of its receptivity to hearing the voice of God and its openness to following the divine mandates. If I might put it this way, Israel's importance will be passive rather than active. Their center of gravity will be outside of themselves, and they will flourish in the measure that they accept commands from another.

Jonathan Sacks famously distinguished between the ancient Greek culture, which is ordered to the visible, and the ancient Jewish culture, which is ordered to the audible.[1] If the eye is the principal organ for Greek wisdom—and indeed the centrality of Plato's *eidos* (form) indicates this—then the ear is the principal organ for Jewish wisdom. Moses clarifies this in the fourth chapter of Deuteronomy, reminding the people: "Then the LORD spoke to you out of the fire. You heard the sound of words but saw no form; there was only a voice" (Deut. 4:12). Since God is the Creator of all finite, conditioned things, he cannot be, himself, a finite, conditioned thing—one being, however exalted, among many. He cannot appear among the items within the universe that he has made in its entirety—and this is why all attempts to see him clearly are forbidden in the biblical literature. The auditory, which is heard and then quickly fades into oblivion, better symbolizes spiritual communication than does the visible, which endures across time.

This preference for hearing rather than seeing is complicated within the Christian dispensation, for the Incarnation constitutes

1. See, for example, Rabbi Jonathan Sacks, "The Meanings of Shema," https://www.rabbisacks.org/covenant-conversation/vaetchanan/the-meanings-of-shema/.

what St. Paul memorably referred to as the formation of an *eikon* (image) "of the invisible God" (Col. 1:15). To be sure, the God of Israel, inasmuch as he is the Creator of the visible universe, remains in his ownmost nature invisible; nevertheless, he has taken to himself, in the humanity of Christ, a visible nature that he uses for his iconic purposes. All of Christian art and iconography follows from this basic Pauline claim, as is evident in the anti-iconoclast writings of John of Damascus: we can make images of Christ and the saints, for God has already fashioned an icon of himself.[2]

Now, from this fundamental truth about God follows the first and most basic command given to the people Israel: "Since you saw no form when the LORD spoke to you at Horeb out of the fire, take care and watch yourselves closely, so that you do not act corruptly by making an idol for yourselves, in the form of any figure—the likeness of male or female, the likeness of any animal that is on the earth, the likeness of any winged bird that flies in the air, the likeness of anything that creeps on the ground, the likeness of any fish that is in the water under the earth" (Deut. 4:15–18). Even the most superficially attentive reader will notice the parallel between this extended articulation of the prohibition against idolatry and the opening verses of the book of Genesis. As I argued above, the creation account amounts to a de-sacralization of creation, even as it demonstrates the goodness of the world and its purpose in God's design. Since no creature is divine, *a fortiori*, no depiction or image of a creature can become the object of worship. If I might state this principle in more psychological and spiritual language, nothing in the visible range could possibly answer the deepest longing of the human heart. Moses concludes that the people ought to avoid all forms of idolatry, "for the LORD your God is a devouring fire, a jealous God" (Deut. 4:24). Once more, I would urge you to read this not so much as a commentary on God's psychology, but rather as an observation regarding spiritual physics. When we turn our

2. John of Damascus, *On Divine Images* 1.4, 1.16.

hearts from God and commence to worship something less than God, we are destroyed; we come apart; we are consumed.

THE *SHEMA*

Chapter 6 contains one of the most significant passages in the entire biblical revelation, an injunction so fundamental that the recitation of it twice a day has been part of Jewish practice for nearly three millennia. I am speaking, of course, of the *shema*: "Hear, O Israel: The LORD is our God, the LORD alone. You shall love the LORD your God with all your heart, and with all your soul, and with all your might" (Deut. 6:4–5). We remark, in the first place, Jonathan Sacks' point about the primacy of hearing in biblical religion. Abram hearkening unto the voice of God was the manner in which the entire Israelite experiment commenced, and it unfolded through a long series of hearings, acts of attention, on the part of Jacob, Joseph, and Moses. So, up and down the ages, the summons goes out: "Listen." It is echoed as well in St. Paul's dictum articulated in the Letter to the Romans to the effect that faith "comes from what is heard" (Rom. 10:17) and in the two-millennia-long tradition of Christian preaching to the new Israel, which is the Church. The fundamental problem is listening exclusively to one's own voice; the solution is attending ("Hear!") to the transcendent voice of God.

Now, whose voice, precisely, is attended to? To which God are we to listen? The *shema* carefully identifies him as "the Lord," the one who spoke to Moses out of the burning bush: YHWH, *Ehyeh-Asher-Ehyeh*, "I AM WHO I AM" (Exod. 3:14). And it furthermore insists that this God is the only God, that he has no ontological rivals, that any other claimant to ultimacy must be an idol, for this God is "Lord alone." As inheritors of the ancient theological tradition that flows precisely from the revelation contained in the Old Testament, we are likely insufficiently appreciative of how radical this claim was. The cultures that environed ancient Israel were almost exclusively polytheist. A given nation typically reverenced a number of its own divinities arranged in a hierarchy, and it was taken for granted that other nations had their distinctive pantheons of gods and goddesses. A military victory of one people over another signaled not only the winner's political superiority; more importantly, it meant that their gods were more powerful than those of their enemy.

But none of this is reconcilable with the claim of the *shema*. As Creator of every existent outside of himself, as the sheer act of to-be itself, God is supremely one and incomparable. No conditioned reality, however exalted, could compare with God since God is the one who fulfills that reality's conditions. The one God is the source of actualization for anything that stands outside of him, and hence he is "Lord alone." It is from this ontological claim that the moral and spiritual demand placed upon Israel follows: "You shall love the LORD your God with all your heart, and with all your soul, and with all your might." If the Lord in question were one reality among many, even one god among many, he could not rightfully claim the allegiance of the *whole* of one's heart, soul, and might. He could demand the better part of our devotion but not the entirety of it.

But from this exclusivity, would it not follow that no merely finite or earthly reality could demand even an ounce of our attention? Does not the *shema* compel us to a *fuga mundi* (flight from the world) spirituality of renunciation of anything creaturely? The answer to these questions is no, but we can understand why only if we grasp the peculiar metaphysics of creation. Since God is entirely responsible for the being of whatever he creates, and since the world adds nothing to the divine perfection, in loving God, one is implicitly loving everything that God sustains in existence. This is why the spiritual masters can speak of loving God in the first place and then loving everything else for the sake of God. If we love created things and then love God as a sort of afterthought, we are getting the metaphysics of creation backward and inviting spiritual distortion. To put this in the language of the book of

Genesis, we can indeed love the Lord with our entire strength and, at the same time, eat of all of the trees of the garden (save one). Nothing prevents the one who utterly and completely loves the one God from loving, simultaneously, the good things to which God continually gives rise. Indeed, this simultaneity is precisely what inspires Jesus' own addition to the *shema* of a second law that is "like" the first—namely, to love one's neighbor as oneself (Matt. 22:39). Again, what is interesting is that Jesus does not feel the slightest compulsion to mitigate the exclusivity of the *shema* when he adds the second commandment: the one who is to love his neighbor is precisely the one who is summoned to love the Lord with *all* his heart, soul, and mind.

So fundamental is this metaphysical and moral intuition to Israel that they are told to "keep these words that I am commanding you today in your heart" and to "recite them to your children and talk about them when you are at home and when you are away, when you lie down and when you rise" (Deut. 6:6–7). Though it is subtly expressed, we can sense here the missionary purpose of Israel, for they are commanded not only to discuss this truth among themselves but also to talk about it when they are venturing away from home. So elemental are the words of the *shema* that they are told to "bind them as a sign on your hand, fix them as an emblem on your forehead, and write them on the doorposts of your house and on your gates" (Deut. 6:8–9). How typically Jewish the nondualist, deeply embodied quality of this recommendation is, and how wonderful and mysterious that these ancient precepts are honored in many Jewish communities around the world to the present day.

BLESSINGS AND CURSES
After articulating the *shema*, Moses spells out the chief implication of obeying it and its attendant commands. Israel is about to enter a land with cities that the people of Israel did not build, with houses filled with good things that Israel did not collect, with

vineyards and olive groves that Israel did not cultivate. If, in the midst of all of this undeserved treasure, they forget the Lord who provided it, they will awaken the anger of God, who will "destroy [them] from the face of the earth." But if they accept the *shema* and all of its ramifications, it will "go well" for them, and they will "go in and occupy the good land that the LORD swore" to give them (Deut. 6:15, 18). This sort of promise/warning is repeated throughout Deuteronomy: "This entire commandment that I command you today you must diligently observe, so that you may live and increase, and go in and occupy the land that the LORD promised on oath to your ancestors" (Deut. 8:1). "If you do forget the LORD your God and follow other gods . . . you shall surely perish" (Deut. 8:19). "Be careful to obey all these words that I command you today, so that it may go well with you and with your children after you forever" (Deut. 12:28). "Choose life so that you and your descendants may live, loving the LORD your God, obeying him, and holding fast to him; for that means life to you and length of days, so that you may live in the land that the LORD swore to give to your ancestors, to Abraham, to Isaac, and to Jacob" (Deut. 30:19–20). Many other similar passages could be cited. In fact, the dichotomy between weal and woe is arguably the central theme of Deuteronomy: follow the commands of the Lord, and you will be blessed; fail to do so, and you will be cursed.

This Deuteronomistic principle runs as a leitmotif through the entire telling of the story of Israel, from the book of Deuteronomy itself to the end of the second book of Kings, giving support to Martin Noth's suggestion that this entire body of literature was written, or at least edited, by a single figure.[3] When Israel obeys the Lord, she prospers; when she abandons the commands of the Lord, she suffers: certainly a neat and simple hermeneutic. And since human beings are always wont to wander from the divine demand, it is easy enough to use this principle to explain even the

3. See Martin Noth, *The Deuteronomistic History* (Sheffield, UK: JSOT, 1981).

terrible disasters that befall Israel throughout its history. However, one of the most remarkable accomplishments of the Bible is to have problematized this interpretive framework, even as it puts it forward. If we look especially in some of the Psalms, in the book of Tobit, and in the book of Job, we will witness the questioning of the principle, at least in its straightforward form. Many times those who follow the Lord strictly (Job is a particularly clear case) nevertheless suffer terribly and those who are wicked do well, despite their wickedness. We might look carefully at the passage from the prophet Jeremiah that Gerard Manley Hopkins took as the prompt for his achingly beautiful poem "Thou art indeed just, Lord": "You will be in the right, O LORD, when I lay charges against you. . . . Why does the way of the guilty prosper? Why do all who are treacherous thrive?" (Jer. 12:1).[4] Why indeed? Anyone who has ever sensed what Hopkins and Jeremiah sensed necessarily feels some uneasiness, at least with a simple application of the Deuteronomistic hermeneutic. Nowhere does this tension come to fuller expression than in the theological literature, written by both Jews and Christians, in the wake of the Holocaust. How could the standard interpretive framework even begin to make sense of a suffering so egregious, so horrific?

I wonder whether we might shed some light on this dilemma by interpreting the curses and blessings mentioned in the book of Deuteronomy in a more symbolic manner. Land, fruitful crops, large families, protection from one's enemies, victory over one's opponents are frequently listed as the blessings that the Lord has in store for those who obey him, and exile, famine, infertility, and defeat in battle are, consequently, construed as the curses that God visits upon the disobedient. But as Job, Jeremiah, and the Psalmist suggest, these worldly advantages and disadvantages are not typically doled out in strict accordance with Israel's moral and ritual performance. Perhaps it would be best to read them,

---

4. Gerard Manley Hopkins, "'Thou art indeed just, Lord,'" in *Ignatian Collection*, ed. Holly Ordway and Daniel Seseske (Park Ridge, IL: Word on Fire Classics, 2020), 189.

consequently, as evocative of blessings and curses in the properly spiritual order of things. It is certainly the case that obedience to the divine command produces peace of soul, even in the midst of the worst calamities, and that disobedience to God's will produces trouble in the soul, even in the best of circumstances. Might the Promised Land, fertility, plentiful crops, and victory over one's enemies, as I have suggested elsewhere in this book, represent the friendship with God that can commence in this life and that reaches fulfillment in the world to come? And might the corresponding curses represent the compromising of that intimacy with the Creator, which can begin here and now and reach an awful culmination in the next life?

One might think in this context of Christian witnesses who maintained peace of soul and spiritual equilibrium even while undergoing years of torture and solitary confinement, or of Viktor Frankl, who found meaning and purpose even while enduring imprisonment in three Nazi concentration camps, including Auschwitz. When St. Teresa of Avila speaks of the "interior castle," or St. John of the Cross of the "inner wine cellar," these mystics are referring to the place of contact, at the depths of the soul, where the creature touches the Creator.[5] The blessings and curses referred to in Deuteronomy sometimes manifest themselves in a morally satisfying way in the worldly realm, but they do so unfailingly at this deeper level. When the soul follows the Law of the Lord, it finds peace; when it deviates from the Law, it suffers. At this metaphysical and spiritual level, the Deuteronomistic principle obtains consistently. In so many of the great spiritual masters, including and especially John of the Cross and Ignatius of Loyola, we find a stress upon detachment—which is to say, an indifference toward the goods and evils of the world—as a spiritual ideal: long life or short life, wealth or poverty, sickness or health, psychological

---

5. Teresa of Avila, *The Interior Castle*; John of the Cross, "The Spiritual Canticle" 26, in *John of the Cross: Selected Writings*, ed. and trans. Kieran Kavanaugh (Mahwah, NJ: Paulist, 1987), 225.

equilibrium or anxiety.[6] Detached from blessings and curses in the conventional sense, attuned to the Law of God, a person reaches the promised land of peace.

A PROPHET LIKE MOSES

The book presently under consideration derives its name, Deuteronomy or "second law," of course, from the fact that it largely repeats the instructions and requirements, both moral and ceremonial, that had been laid out already in Exodus and Leviticus. I will not, accordingly, provide detailed commentary on those chapters, roughly eleven through twenty-six, in which these precepts are presented. But there are some insights and observations in these chapters that are unique to Deuteronomy and worthy of special consideration. One of these is found in chapter 18, and it seems, at first glance, a tossed-off remark. Moses tells the people that, when they enter the Promised Land, they must not indulge in the superstitious religious practices of the native people: divination, soothsaying, the casting of spells, and consultation with ghosts or spirits. All of this is quite familiar. But then he adds, "The LORD your God will raise up for you a prophet like me from among your own people; you shall heed such a prophet" (Deut. 18:15). When God further specifies the nature of this coming prophet's speech, we understand how distinctive this figure will be: "I will put my words in the mouth of the prophet, who shall speak to them everything that I command. Anyone who does not heed the words that the prophet shall speak in my name, I myself will hold accountable" (Deut. 18:18–19). Since the Lord has spoken abundantly indeed to Moses, even definitively so, we can only imagine that this predicted prophet's speech will be, somehow, qualitatively different than Moses', more than simply further moral and ceremonial instruction. If he were but another Moses, why would God specially clarify that he (God) would put his own words

6. For example, John of the Cross, *Ascent of Mount Carmel* 1.11.1–6; Ignatius of Loyola, *Spiritual Exercises*, in *Ignatian Collection*, ed. Holly Ordway and Daniel Seseske (Park Ridge, IL: Word on Fire Classics, 2020), 22–23.

in the mouth of this prophet? And lest we are tempted to interpret this passage as simply a prediction of the great prophetic tradition that would follow after Moses, including such unquestionably great characters as Elijah, Elisha, Isaiah, Jeremiah, Ezekiel, Amos, and Zechariah, we must pay careful attention to some lines for the very last book of Deuteronomy.

In chapter 34, after the death of Moses has been narrated, we find this observation: "Never since has there arisen a prophet in Israel like Moses, whom the LORD knew face to face" (Deut. 34:10). Presuming that Deuteronomy was finally edited in the post-exilic period, the author/editor knew the entire prophetic tradition—and yet he could say that this prophet like Moses, long predicted and awaited, had not yet arrived. This is precisely why the passage from chapter 18, coupled with this contention from chapter 34, led some to presume that this prophet like Moses would be the Messiah, and why the first Christians understood it as a foreshadowing of Jesus. In his multivolume study of Jesus, Joseph Ratzinger / Pope Benedict XVI identified this text from Deuteronomy as the interpretive key to his work.[7] The only one who could be greater than Moses, who knew God "face to face," would be he who is God himself, he whose human face was perfectly iconic of God's own face.

"CURSED IS EVERYONE WHO HANGS ON A TREE"
The second passage in this lengthy middle section of Deuteronomy upon which I should like to comment is a peculiar one. It has to do with the disposition of the body of an executed man that has been displayed upon a cross or a gibbet of some kind, likely as a disincentive to others: "When someone is convicted of a crime punishable by death and is executed, and you hang him on a tree, his corpse must not remain all night upon the tree; you shall bury him that same day, for anyone hung on a tree is under God's

---

7. Benedict XVI, *Jesus of Nazareth: From the Baptism in the Jordan to the Transfiguration*, trans. Adrian J. Walker (New York: Doubleday, 2007), 1–5.

curse" (Deut. 21:22–23). One might be tempted to read this as simply one more in a long line of commands dealing with ritual purity, but the Christian interpreter cannot possibly overlook the use that the Apostle Paul made of this obscure passage. In his Letter to the Galatians, Paul said, "Christ redeemed us from the curse of the law by becoming a curse for us—for it is written [and here he quotes Deuteronomy], 'Cursed is everyone who hangs on a tree'" (Gal. 3:13). Death on a Roman cross was not only horrifically painful; it was also deeply humiliating, and meant to be so. To die publicly on such a dreadful instrument of torture was so shameful that it is easy enough to see why it would be considered not only the capital punishment of the state but also as the curse of God himself. Paul sees this as appropriate in the measure that Jesus, taking upon himself the sin of the world, *became* sin on the cross (2 Cor. 5:21) and hence endured the curse for us. N.T. Wright comments that Jesus' remark to the effect that he longed to gather the children of Israel together as a mother hen gathers her chicks under her wings is a pithy description of what happens on the cross (Matt. 23:37; Luke 13:34).[8] As the hen protects her young from a barnyard fire, taking the full effect of the blast on herself, so Jesus protected Israel by taking the full fury of sin upon himself. In this sense, he took the curse that was meant for us. Utterly obedient to the Father, he endured the effects of human disobedience to God—in Paul's terms, "the curse of the law."

This magnificent reversal provides in turn the interpretive key to all of the language of blessing and cursing in Deuteronomy. In chapter 28, we find one of the most thorough descriptions of the blessings that will accrue to Israel if she is obedient to the commands of the Lord upon entering the Promised Land. She will be blessed "in the city" and "in the field," blessed too in "the fruit of your womb, the fruit of your ground, and the fruit of your livestock," blessed as well "when you come in" and blessed "when

---

8. N.T. Wright, *Jesus and the Victory of God* (Minneapolis, MN: Fortress, 1996), 570–572.

you go out." Moreover, "the LORD will cause your enemies who rise against you to be defeated before you"; "all the peoples of the earth shall see that you are called by the name of the LORD, and they shall be afraid of you"; and finally, "the LORD will make you the head, and not the tail; you shall be only at the top, and not at the bottom" (Deut. 28:3–7, 10, 13). The most obvious reading of these passages is that Israel is being promised political and economic well-being, even dominance over other nations, if it follows God's commands.

And as has been often pointed out, the curses promised to a disobedient Israel are even more elaborately laid out than the blessings: "Cursed shall you be in the field. Cursed shall be your basket and your kneading-bowl. Cursed shall be the fruit of your womb, the fruit of your ground. . . . Cursed shall you be when you come in, and cursed shall you be when you go out. The LORD will send upon you disaster, panic, and frustration in everything you attempt to do, until you are destroyed and perish quickly. . . . The LORD will make the pestilence cling to you until it has consumed you from the land that you are entering to possess" (Deut. 28:16–21); and on and on. Once more, these maledictions, *prima facie*, have to do with the material and political fate of the nation. Now, it would be easy enough, as I suggested, to read the subsequent history of Israel, which includes successes, to be sure, but predominantly shame, exile, and subjugation, as the working out of these predictions. But it would be far more accurate to interpret both the blessings and the curses as pertaining to the spiritual order—material success representing the fruits of friendship with God, and material disaster symbolizing the effects of losing intimacy with God. The Christian, accordingly, reads this program in a Christological manner, with Jesus representing both the weal and the woe that appertain to humanity vis-à-vis the Creator. As the great representative of the human race, Jesus embodies, to be sure, the myriad blessings that come to us through obedience, but also the curses that flow from disobedience—not, mind you, that he is ever personally disobedient to his Father, but that he willingly *becomes* sin on the cross and endures the effects of our disobedience. If I might press this matter: on the cross, even as he endures the curses due to sin, Jesus exhibits perfect acquiescence to the will of the Father and hence shows that the blessing overwhelms the curse. In the language of St. Paul, "where sin increased, grace abounded all the more" (Rom. 5:20). Following the suggestion of Michael Dauphinais and Matthew Levering, I might argue that the Promised Land, with all its attendant benefits, is ultimately a symbolic anticipation of Jesus and his Mystical Body.[9] Within the life of the Church—which is to say, *in Christ*—we find the blessings promised to ancient Israel; in alienation from it (from him), we experience the curses.

9. Michael Dauphinais and Matthew Levering, *Holy People, Holy Land* (Grand Rapids, MI: Brazos, 2005).

Joshua

The book of Joshua, which picks up the story of Israel after the death of Moses, presents the interpreter with a number of problems. A first is the historicity of the account. Many biblical specialists and archeologists believe that the sort of conquest described in the pages of the book of Joshua almost certainly did not happen.[1] There is practically no evidence, and plenty of counterevidence, for the massive invasion and suppression of the peoples of the region during the time of Joshua.

A second and more serious difficulty is the frankly jingoistic and racist tone of the narrator of the book. The peoples already inhabiting the Promised Land are presented, almost uniformly, as morally depraved and eminently worthy of being supplanted by the invaders.

A third and related problem is what, at the very least, appears to be a celebration of genocidal imperialism on the part of Israel. Time and again, God himself gives the command to put the ban on the conquered people of Palestine. How, especially in our cultural moment, when the rights and dignity of the "other" are so valued and when schemas of religiously motivated violence are so justly excoriated, are we to make any sense of the narrative and moral thrust of the book of Joshua? Does this book, perhaps more than

1. Martin Noth, *The History of Israel* (London: SCM, 1983), 68–84.

any other in the Bible, not lend support to the very worst impulses within biblically formed people up and down the ages?

I should like to suggest, at the outset, that the very title of the book, at least for Christians, is a key to a correct interpretation of its contents. "Joshua," a common enough name among Jews in both Old Testament and New Testament times, means "Yahweh saves," and of course it is the name borne by the Savior. Therefore, we are meant to understand the Old Testament Joshua and his exploits in light of the definitive Joshua who reveals Yahweh's person and intention in the fullest possible sense. If we find something in our reading of the book of Joshua that is fundamentally at odds with what we know about Jesus of Nazareth, we have, *ipso facto*, read that book inadequately. Or to state the principle more positively, we ought to interpret Joshua as a type or symbolic anticipation of *Yeshua* of Nazareth. This principle was followed, with extraordinary enthusiasm and insight, by the Fathers of the Church, and it will inform my own reading.

The book opens with the assertion that the Lord spoke to Joshua "after the death of Moses the servant of the LORD," commanding him to prepare the people for their entry into the Promised Land (Josh. 1:1). According to our Christological hermeneutic, this signals that Jesus' leadership of the human race into the final Promised Land of heaven follows upon the era of the Law associated with Moses. I am by no means adopting a Marcionite perspective here, as though the Mosaic Law is of no salvific significance, but I am indeed signaling that the definitive Joshua accomplishes a work that goes beyond what the Law, on its own, could effect. He will lead them in a battle that Moses, on his own, could never have won.

ENTERING THE PROMISED LAND

In imitation of Moses, Joshua sends spies into the land. We recall that the earlier undertaking of espionage resulted in disaster, as the spies returned with a discouraging message that led to a general rebellion. Things go considerably better this time, for upon their return, the spies inform Joshua, "Truly the LORD has given all the land into our hands; moreover, all the inhabitants of the land melt in fear before us" (Josh. 2:24). Might we read this as the powers of negativity and sin, the *tohu wabohu*, trembling in the presence of Christ and his company? The timorous tribes of Canaan anticipate the teaching of Jesus that the gates of hell will not prevail against the Church (Matt. 16:18).

We hear that the spies are aided by Rahab, a prostitute living and working in Jericho. In exchange for a guarantee of safety for her and her family when Israel invades, she agrees to hide the two Israelite scouts. The episode concerning Rahab is of considerable interest, not least because she is mentioned in the Gospel of Matthew as one of the ancestors of Jesus (Matt. 1:5). One would suppose that, were Matthew motivated by a desire to preserve the respectability of the Lord, he would have managed to leave Rahab out of the genealogy. But God is pleased to enter into the human condition in all of its ambiguity and moral depravity, precisely because he has come not for the well but for the sick (see Matt. 9:12; Mark 2:17; Luke 5:31). How could a reader of the New Testament not appreciate a link between the prostitute who helps the Israelite spies in the book of Joshua and the prostitutes whom Jesus predicts will enter the kingdom of heaven before the scribes and Pharisees (Matt. 21:31)?

A second reason why Rahab is of importance is that she is yet another instantiation of the principle, rather steadily maintained throughout the Old Testament, that Israel was chosen not for itself but for the nations. Whenever a righteous figure among the "Gentiles" emerges in the pages of the Bible, we are reminded that the revelation given to Israel has a finally universal destination. Though, as we will see, Jericho is obliterated by the invading tribes of Israel, Rahab and her family are spared, and were she not protected, the Messiah himself would not have appeared. On St. Augustine's reading, she functions, therefore, as a type of the Church, somewhat in the manner of the Samaritan woman at the well.[2] Even after a lifetime of sin and ignorance, a person can turn to the God of Israel and find a place around the table with Abraham, Isaac, and Jacob.

The invasion of the Promised Land commences with the crossing of the River Jordan from its east bank. Joshua is instructed to have priests carry the ark of the covenant to the edge of the water, at which point, the flow from the north is halted, enabling the people to cross. The symbolic link to the crossing of the Red Sea at the behest of Moses is obvious and was designed to instill in the people a reverence for Joshua that equaled their reverence for Moses. This sacramental reiteration of the Exodus would be itself reiterated many centuries later when John the Baptist, operating on the banks of that same Jordan River, would lead the people, through the water, from slavery to spiritual freedom and would announce the new Joshua, standing in the river water shoulder to shoulder with sinners, as the leader of the renewed tribes.

Just as the coming forth of creatures from the Creator is presented as a sort of liturgical procession, so here, the entry of Israel into the land of God's promise is a stately march under the watchful eyes of the priests and in the presence of the sacred tabernacle. Though they do indeed carry swords and will indeed eventually wield them, the holy people of God make their entrance into the land of their inheritance as a priestly nation. Joshua selected twelve men, evocative of the twelve tribes, and instructed them to take stones from the bed of the Jordan and to erect them as a monument, thereby calling to mind Jacob's designation of the stone on which he had slept while dreaming of the sacred ladder (Gen. 28:10–19). The clear implication is that all of Israel ought to remember, in a liturgically focused way, this place of privileged encounter with God: "When your children ask their parents in time to come, 'What do these stones mean?' then you shall let your

---

2. Augustine, *Expositions on the Psalms* 87.6, in *Saint Augustine: Expositions on the Book of Psalms*, ed. Philip Schaff, trans. A. Cleveland Coxe, vol. 8, A Select Library of the Nicene and Post-Nicene Fathers of the Christian Church, First Series (New York: Christian Literature Company, 1888), 422.

children know, 'Israel crossed over the Jordan here on dry ground.' For the LORD your God dried up the waters of the Jordan for you until you crossed over" (Josh. 4:21–23).

Continuing the liturgical/ritual motif, the narrator tells us that, before the city of Jericho is to be engaged, Joshua should preside over a "second circumcision" of Israelite males (Josh. 5:2). The generation of males who came with Moses out of Egypt and had wandered for decades in the desert had now died off, and their descendants had, evidently, not been formally consecrated to the covenant through circumcision. This carving of fidelity to Yahweh into the very flesh of Israel will prove essential to their taking possession of the Promised Land, and it symbolically anticipates the circumcision of the heart that takes place through Baptism and that permits entry into the transcendent Promised Land of heaven. Once the men were healed from the wound of circumcision, the entire community gathered for the Passover meal, thereby further consolidating their liturgical identity, and after the Passover, they ate from the fruit of the land flowing with milk and honey for the first time, at which point, the manna ceased to fall. In accord with Jesus' own words in the synagogue discourse recorded in the sixth chapter of John's Gospel, the Church has appreciated the Eucharist as symbolically related to the manna, both being bread for the journey. Once a person arrives in the final Promised Land of heaven, sees God face to face, and eats of the eschatological banquet, the Eucharist, a sign of the Real Presence of Christ, will indeed fade away.

Just before the conquest of Jericho, Joshua has a peculiar encounter. Looking up, he spies a man standing with drawn sword. When he enquires whether the swordsman is of their company or of the enemies, the man responds, "Neither; but as commander of the army of the LORD I have now come" (Josh. 5:14). A fundamental biblical teaching is that spiritual warfare involves enemies we can see but also enemies that we cannot see. Behind the obvious struggles against the forces of sin and death, we also confront, as St. Paul put it, powers and principalities—which is to say, immaterial realities endowed with intellect and purpose. We are also meant to see in this angelic commander a clear indication that the deepest meaning of Israel's conquest is moral and spiritual rather than strictly military. The various battles waged by Israel in the book of Joshua are to be read as symbolic of the spiritual combat against sin in its many aspects.

The Lord announces to Joshua that Jericho will be given over to Israel, but God does not command a military invasion. Instead, he suggests something along the lines of a liturgical procession: "You shall march around the city, all the warriors circling the city once. Thus you shall do for six days, with seven priests bearing seven trumpets of rams' horns before the ark" (Josh. 6:3–4). Movement, music, priests, and the sacred ark take the place of swords, spears, and fire. This liturgical attack culminates on the seventh day, the day of worship *par excellence*, when the people, led by the priests, march seven times around Jericho and then, at the sound of trumpets, shout mightily. Under the pressure of this Israelite orthodoxy, the walls of the city give way and Israel enters in. What should be clear is that we are dealing with a symbolic account of how the earthly city, from the time of Cain and the Tower of Babel predicated upon sin, collapses through the sheer force of a people ordered through right praise. In making this observation, I move very much within the ambit of Augustine's analysis of the "earthly city" and the "City of God," the former invariably marked by some form of self-love and hence faulty praise.[3]

Sparing only Rahab and her family, Israel then utterly destroys Jericho, though she preserves "silver and gold, and the vessels of bronze and iron" for the treasury of the Lord. When the conquest is complete, Joshua pronounces a formal oath: "Cursed before the LORD be anyone who tries to build this city—this Jericho! At the cost of his firstborn he shall lay its foundation, and at the cost of his youngest he shall set up its gates!" (Josh. 6:22–26). A bit later,

3. Augustine, *The City of God* 14.28.

we shall examine the massively complex issue of Israel's brutal elimination of its enemies, but for the moment, I should like to draw attention to the rather obviously symbolic charge of the destruction of Jericho, which is signaled by Joshua's oath. Why would such a devastating promise be made? Why would the rebuilding of a particular city in ancient Canaan awaken such resistance unless Jericho was functioning within this narrative as a symbolic evocation of sin? In the tenth chapter of the Gospel of Mark, we find the story of blind Bartimaeus, whom Jesus encounters on the outskirts of Jericho. Jesus summons the man and asks him what he wants. When Bartimaeus responds, "My teacher, let me see again," Jesus answers, "Go; your faith has made you well" (Mark 10:51–52). With that, the blind man recovers his sight. The rather clear implication of this story is that Bartimaeus' malady, evocative of his spiritual blindness, comes from his proximity to the paradigmatic city of sin. What God had effectively destroyed in the time of Joshua had been, sadly, in the course of many centuries, rebuilt. Jesus has come definitively to knock down the walls of the corrupt city.

Next, we hear of the attack on the city of Ai. As a preliminary move, Joshua sends a small contingent of about three thousand men against the Amorite city, but the force is easily repulsed, sending Joshua and all of the Israelite leadership into a depression: "Then Joshua tore his clothes, and fell to the ground on his face before the ark of the LORD until the evening, he and the elders of Israel; and they put dust on their heads" (Josh. 7:6). It soon becomes apparent that the reason for the debacle was that Israel "broke faith in regard to the devoted things" taken at the conquest of Jericho (Josh. 7:1). The entire population had been placed under the ban, and all of the silver and gold recovered from the conquered city was meant to be consecrated to the Lord. Since Israel was derelict in following this latter command, they were punished at the gates of Ai. Once again, I would strongly suggest a liturgical interpretation of this military enterprise. Whatever in Jericho smacked of unorthodox praise was meant to be obliterated, and whatever remained morally and spiritually neutral was to be turned to the worship of God. When certain Israelites used the wealth of Jericho, therefore, for their own private gain, they were failing to live up to their proper vocation as a priestly people. We notice how the Lord explains the setback at Ai: "They have taken some of the devoted things; they have stolen, they have acted deceitfully, and they have put them among their own belongings. Therefore the Israelites are unable to stand before their enemies. . . . They have become a thing devoted for destruction themselves" (Josh. 7:11–12). In a word, the sacred people had caught some of the virus of the fallen world's false praise—a perennial problem throughout the history of Israel.

Consequently, the tribes are brought before the Lord and by a winnowing process the culprit, Achan, is discovered and the devoted things uncovered. Subsequently, Achan is stoned to death and his entire family and household are burned by fire, which causes the Lord to turn from his terrible anger. In the wake of the cleansing—so similar to the punishment of Korah and his followers in the book of Numbers—Israel advances successfully on Ai and brings it to submission: "Then the LORD said to Joshua, 'Stretch out the sword that is in your hand toward Ai; for I will give it into your hand.' . . . They entered the city, took it, and at once set the city on fire" (Josh. 8:18–19). So total is the conquest that, after the battle, twelve thousand people, both men and women, the entire population of Ai, lay dead. For the next several chapters of the book of Joshua, we find accounts of very similar Israelite attacks and victories. Despite the concerted efforts of a number of the environing tribes and nations, Israel makes its sure and brutal way through the Promised Land, effecting what no one today would hesitate to describe as genocide or ethnic cleansing. All during the rampage, God fights for Israel, nowhere more famously than at the victory over the Amorites at Gibeon, when "the sun stood still, and the moon stopped, until the nation [Israel] took vengeance on their enemies" (Josh. 10:13).

HEREM WARFARE

At this point, we should address with focus and care this issue that bedevils many commentators today and gives fuel to the enemies of religion: How could the God who presides serenely over the bloody conquest of the Promised Land be anything other than a moral monster? The "new" atheists of the early twenty-first century—Christopher Hitchens, Sam Harris, and especially Richard Dawkins—obsessively turned to these and other similar texts to show what they took to be the moral ambiguity of the portrait of God in the Bible. To be sure, the question presents itself frequently throughout the Scriptures, but perhaps nowhere more pointedly than in these opening chapters of the book of Joshua. Before looking at some of the classic attempts to solve this problem, it is worth pointing out that the dilemma is hardly of recent discovery. The great Christian tradition, from ancient times, has wrestled mightily to reconcile these "darker" texts with the New Testament revelation that God is best described as merciful love.

One manner of approach, drawing inspiration from St. Irenaeus, emphasizes the "divine pedagogy" on display in the biblical narratives.[4] The great bishop of Lyon stressed that, in the course of salvation history, God is gradually revealing his nature and purpose to Israel and that this progressive unfolding is reflected in the texts of Scripture. Thus, for example, in certain stories of the Bible, especially from the books of Genesis and Exodus, God is presented rather straightforwardly as an embodied, human-like being, while in later texts, especially in the great prophets, God's immateriality and essential unknowability are insisted upon. On the surface, of course, these descriptions are in direct contradiction with one another, but might they reflect Israel's deepening understanding of God? At an earlier stage of its development, the holy people, borrowing liberally from the theologies of neighboring peoples, pictured God in a relatively crude manner, but in time, under the

4. Irenaeus, *Against Heresies* 3.20.2, 4.21.3.

influence of grace, they saw ever more clearly. By the same token, might the "commands" of God reported in the book of Joshua reflect Israel's relatively primitive comprehension of the true will of God? Thus, of course, the directives given in Joshua are in contradiction to the directives provided by the Son of God in the Sermon on the Mount (Love your enemies; bless those who curse you; turn the other cheek, etc. [see Matt. 5]), but this discrepancy represents an evolution in religious and moral consciousness.

A second mode of interpretation, adopted by the greatest of the Western theologians—namely, St. Augustine and St. Thomas Aquinas—sees the *herem* (ban) carried out against the Canaanite peoples as a delegated exercise of the divine justice.[5] With typical understatement, Aquinas argues that since all people have merited physical death through original sin, God is justified in bringing about their death in any manner that he chooses. In the book of Joshua, this working out of God's justice takes place through the delegated ministrations of his holy people Israel. Hence, the *herem* does not represent a violation of the commandment not to kill and in fact incarnates the divine intention to set the world aright. We might nuance this view by adding that all life here below belongs to God, and hence God can take it as freely as he gives it. Within this Augustinian/Thomistic framework, one might argue that the problem arises, falsely, from applying the same moral principles to the author of life as to human agents. To be sure, it is by no means the prerogative of a human being to take life arbitrarily or without sufficient cause, but the one who is the Lord of life is under no such constraints. In the long run, God, as the ultimate source of being and action, "kills" every human person, violently or nonviolently, by the sword or through disease; therefore, the command not to kill does not apply to him in anything like a univocal manner. Thomas Aquinas utilizes this style of argumentation in justifying God's order

5. Augustine, *The City of God* 1.21; Thomas Aquinas, *Summa theologiae* 1-2.94.5 ad 2.

to Abraham—every bit as shocking as the order to impose the *herem*—to sacrifice his innocent son.[6]

A third patristic strategy—and one with which I most sympathize—is associated with Origen of Alexandria, significantly the Church Father probably best acquainted with Scripture and with the wide variety of interpretive methods applied to it in both the Jewish and Christian contexts. Acutely aware that the brutal instructions given to Israel by God seem dramatically at odds with the God disclosed in the New Testament, Origen makes a crucially important hermeneutical move. He argues that the whole of the Bible should be read from the standpoint of an event narrated in the last book of the Bible—namely, the appearance of the Lamb standing as though slain.[7] We recall the setting: in the heavenly throne-room, the one seated on the throne holds in his hand a scroll sealed by seven seals. An angelic voice cries out, "Who is worthy to open the scroll and break its seals?" (Rev. 5:2). We might reasonably construe the scroll in question as the Scriptures in their entirety, and we might therefore understand the one capable of opening the seals as the correct interpreter of the sacred contents. At first, no one comes forward, but then one of the elders says, "Do not weep. See, the Lion of the tribe of Judah, the Root of David, has conquered, so that he can open the scroll and its seven seals" (Rev. 5:5).

Though we are expecting a lion to appear, in fact "a Lamb standing as if it had been slaughtered" comes forward (Rev. 5:6). The reference, obviously enough, is to Jesus the Lamb of God, who was not a conquering military hero but rather a crucified victim, raised nonetheless to life. Since it is precisely this figure who commences to open the seals and reveal the contents of the scroll, we understand that we are to read the whole of the Bible through the lens that he provides. It is the weakest of animals, the lamb, whose weakness is accentuated through being slain, who opens the meaning of the book and of salvation history. Therefore, any

6. Thomas Aquinas, *Summa theologiae* 1-2.94.5 ad 2.
7. Origen, *Homilies on Joshua* 12.1.

THE GREAT STORY OF ISRAEL

interpretation of any section of the Bible that leads to the conviction that God is an avenging, violent tyrant is, *ipso facto*, incorrect. The pithy summary in the First Letter of John to the effect that "God is love" (1 John 4:8) is the three-word encapsulation of what was disclosed in the cross of the Lamb, and hence it can function as a kind of canon within the canon of Sacred Scripture.

How, therefore, does this Origenistic hermeneutic apply to the texts presently under consideration? We must read the accounts of invasion, conquest, and the placing of the ban as allegories, Origen says, of the spiritual struggle. Here is one fairly representative text from Origen: "If those things that were dimly sketched through Moses concerning the tabernacle or the sacrifices and the entire worship are said to be a 'type and shadow of heavenly things,' doubtless the wars that are waged through Joshua and the slaughter of kings and enemies must also be said to be 'a shadow and type of heavenly things,' namely, of those wars that our Lord Jesus with his army and officers . . . fights with the Devil and his angels."[8] Origen, of course, was one of the earliest and most creative proponents of exploring the spiritual sense of a biblical text—which is to say, the allegorical, tropological, and anagogical meanings that lie behind the literal meaning. Typically, the allegorical has to do with a Christological dimension of the text, and this is what we see in the proposal just made. Joshua (naturally) evokes and anticipates Jesus (*Yeshua*), and the Israelites evoke the Church, the Mystical Body that Jesus uses to effect his purposes in the world. Accordingly, the peoples of the Promised Land are all of the vices that stand opposed to Christ's intention and that have to be crushed in the spiritual combat.

A particular virtue of this style of interpretation is that we can make perfect sense of the thoroughness and seeming brutality of the Israelite invasion, including the practice of the ban. When dealing with moral and spiritual evil, compromise and halfway measures are not called for; on the contrary, these enemies should

---

8. Origen, *Homilies on Joshua* 12.1.

be met with a certain ruthlessness. They should be battled all the way down, even, so to speak, to the last man; for evil left unaddressed has a way of reasserting itself, something like a cancer that has been extricated, except for a few errant cells. I believe it is extremely useful to apply this Origenistic allegorical hermeneutic to most of the "dark" texts of the Old Testament, interpreting those puzzling passages in a radically Christological manner.

"CHOOSE THIS DAY WHOM YOU WILL SERVE"

The bulk of the rest of the book of Joshua is given over to lists, first of the kings conquered by Israel and next of the locales assigned to the individual tribes within the Promised Land. This lengthy and somewhat tedious section of the book calls for no extensive theological commentary. But chapter 24, the final chapter of the text, draws our attention, for it functions as a pithy summary of the moral and spiritual character of the people Israel. More precisely, it compels us to see Israel as a people to whom a stark choice is offered: the service of God or the service of false gods. As we have seen, this theme has been front and center from the opening chapters of the book of Genesis, and indeed it sounds like a refrain throughout the whole of the Pentateuch. Chapter 24 commences with Joshua gathering the entire nation—the elders, the heads, the judges, and officers of Israel, as well as the tribes themselves—and rehearsing for them the story of their people, which culminated in the provision of the land: "I gave you a land on which you had not labored, and towns that you had not built, and you live in them; you eat the fruit of the vineyards and olive groves that you did not plant" (Josh. 24:13). In other words, I have rescued you from slavery and given you, as a sheer grace, the Promised Land, which you now inhabit.

As is always the case in the biblical narratives, grace calls forth cooperation and hence a command is sounded: "Now therefore revere the LORD, and serve him in sincerity and in faithfulness; put away the gods that your ancestors served beyond the River and in

Egypt, and serve the LORD" (Josh. 24:14). Once again, orthodoxy is the spiritual desideratum and the suspension of orthodoxy is the fundamental spiritual problem, the former resulting in blessing and the latter in a curse. Laying the matter unambiguously on the line, Joshua says, "Now if you are unwilling to serve the LORD, choose this day whom you will serve, whether the gods your ancestors served in the region beyond the River or the gods of the Amorites in whose land you are living; but as for me and my household, we will serve the LORD" (Josh. 24:15). Bob Dylan famously riffed on this admirable Kierkegaardian either/or with his "It may be the devil or it may be the Lord / But you're gonna have to serve somebody."[9] There are indeed many subtleties and ambiguities in the spiritual order; there is indeed much that we do not see clearly in the theological realm. But on this absolutely crucial point, there is no confusion, uncertainty, or equivocation. Either the Creator God receives our highest praise or something less than the Creator God receives that praise. In Augustine's language, we worship either God or creatures—and everything else will follow from this elemental determination. Another fundamental biblical motif is highlighted here—namely, the role of freedom in our relationship with God. God, who is infinite freedom, wants always to engage the finite freedom of his rational creatures. He does not want abject servility, nor does he want to preside over automatons; rather, he wants to lure, draw, and beguile properly free agents. And so acquiescence is not imposed, but rather a choice is proposed. Though he is, like all of Israel's leaders, a flawed character, Joshua enunciates the decision that marks Israel at its best, the decision the implications of which continue to reverberate throughout the world. To be sure, Israel wrestles with the Lord, but when it is true to itself and its spiritual identity, it chooses the Lord. How can the Christian reader miss the Christological typology at work here? The true Joshua, Jesus of Nazareth, who consistently follows

9. Bob Dylan, "Gotta Serve Somebody," track 1 on *Slow Train Coming*, Columbia, 1979.

the will of his Father, even unto death, is the definitive breaker of idols. And it is he, accordingly, who, with the most authoritative voice, calls his followers to conform their decisions to his.

Judges

The book of Judges is perhaps the most brutal and violent in the Bible, which is saying quite something, given that we have just considered the book of Joshua. I doubt there is another biblical text that portrays human depravity quite as consistently and honestly as the book of Judges. Many of its stories call rather vividly to mind *Game of Thrones* episodes, or perhaps Scorsese films. Murder, rape, evisceration, the nailing of a peg through a man's skull, and the dismemberment of a woman are but some of the horrors featured in this book. To state it simply, Judges shows what happens to Israel when it wanders from the commands of God, and its overall trajectory is in the direction of kingly rule that would restore something like moral and political order to the nation. It is easy enough to articulate the cyclical pattern that obtains throughout the text. Israel forgets the laws of the Lord; they are, accordingly, handed over to their enemies for chastisement; they cry out to God; God sends "judges"—tribal chieftains—to help them and to deal with their enemies; peace is briefly restored; and Israel falls again into sin, prompting a repeat of the cycle.

A grand question prompted by this book in particular but frankly present throughout the Old Testament is this: What good finally are the laws, covenants, prophetic warnings, and liturgies of Israel? Do they ever effect what they are intended to? Do the people ever really become more attuned to God under their influence? There might be—as there are in Judges—occasional glimmers of hope, but these fade quickly enough. The attentive Christian reader senses that all of the institutions and laws just referenced anticipate Christ, for by their very inefficacy, they point to the one who will be the true Torah, the fulfillment of the covenants, the most authentic prophet, the true high priest. In the language of the prophet Jeremiah, the Lord will, in time, write the law upon the hearts of his people, taking the external commands written on stone and embodied in institutions and inscribing it within the souls of those who are grafted onto Christ Jesus. Thus, it is true that, in a sense, the entire revelation contained in the Old Testament leaves us, spiritually speaking, in a state of suspense. We know what God wants us to do, but, with a handful of exceptions, we are not able to do it.

DEBORAH

The book of Judges lays out the stories, sometimes in very brief compass, of twelve of these tribal leaders, but it focuses in on four of them: Deborah, Gideon, Jephthah, and Samson. Therefore, I will follow this prompt and concentrate my attention on these four flawed heroes of Israel. It is first of all of considerable note that one of the most celebrated leaders of this roiled period of Israelite history was a woman. Deborah is not only a judge—which is to say, a political leader—but a "prophetess" as well, and her leadership indeed involves both practical wisdom and intuition into the purposes of God. Certainly, within the culture of that time and place, the choice of a woman to act as leader was an indication that God typically selects the least likely and most marginal figures to work his will. At the prompting of the Lord, she summons Barak, son of Abinoam, a military commander from Naphtali, in order to take on a Canaanite people who had remained unsubdued. Supported by the personal presence of Deborah, Barak goes out against the enemy forces, who are led by Sisera, and routs them. Fleeing for his life, Sisera comes to the tent of one Jael, wife of a man that he considers an ally. After calming him with soothing words and nourishing him with a skin of milk, Jael urges Sisera to lie down and rest. While he sleeps, she blithely drives a tent peg through his temple and into the ground. Therefore, the mighty warrior is done in, effectively, by two women. Following their consistently allegorical inclinations, the Church Fathers saw Deborah and Jael as evocative of the Church itself, the Mystical Bride of Christ. As a foreigner, a non-Jew, Jael functioned especially well as a symbol of that community that would be gathered around Christ from all the nations. Further, her wooden peg, used to snuff out the life of one of Israel's enemies, was compared to the wooden cross of Jesus by which the dark powers of sin and death were defeated.[1]

GIDEON

The victories of Deborah bring about forty years of peace for Israel, symbolically suggestive, obviously, of the eschatological rest that will come at the end of time with the definitive defeat of God's enemies. But soon enough, in line with the inevitable pattern, Israel falls into sin again, and the Lord turns them over to the oppressive rule of the Midianites. After his people cries out in distress, God sends an angel to a young and obscure figure, Gideon, the son of Joash the Abiezrite. The messenger of the Lord says to Gideon, "The LORD is with you, you mighty warrior" (Judg. 6:12). All we know at this point is that Gideon is threshing wheat near a winepress, and we have no indication whatsoever that he is a military man or even someone who aspires to such a life—which proves that God tends to name us not in accord with who we are, but rather in accord with who he wants us to become. The Church Fathers exploited Gideon's association with both threshing floor and winepress to show him as a Christological type as well as a type for the Church, for Jesus would indeed separate wheat from chaff, saint from sinner, and the Church would be "the winepress of the eternal fountain in which abounds the fruit of the heavenly vine."[2]

1. Origen, *Homilies on Judges* 5.5; Ambrose, *Concerning Widows* 8.47–50.
2. Caesarius of Arles, *Sermons* 117.1, in *Sermons: Volume 2 (81–186)*, trans. Mary Magdaleine Mueller (Washington, DC: The Catholic University of America Press, 1964), 177.

These exalted associations, to be sure, do not disguise the fact that Gideon is a limited and morally imperfect man, which becomes evident in his supreme reluctance to take on the task assigned to him: "But sir [he said to the angel], how can I deliver Israel? My clan is the weakest in Manasseh, and I am the least in my family" (Judg. 6:15). When the angel insists that God will be with the young man, Gideon remains hesitant and asks for a confirming sign. Even after this is given, Gideon is unsure. On the eve of the great battle, he poses another sort of challenge to God: "I am going to lay a fleece of wool on the threshing floor; if there is dew on the fleece alone, and it is dry on all the ground, then I shall know that you will deliver Israel by my hand." When God rose to this challenge, Gideon, remaining unconvinced, offered another: "Let it be dry only on the fleece, and on all the ground let there be dew" (Judg. 6:37–39). When God responded favorably to this request, the young man was ready to fight. Though it is certainly true that this episode has inspired, especially in evangelical circles, the pious practice of "laying out the fleece"—which is to say, looking for a concrete sign of God's approval—it does not reflect well on Gideon. Instead of answering the Lord with a prompt "Here I am!" he requires repeated assurances. The greatest heroes of Israel and the holiest saints of the Church are those who did the will of God, even in the face of rejection and even without confirming signs.

As the time for battle approaches, God is eager to whittle down in size the army of Gideon, lest the impression be given that the victory came not through God's power but through force of arms.[3] The Lord's first move is to encourage Gideon to sift out the fearful: "Whoever is fearful and trembling, let him return home" (Judg. 7:3). The Church Fathers were quick to see a symbolic link here to the fighting church, which must purge from its ranks the faint of heart. Origen's reflection is typical: "Does not the leader of our army, the Lord and Savior Jesus Christ, call out now to

3. Salvian the Presbyter, *The Governance of God* 7.9–9.

his soldiers and say, 'Whoever is fearful and anxious of heart, let him not come to war with me'?"[4] After this initial winnowing, twenty-two thousand of Gideon's troops melt away. But the Lord was not satisfied: "The troops are still too many; take them down to the water and I will sift them out for you there" (Judg. 7:4). The proposed process turns out to be peculiar, to say the least. The Lord orders Gideon to separate out those who drink from the river in the manner of a dog, lapping the water with their tongues, from those who bend down and quench their thirst by putting hand to mouth. The mere three hundred who drink like dogs are to be the army with which Gideon fights. How could poetically minded interpreters possibly miss the opportunity to interpret this strange means of choosing Gideon's fighting men? So St. Augustine proposes this symbolic reading: "Dogs are commendable, not abominable. They observe fidelity toward their master, and before his house they bark against enemies."[5] And Gregory the Great concentrates on the posture of those whom God rejects: "Therefore those who are reported to have bent their knees while drinking the water retired from the strife of battles, having been forbidden because Christ proceeds to battle against the enemies of the faith with those who, when they drink the streams of doctrine, do not distort the uprightness of their actions."[6] The point is that the army of God, even if it is small, must be focused, disciplined, and virtuous, in which case, God can accomplish great things through it.

The battle itself, conducted by this tiny army against a far larger enemy contingent, is reminiscent of the taking of Jericho. We are told that the three hundred are armed, not with swords

---

4. Origen, *Homilies on Judges* 9.1, in *Origen: Spirit and Fire: A Thematic Anthology of His Writings*, ed. Hans Urs von Balthasar, trans. Robert J. Daly (Washington, DC: The Catholic University of America Press, 1984), 225.

5. Augustine, *Expositions on the Psalms* 68.29, in *Old Testament IV: Joshua, Judges, Ruth, 1–2 Samuel*, ed. John R. Franke, Ancient Christian Commentary on Scripture (Downers Grove, IL: InterVarsity, 2005), 129.

6. Gregory the Great, *Morals on the Book of Job* 30.25.74, in *Old Testament IV: Joshua, Judges, Ruth, 1–2 Samuel*, 129.

and spears, but with trumpets in one hand and empty jars with torches inside in the other. At Gideon's signal, they blow the trumpets, shout, and smash the jars, uncovering the lights, thereby frightening the Midianites and starting a kind of stampede among them. In the ensuing confusion, the Midianites turn upon one another in violence, lose their corporate cohesion, and commence to flee. Just as Jericho fell without violent intervention on the part of Israel, but rather through something akin to a liturgical exercise, so here lights, musical instruments, and raised voices—all liturgical expressions—produce the victory. With typical poetic exuberance, Gregory the Great interprets trumpet, jar, and lights as follows. The trumpets represent the loud and enthusiastic proclamation of evangelical preachers; the jars stand for the frail human flesh of those martyrs who gave themselves for the faith; and the torches indicate the power and illumination of the spirit unleashed precisely through the death of brave evangelizers.[7] The point, once again, is that the forces of sin and wickedness are conquered not through the weapons of the world, but through prayer, praise, and proclamation. Not to be overlooked is the general patristic insistence that Gideon, despite his rather obvious failings, functions as a kind of anticipation of Christ, the crucified Lord who will lead his nonviolent army of evangelizers and martyrs into battle.[8]

In the wake of the great and surprising victory over the Midianites, the people of Israel turn to Gideon and beg him to become their king. Gideon's response gives voice to a consistent biblical reticence in regard to kings: "I will not rule over you, and my son will not rule over you; the LORD will rule over you" (Judg. 8:23). The admirable conviction that God alone is the ruler of his people will be eloquently articulated later by the prophet

7. Gregory the Great, *Morals on the Book of Job* 30.25.75, in *Old Testament IV: Joshua, Judges, Ruth, 1–2 Samuel*, 131–132.

8. Gregory the Great, 30.25.73, in *Old Testament IV: Joshua, Judges, Ruth, 1–2 Samuel*, 131.

Samuel, though that prophet does become the reluctant anointer of King Saul and later of King David. That an ambiguity, a back-and-forth ambivalence, regarding kings obtains in the Bible is without question. On the one hand, the biblical authors are painfully aware of the dangers that kings represent; on the other hand, they also appreciate virtuous kings as new Adams, presiding over the new Eden of Israel. Since even the best of the Old Testament kings—David, Solomon, Josiah—are flawed, even deeply so, the ambivalence about kings will not be resolved definitively until Christ the King presents himself, crucified and crowned with thorns, as ruler to be sure, but in an attitude of nonviolence and forgiving love. This is precisely why the placard that Pontius Pilate places over the cross of Jesus—"Jesus of Nazareth, the King of the Jews" (John 19:19)—is so significant. Since it shows, at long last, what the King of Israel looks like, and declares it in the major languages of that time and place, it functions as the first piece of truly evangelical writing.

We learn that Gideon, with a number of wives, gave rise to seventy sons, as well as another son, Abimelech, born of a concubine. When the great warrior died, Israel, according to the well-established pattern, relapsed almost immediately into moral disarray and "prostituted themselves with the Baals, making Baal-berith their god" (Judg. 8:33). It was precisely this fundamental spiritual distortion that conduced toward disastrous developments on the political front. Consumed with ambition, Abimelech conspired with his mother's family to maneuver himself into position as Gideon's successor, but he faced the rather formidable obstacle of seventy candidates that stood ahead of him in the order of succession. And so, with ruthless efficiency, Abimelech employed the services of some "worthless and reckless fellows" and put to death all seventy of his half-brothers "on one stone." (Judg. 9:4–5). Though it is told with typical biblical laconicism, the unfolding of this mass execution must have been horrific in the extreme. One is put in mind of Mafiosi featured in contemporary films, those desperate and canny men who simply eliminate their competitors for power. Unsurprisingly, in the wake of this rub-out, "all the lords of Shechem and all Beth-millo came together, and they went and made Abimelech king" (Judg. 9:6). In a fallen world, it is not the best and brightest, but rather the one who displays fearlessness and raw power who typically wins the allegiance of the masses.

We are told that the one survivor of the Abimelech massacre was Gideon's youngest son, Jotham. This figure is on the biblical stage for only a very short time, but he manages to deliver himself of one of the most memorable critiques of tyranny in the Bible, ranking with the prophet Samuel's alarming description of the evil that kings do. Climbing to the top of Mt. Gerazim, and hence symbolically addressing all of Israel, this sole survivor of a murderous usurpation of power enunciates the parable of the bramble—which is, by the way, one of the few examples of this type of literature in the Old Testament. Seeking a king to reign over them, the trees, Jotham says, enquire of the olive tree, but the olive tree declines; then they ask the fig tree, and they get the same negative response; then they seek out the vine, but the vine says no. Finally, they resort to bramble, which is only too willing to reign: "If in good faith you are anointing me king over you, then come and take refuge in my shade" (Judg. 9:15). The irony, of course, is that the thornbush, growing close to the ground, provides precious little shade; and whereas the other plants— olive, fig, and vine—offer something of real value, the bramble gives nothing. On the contrary, its rapid growth and insinuating tendency compromise plants in its vicinity. So it goes, Jotham is suggesting, with kings, who take rather than give, who provide no shelter and in fact worm their way aggressively into the lives of those over whom they reign. So it has indeed gone with the murderous Abimelech.

The usurper's reign was brief, only three years, and it came to an abrupt end with the ignominious death of Abimelech. Standing at the foot of a tower in the town of Thebez, seeking to burn the structure down, Abimelech was struck in the head by a millstone dropped by a woman on the ramparts. Ashamed that he was dying at the hand of a woman, the ruler asked one of his troops to run him through so that "people will not say about me, 'A woman killed him'" (Judg. 9:54). Of course, through the biblical narrative, the entire world knows it—and this, the author of Judges assures us, is payback for Abimelech's murder of his brothers.

JEPHTHAH

The third judge upon whom the book specially concentrates is Jephthah the Gileadite, described as "a mighty warrior" and "the son of a prostitute" (Judg. 11:1). Spurned by his family because of his questionable origin, Jephthah withdrew to the wilderness, where he eventually attracts to himself outlaws and marginalized persons, becoming a kind of rough and ready gang leader. When Israel is threatened by the Ammonites, Jephthah's relations come to him, seeking his aid. Sensing their desperation, he cuts a deal with them: "If you bring me home again to fight with the Ammonites, and the Lord gives them over to me, I will be your head" (Judg. 11:9). Inspired by the prospect of becoming chief warlord, Jephthah engages the Ammonites, but not before making a fateful vow: "If you will give the Ammonites into my hand, then whoever comes out of the doors of my house to meet me, when I return victorious from the Ammonites, shall be the Lord's, to be offered up by me as a burnt offering" (Judg. 11:30–31). The battle goes decisively his way, and Jephthah goes back to his home at Mizpah. As he approaches the residence, his daughter, his only child, comes to meet him, dancing and shaking a tambourine, and Jephthah realizes, to his infinite chagrin, that he is now obligated to sacrifice her to the Lord.

Incredibly (at least to our sensibilities), Jephthah's daughter acquiesces to the implications of her father's vow and asks only for two months to "go and wander on the mountains, and bewail" her virginity with her companions (Judg. 11:37). One cannot help but think here of Abraham's willingness to sacrifice his only son and Isaac's compliance with the divine command. But that particular narrative might help us to interpret the Jephthah story in the measure that God clearly did not want the sacrifice of Isaac—and indeed, human sacrifice is explicitly forbidden in the law of Moses. Therefore, might we read this story as a tragic cautionary tale, which makes clear the folly of formulating precisely the kind of vow that Jephthah made? Making arrangements with God on our terms, or using the name of the Lord in incantations and spells, or undertaking vows without any prompting from God—it all amounts to a manipulation of the one who, in principle, should never be manipulated. We are indeed to cooperate actively with God's providence, but we ought never attempt to arrange that providence according to our desires. St. Augustine observes that the Bible does not explicitly evaluate the vow of Jephthah, leaving open at least the possibility of this line of interpretation.[9]

SAMSON

The tribal chieftain to whom the book of Judges pays most attention is Samson, a figure whose mythic and archetypal qualities have guaranteed him a privileged place in the cultural imagination of the world. The author of Judges is particularly interested in the manner of Samson's birth, which calls to mind those of Isaac, Samuel, and John the Baptist. His mother, who remains unnamed throughout the narrative, is described as barren, but she receives an unexpected visit from a divine messenger who tells her that she will have a child. The angel then gives specific instructions to the mother: "Now be careful not to drink wine or strong drink, or eat anything unclean, for you shall conceive and bear a son. No razor is to come on his head, for the boy shall be a nazirite to God from birth" (Judg. 13:4–5). The angel's reference here is to a form of radical dedication to the Lord, described in the book of Numbers (Num. 6:1–21). It is crucial that we bear this dedication

9. Augustine, *Questions on Judges* 49.7.

in mind as we read the story of Samson, for his eventual fall from grace will be tied to his failure to live up to the expectations of his nazirite vocation.

But for the moment, we should attend to the theological significance of his coming to be born. The birth of a hero from a woman considered incapable of having children is, in the Bible, an indication of the primacy of grace. What presses the history of salvation forward is never primarily human activity, but rather the unmerited gift of God's love. To be sure, the God of Israel, never a rival with his creation, calls forth our cooperation and response; we are summoned to participate actively in a play and not to be marionettes. But the initiative always belongs to God.

When Samson came of age, he journeyed with his parents to a town called Timnah, where he spied a Philistine woman. This was during a period when the Philistines were dominating Israel. Without hesitation, he asked his parents to "get her" as his wife (Judg. 14:2). We are told that this had little to do with love and much to do with Samson's desire to undermine Philistine power—to move, as it were, behind enemy lines. On his way to marry the woman, he is accosted by a fierce lion, whom he dispatches with his bare hands, thus revealing, for the first time, his prodigious strength. Later he spies the carcass of the lion and finds within it a swarm of bees and honey. He tastes of the honey and then brings some of it to his father and mother, though he does not tell them whence it came. At the wedding banquet, he beguiles his wife's entourage with a riddle that references this odd episode: "Out of the eater came something to eat. Out of the strong came something sweet" (Judg. 14:14). Anticipating the Delilah episode, the relatives of Samson's wife pressure her to get the secret to the riddle out of Samson. Why, we might wonder, would the author of Judges tell this peculiar story and bother to look at it from a number of angles?

Unsurprisingly, the Church Fathers eagerly explored the symbolic overtones of the tale. In the allegorical sense, the lion represents Christ, the Lion of Judah, who died, but from whose death came the swarming bees of Christian evangelizers and the sweet honey of the Gospel word.[10] Caesarius of Arles riffed as follows on the riddle proposed by Samson: "What else does it signify but Christ rising from the dead? Truly, out of the eater, that is, from death which devours and consumes all things, came forth that food which said: 'I am the bread that has come down from heaven.'"[11] On a somewhat more mundane level, we remark that this is the first violation of Samson's nazirite vow, for he came into contact with a dead animal. Even as he accomplishes great things for his people, he gradually undermines himself, compromising his sacred identity.

Samson's endeavoring to undermine the power of Philistia comes to the fore in the next tale told of him. Having heard that his father-in-law had given his wife to a companion, Samson flies into a rage and seizes upon the truly bizarre strategy of attaching burning torches to the tails of foxes and letting the animals loose through the standing grain of the Philistines. This procedure anticipates a very similar one that David's son Absalom would employ in 2 Samuel, and it also brings to light the curious connection between Samson, the feral man, and animals: lion, foxes, and a donkey. In retaliation, the Philistines, brutally enough, burned Samson's wife and father-in-law to death, which prompted the strong man to effect "a great slaughter" on his enemies (Judg. 15:8). Following the awful logic of eye for eye, the Philistines then come after Samson and persuade a number of his countrymen to bind him and hand him over. But when they sought to seize him, he effortlessly broke his bonds, grabbed the jawbone of a donkey and, blithely, killed a thousand Philistines. The hero's desire to break the power of his enemies has now come to satisfying fruition. Once again, however, we must not overlook his contact with the flesh of a dead animal, which violates his sacred vow, so that even as he conquers, he is conquered.

10. Caesarius of Arles, *Sermons* 118.3, 119.1.
11. Caesarius of Arles, 118.3.

Chapter 16 commences with still another story of Samsonian Philistine infiltration. Arriving in Gaza, the principal city of the enemy nation, Samson takes up with a prostitute. Hearing of this, a small army of Philistines surround the woman's residence, waiting until morning to waylay the Israelite hero. Learning of their presence, Samson rises at midnight, evades his opponents, and takes "hold of the doors of the city gate and the two posts," subsequently carrying them, incredibly, "to the top of the hill that is in front of Hebron"—which is to say, a place roughly forty miles away (Judg. 16:3). Once more, the very peculiarity of the tale invites the introduction of a symbolic hermeneutic. The Fathers of the Church tended to interpret Samson's stay in Gaza, the capital of Philistia, as an anticipation of Jesus' journey, after his death, to hell, the capital of the kingdom of darkness. The band of marauders who surrounded the prostitute's home is evocative of the band of Roman soldiers assigned to guard the tomb of the crucified. The taking of the gates of Gaza, of course, anticipates Jesus' harrowing of hell, his breaking down of the gates of that eschatologically sad place, and the triumphant journey to Hebron is a sign of Christ's definitive victory.[12] That Hebron is associated strongly with David, who first reigned there as king before taking his seat in Jerusalem, only solidifies this interpretation, which centers on the new and definitive David.

To this point, Samson has been largely successful in his campaign of infiltration, using his various intimacies with Philistine women to undermine the strength of his enemies and, in this last instance, taking away the gates of their capital city and hence exposing it to ruin. And the last and most famous of his encounters behind enemy lines proves to be, at the same time, his most ruinous and most victorious. We are told that the great judge "fell in love" with a woman named Delilah. Though she comes from an area in Israelite territory, her close affiliation with

12. Caesarius of Arles, *Sermons* 118.5; Gregory the Great, "Homily 21," in *Forty Gospel Homilies*, trans. Dom David Hurst (Kalamazoo, MI: Cistercian, 1990), 162–163.

"the lords of the Philistines" seems to indicate that she is, at the very least, a Philistine fellow-traveler (Judg. 16:4–5). According to the now-familiar pattern, these "lords" press her to trip up Samson by finding out the source of his strength. Toying with her, the strong man makes a number of misleading indications, and his enemies are foiled. Finally, employing all her skills as both seductress and nag, Delilah wears down his resistance: "So he told her his whole secret, and said to her, 'A razor has never come upon my head; for I have been a nazirite to God from my mother's womb. If my head were shaved, then my strength would leave me'" (Judg. 16:17). Though he has violated his nazirite vow by associating with prostitutes, drinking alcohol, and coming into contact with the carcasses of animals, he now prepares the way for the final infidelity. Convinced that he has finally spoken the truth, Delilah lulls him to sleep on her lap, cuts off his flowing locks, and then summons his Philistine enemies to take him. This time, he truly was disempowered, and his persecutors gouged out his eyes, dragged him back to Gaza, shackled him, and put him to work turning a mill like an animal, his humiliation now complete.

Perhaps the most important theological point to understand is that whatever strength we have comes ultimately from God and is enhanced by our devotion to God. Just as things exist and live only through the causal influence of God, so heroes are able to do the work of the Lord only through his influence and at his pleasure. A second insight, brought forward by any number of the Church Fathers, is that Samson—betrayed, corralled by his enemies, tortured, and mocked—is an anticipation of Christ in his Passion.[13] To be sure, Samson is no morally flawless Christ, but in his suffering, he symbolizes the participation of every Christian in Jesus' manner of being during the last days of his life. But as before, Samson's involvement with the Philistines conduces toward Israelite victory. To celebrate and to offer sacrifice for the

13. Caesarius of Arles, *Sermons* 118.6, 120.4; Ephrem the Syrian, *Hymns on Paradise* 13.12–13.

deliverance of their enemy into their hands, the Philistines gather in great numbers within a spacious house. In high spirits, they bring Samson before them to play the fool. But they make the fatal mistake of placing their victim between two of the supporting pillars of the structure. Samson asks the Lord to give him, once more, great strength and then, pressing hard against both pillars, he brings the entire house down upon himself and upon the three thousand gathered there, so that "those he killed at his death were more than those he had killed during his life" (Judg. 16:30). We might say that this horrific act represented the culmination of Samson's many-years'-long campaign against Philistia. How could the Church Fathers not see this act as symbolic of Christ's Passion? By an act of supreme self-sacrifice, Samson put to death those myriad Philistines who, in their worship of a false god, are evocative of sin and rebellion against the true God. The meditation of Caesarius of Arles is representative of the patristic consensus: "Notice here an image of the cross. Samson extends his hands spread out to the two columns as to the two beams of the cross. Moreover, by his death he overcame his adversaries, because his sufferings became the death of his persecutors. . . . This mystery was clearly fulfilled in our Lord Jesus Christ, for at his death he completed our redemption."[14]

After the death of Samson, the tribes of Israel seemed to drift into disunity and to manifest shocking violence to one another. The most remarkable and frankly sickening story concerns the Benjaminites and the outrage at Gibeah. We hear of a Levite from Ephraim who had taken a concubine from Bethlehem. When the woman escaped and returned home, the Levite came after her. After tolerating some stalling tactics on the part of the woman's father, he set out with her and came to the town of Gibeah, hoping to find shelter for the night and a kindly reception. Instead, "a perverse lot" from the city surrounded

14. Caesarius of Arles, *Sermons* 118.6.

the house of an old man who had taken in the Levite and his concubine. Exactly duplicating the infamous tale from the book of Genesis, the mob shouts: "Bring out the man who came into your house, so that we may have intercourse with him" (Judg. 19:22). With astonishing moral turpitude, the owner of the abode replied, "Do not do this vile thing. Here are my virgin daughter and his concubine; let me bring them out now. Ravish them and do whatever you want to them; but against this man do not do such a vile thing" (Judg. 19:23–24). At that, the Levite shoved his concubine outside and the men, we are blithely informed, "wantonly raped her, and abused her all through the night until the morning" (Judg. 19:25).

Utterly indifferent to her suffering and humiliation, he placed her, next morning, on his beast of burden and commenced the journey to Ephraim. When he arrived home, "he took a knife, and grasping his concubine he cut her into twelve pieces, limb by limb, and sent her throughout all the territory of Israel" (Judg. 19:29). Was she dead when he found her that morning? Did she die on the way? Did he kill her? We're not told, and this adds to the horror of the narrative. When the gruesome message was received across the nation of Israel, the elders assembled an army and attacked the Benjaminites at Gibeah, effecting a general slaughter of the enemy. Though there is a good deal of competition for the distinction, this gruesome and cruel episode might represent the low point of human behavior described in the Bible. And it followed from the disappearance of the judges and hence of anything approaching kingly leadership within the nation. Rudderless and without a captain, the ship simply smashes into the rocks. The final line of the book of Judges sums up the spiritual situation: "In those days there was no king in Israel; all the people did what was right in their own eyes" (Judg. 21:25). Though we utterly valorize self-determination and the finding of one's own voice, the Bible sees these as hopelessly dysfunctional. The needful thing is the leadership of God mediated typically through the leadership of those who act according to God's heart. When the historical narrative is picked up with the books of Samuel, we will see precisely how the God of Israel begins the process of finding right government for his people.

Ruth

The book of Ruth is anomalous. It is extremely rare in the biblical canon in the measure that everyone in it is good. Some characters are indeed better than others, but there are no real villains in the story. And though there is a tension at the heart of the narrative, it is beautifully and happily resolved at the end. Though in the Hebrew canon it is placed among the "writings," in the Septuagint and in the Christian Bible, it follows immediately upon the horrific book of Judges and precedes the books of Samuel. Perhaps the assemblers of the collection felt that some sort of reprieve was needed before heading back into the muck and ambiguity of the human condition that is on clear display in the Samuel literature.

The story commences in Bethlehem, which right away puts us in mind of King David and Jesus, both of whom were born in that small town near Jerusalem. A man named Elimelech (which has the sense of "God is my king") sets out with his wife Naomi and his two sons for the land of Moab, for there was a famine in Bethlehem. While in Moab, Elimelech dies and his sons, who had taken Moabite women for their wives, also die. So the three widowed women—Naomi, Orpah, and Ruth—are left to fend for themselves. Hearing that the famine in her home country was over, Naomi resolves to return to Bethlehem, but she urges her daughters-in-law to remain in Moab. Even with tears of regret, Orpah obeys this command and stays, but Ruth determines to journey to what is, to her, a foreign land. When Naomi presses the matter, Ruth delivers a lovely speech, presented in nearly poetic form: "Do not press me to leave you or to turn back from following you! Where you go, I will go; where you lodge, I will lodge; your people shall be my people, and your God my God. Where you die, I will die—there will I be buried" (Ruth 1:16–17).

We have already come across a number of times the theme of Israelites, as it were, behind enemy lines and also the related motif of foreigners coming under the aegis of the God of Israel. The tale of Ruth is an example of the latter. Once we see this, we can understand the patristic instinct to read this as a story of the Church[1]—which is to say, the Gentiles being drawn to the God of Abraham, Isaac, and Jacob. When the two women arrive in Bethlehem, there is general rejoicing and fascination: "Is this Naomi?" Playing on her name, which has the sense of "sweet" or "pleasant," Naomi replies, "Call me no longer Naomi, call me Mara, for the Almighty has dealt bitterly with me" (Ruth 1:19–20). "*Mara*" means something like "harsh." She still has her faith of course, but it has been sorely tested. We will see, in the strange workings of God's providence, that famine, exile, and the loss of her husband and sons is precisely what has permitted Ruth to come to Bethlehem, there to serve God's purposes in an absolutely decisive way.

Soon after her arrival, Ruth learns of a certain Boaz (the name means something like "strength"), a prosperous man and a relative of Naomi's late husband Elimelech. Obviously interested in him, she manages to find employment gleaning one of his fields. A hard worker, she comes to the attention of Boaz, and the two commence a tentative courtship. Overjoyed at the prospect of this union, Naomi encourages Ruth to move rather boldly into Boaz's space: "When Boaz had eaten and drunk, and he was in a contented mood, he went to lie down at the end of the heap of grain. Then she came stealthily and uncovered his feet, and lay down" (Ruth 3:7). When he wakens and sees a woman at his feet,

1. Isidore of Seville, *On Ruth*; Ambrose, *Exposition on the Gospel of Luke* 3.30; John Chrysostom, *Homilies on the Gospel of Matthew* 3.5.

he asks her name. When told it is Ruth, he says, "I will do for you all that you ask, for all the assembly of my people know that you are a worthy woman" (Ruth 3:11). Once it is clarified that an even closer relative of Elimelech is not interested in Ruth, Boaz and the Moabite woman marry. This union so delights the people of Bethlehem that they, unusually enough, offer a formal benediction to a foreign woman, likening her to some of the heroes of Israel: "We are witnesses. May the LORD make the woman who is coming into your house like Rachel and Leah, who together built up the house of Israel. May you produce children in Ephrathah and bestow a name in Bethlehem; and, through the children that the LORD will give you by this young woman, may your house be like the house of Perez, whom Tamar bore to Judah" (Ruth 4:11–12). The marriage of Boaz and Ruth bears fruit promptly, giving rise to a son named Obed who, we are told, became "the father of Jesse, the father of David" (Ruth 4:17).

And now we understand the purpose of the wanderings and trials of Naomi and Ruth. Though what they endured must have seemed to them like so much dumb suffering, in point of fact, God was, precisely through those trials, expressing his saving will. Had there not been a famine many years before in Bethlehem, had Naomi not journeyed into a foreign land, had one of Naomi's sons never met Ruth, and had that son never died, Ruth would never have come to Bethlehem and would never have met Boaz and hence would never have become the great-grandmother of Israel's greatest king.

The Fathers of the Church typically saw marriages in the Old Testament as predictive of the definitive marriage of heaven and earth that would take place in Christ the Bridegroom and his Bride the Church, especially when the Old Testament antecedent involved the coming together of an Israelite and a foreigner. Thus, they took Boaz the Israelite and Ruth the Moabite as a particularly apt symbol of Christ joining himself in the Church to the Gentiles. This passage from a homily of John Chrysostom is representative: "See, for instance, what befell Ruth, how like it is to the things which belong to us. For she was both of a strange race, and reduced to the utmost poverty, yet Boaz when he saw her neither despised her poverty nor abhorred her mean birth, as Christ having received the Church, being both an alien and in much poverty, took her to be partaker of the great blessings."[2] The "meanness" of her birth has to do, of course, not simply with her being a non-Israelite, but an *enemy* of Israel, a daughter of Moab. In a similar manner, Christ can make of his enemies brides to himself.

In terms of the narrative thrust of the historical books of the Bible, the book of Ruth serves as a transition to the marvelous Samuel literature, which centers around the indispensably important figure of Ruth's great-grandson.

2. John Chrysostom, *Homilies on the Gospel of Matthew* 3.5.

1 Samuel

With the books of Samuel, we come to some of the most impressive texts in the Old Testament, indeed to some of the most impressive literature that has come down to us from the ancient world. In its literary craft, its psychological perceptiveness, its narrative verve, and its memorable characterizations, it ranks easily with the *Iliad* and the *Odyssey*. But then, of course, it far surpasses even these masterpieces in its rich theological content. The Samuel literature includes a number of important theological motifs, and they will all be discussed in due course, but at the outset, I might draw attention simply to this master theme, which represents a major leap forward in theological consciousness.

1 and 2 Samuel are remarkably free of what we might call "direct" divine interventions. And God never appears, as he sometimes does in the Torah, as an anthropomorphic figure. Rather, practically the entirety of the narrative could be understood in conventional political, familial, and psychological terms. But what the author takes for granted is that God is indirectly operative in the whole of the story, not so much as a participant in it, but as the master storyteller. To state this in more abstract terms, God is presented as noncompetitively transcendent to the narrative and hence as capable of expressing himself through the entirety of it, without once "interrupting" it or "intervening" as one cause among many.

The central figure in both 1 and 2 Samuel is not, of course, the prophet Samuel himself, but rather David the King, the one who is, along with Abraham and Moses, the most significant personage in the Old Testament. Though these books contain fascinating portraits of Samuel, Saul, Absalom, Jonathan, Eli, and Hannah, among many others, it is fair to say that all of these figures center around David, either anticipating him or reacting to him. Within the grand sweep of the biblical revelation, David is pivotal in the measure that he turns to look back to Adam, the failed king of the Garden of Eden, and turns toward Jesus, the New Adam, the Son of David, who would achieve the kingship that both his predecessors failed to achieve.

Before getting into our theological exegesis, it might be worthwhile to observe that the texts we refer to as 1 and 2 Samuel were originally one text. The division in two took place when the Hebrew was rendered into Greek at the time of the Septuagint translation. Thus, we should treat these two "books" as a literary unit and as manifesting a unified theological perspective. Moreover, in line with the commonly accepted proposal of Martin Noth in the middle of the twentieth century, the Samuel literature is part of a greater whole—namely, the "Deuteronomistic history" that includes the books of Deuteronomy, Joshua, Judges, 1 and 2 Samuel, and 1 and 2 Kings.[1] Thus, we are warranted in seeing connections and hearing echoes between and among these disparate texts.

If, as we have argued, the book of Ruth represents something of an interruption in the narrative flow, we should consult the very end of the book of Judges in order to understand the commencement of the books of Samuel. That particularly gruesome text ended with the despairing observation, "In those days there was no king in Israel; all the people did what was right in their own eyes" (Judg. 21:25). Though this reference to absolute autonomy might appeal to many in our cultural context, within a biblical framework, this is about as hopeless a scenario as could

---

1. Martin Noth, *The Deuteronomistic History* (Sheffield, UK: JSOT, 1981).

be imagined. The biblical authors never valorize autonomy, but rather something like theonomy, or the rule of the self by God. Everyone doing as he pleases, with no direction, either earthly or heavenly, is a picture of utter moral chaos. Therefore, a principal preoccupation of the Samuel literature will be the question of kingship, both earthly and heavenly—that is to say, the manner in which people ought to be directed and governed. That this is anything but straightforward becomes painfully clear throughout the narrative, as God endeavors to govern his people precisely through the awkward and unreliable instruments of human rulers.

HANNAH AND THE BIRTH OF SAMUEL

The story of David the King commences not with the mighty of the world, and not with impressive displays of divine power, but with one of the humblest people within the context of ancient Israelite culture—namely, a childless woman of an insignificant husband. From the beginning to the end of the Scriptures, this theme is hammered again and again: the humble person is the one through whom and with whom God can work most efficaciously. We are told of Elkanah and his two wives, Peninnah and Hannah, the first of whom has borne children and the second of whom is barren. Each year, when the family goes to the tabernacle in Shiloh, Hannah fervently prays for a son, but to no avail. Making matters worse, she has to endure the taunts of Peninnah.

On one of their visits to the sacred precincts, Hannah presented herself before the Lord and prayed so intensely that her lips moved in accompaniment to her thoughts. Thinking her drunk, the high priest, Eli, upbraided her, "How long will you make a drunken spectacle of yourself? Put away your wine" (1 Sam. 1:14). But Hannah patiently explained that she was not inebriated, only a passionate and troubled woman, begging the Lord for a child. Impressed, and we presume a bit chastened, Eli makes the prophetic prediction that God will grant the petition. What we are meant to see in this deftly composed narrative is a principal theme of the Samuel books—namely, that official religion tends toward corruption and that God frequently is compelled to work around it and act through unexpected vehicles. Eli's arrogance, lack of pastoral sensitivity, and plain obtuseness are representative of the tendency.

In time, Hannah did indeed conceive, and she gave birth to a son whom she named Samuel (*shemu'el* in Hebrew, carrying the sense of "God hears"). But in a move that certainly confounds present sensibilities but which is perfectly congruent with biblical spirituality, she resolved, almost immediately, to return the child to the Lord as a gesture of gratitude: "As soon as the child is weaned, I will bring him, that he may appear in the presence of the LORD, and remain there forever; I will offer him as a nazirite for all time" (1 Sam. 1:22). The principle, on display everywhere in the biblical texts, is that the divine grace, once received, should be given away as a gift, thereby prompting an even greater outpouring of grace. This paradox is but the translation into spiritual terms of the metaphysical language of God's noncompetitive transcendence. Since God has no needs vis-à-vis his creation, a gift returned to him redounds to the benefit of the giver. Because of Hannah's gift, the history of salvation moved forward, for without this generous offering, the prophet Samuel never would have emerged, and he never would have anointed David as king.

How wonderful that *after* leaving her child in the tabernacle under the care of the high priest, Hannah sings a song of exultant thanksgiving to God, the central theme of which is God's elevation of the lowly: "The bows of the mighty are broken, but the feeble gird on strength. Those who were full have hired themselves out for bread, but those who were hungry are fat with spoil. The barren has borne seven. . . . The LORD makes poor and makes rich. . . . He raises up the poor from the dust; he lifts the needy from the ash heap, to make them sit with princes" (1 Sam. 2:4–8). Hannah was raised up, not only in the measure that God provided a child for her, but inasmuch as she made a gift of that child back to God.

St. Luke, of course, uses this song of Hannah as the model for Mary's great "Magnificat" in the first chapter of his Gospel. Like her Old Testament antecedent, Mary received a child in a most unexpected way, and then, as the Gospel delineates, she offered the baby to God, resulting in an explosion of grace that indeed, "brought down the powerful from their thrones, and lifted up the lowly" (Luke 1:52).

Just after the exultant song of Hannah, we hear of Eli's sons Hophni and Phineas, who serve under their father as priests in the Shiloh tabernacle. The corruption at least indirectly indicated in Eli's deep pastoral insensitivity to Hannah is on full offer in his sons, who are described as abusive to the people both financially and sexually. When concerns about them are brought to Eli, the high priest speaks bluntly enough to Hophni and Phineas but takes no significant action against them. During this period of spiritual decline among the leadership of Israel, Samuel is coming of age. Chapter 3 of 1 Samuel commences with the charming but finally hard-edged story of the call of Samuel to prophecy. We are informed that "the word of the LORD was rare in those days" and that "visions were not widespread" (1 Sam. 3:1). Moreover, we are told that Eli's eyesight had grown dim, a consequence, on the literal level, of old age, but on the symbolic level perhaps an indication that the one meant to be a seer had become blind to the movement of God. Of course, it remains the prerogative of God to determine when and how he will manifest himself, but we might be permitted to wonder whether the absence of divine communication was a function of the corruption that had taken hold at that time.

THE CALL OF SAMUEL

After Eli and Samuel had retired for the night, the boy hears a voice: "Samuel! Samuel!" Presuming it is his master, the young man says to Eli, "Here I am!" But the old man denies that he had summoned his apprentice. After this same sequence unfolds twice more, Eli understands what is happening and tells the boy, "Go, lie down; and if he calls you, you shall say, 'Speak, LORD, for your servant is listening'" (1 Sam. 3:4–9). At this point, the Lord speaks again, and this time Samuel listens. When this passage is read liturgically, it ends at this point: the young man, having taken spiritual direction from his master, is poised to hear the word of the Lord. I imagine that most people, who are acquainted with this story only from the liturgy, would appreciate it, accordingly, as reassuring and spiritually uplifting, and they wouldn't be wrong. But they also would not sense the true power of the account, for they wouldn't know what precisely God said to young Samuel.

What the Creator in fact says is this: "See, I am about to do something in Israel that will make both ears of anyone who hears of it tingle. On that day I will fulfill against Eli all that I have spoken concerning his house, from beginning to end. For I have told him that I am about to punish his house forever, for the iniquity that he knew, because his sons were blaspheming God, and he did not restrain them" (1 Sam. 3:11–13). And the Lord proves true to his word, for not long after this revelation, Israel found itself at war with the Philistines. After a serious setback, the Israelites determined to carry the ark of the covenant itself into battle, but this was to no avail. The army was routed, and the ark was captured by Israel's enemy, the first time it had ever been taken from the holy people. Moreover, both Hophni and Phineas, the wicked sons of Eli, fell in battle. And when news of this utter disaster reached Eli, he fell backward in shock, broke his neck, and died. The terrible swift sword, about which the Lord warned young Samuel, fell as a punishment for Israel's sins of commission and omission.

As I compose these words, the Catholic Church worldwide is still reeling from the clergy sex abuse scandal, which ranks among the greatest moral and spiritual disasters in the history of the Church. How fascinating that this story, recounting events from over three thousand years ago, serves as a distant but remarkably clear mirror. Priests were engaging in abusive behavior; their superior was contacted; he responded with words of admonition but with no effective action; and the result was a disaster for Israel. One would have to be blind not to see a startling parallel to our own situation. The Church's present-day loss of prestige and respect—not to mention enormous amounts of money and property—is analogous to Israel's disastrous defeat in battle and the capture of the ark. That many of the enemies of the Church have gleefully witnessed and participated in the compromising of the Church shouldn't surprise us, for Israel, God's specially chosen people, had been delivered, precisely according to God's purifying purpose, into the hands of its enemies.

THE PEOPLE ASK FOR A KING

After the death of Eli, Samuel emerges as the principal judge or ruler of Israel, combining in his own person both religious and political leadership. But when he grows old, and the people sense that his sons do not possess their father's virtues, they commence to clamor for a king. We are, at this point, on a crucial fault line of biblical revelation. As we have seen, kingship belonged to God's original plan in the measure that Adam himself was meant to be king, or prudent steward, of creation. One of the effects of the fall is a compromising of this good governance. In establishing a holy people Israel, therefore, God was endeavoring to form a sort of kingly nation that would provide right leadership for all of the tribes of the world. But in order to shape that nation in its entirety, he raised up particular rulers—Abraham, Jacob, Joseph, Moses, Joshua, and Samuel, among others. So in asking for a king, the people, in one sense, were following a basic and admirable impulse.

But when we attend to the precise nature of their petition, we understand that the matter has become much more ambiguous: "Appoint for us, then, a king to govern us, like other nations" (1 Sam. 8:5). Instead of asking for a ruler after the heart of the Lord, they are seeking a king who would rule in the manner of other earthly kings, and this displeases God, for Israel is meant to be a people set apart. As we have seen innumerable times in our survey of the previous books of the Bible, whenever Israel apes the other nations, it falls away from its proper calling.

So the Lord, through Samuel, issues a warning to the people, and it constitutes one of the greatest condemnations of tyranny anywhere in the literature of the world. In the context of a general culture that tended to apotheosize political leadership, this passage from the eighth chapter of 1 Samuel is wonderfully egregious: "These will be the ways of the king who will reign over you: he will take your sons and appoint them to his chariots and to be his horsemen, and to run before his chariots; and he will appoint for himself commanders of thousands and commanders of fifties, and some to plow his ground and to reap his harvest. . . . He will take your daughters to be perfumers and cooks and bakers. He will take the best of your fields and vineyards and olive orchards and give them to his courtiers." And then Samuel draws the inevitable conclusion: "And in that day you will cry out because of your king, whom you have chosen for yourselves; but the LORD will not answer you in that day" (1 Sam. 8:11–14, 18). Anticipated here is practically the entire course of Israel's history under the kings who proved indeed to be like those of other nations. Even the greatest of Israel's kings—David and Solomon—committed heinous crimes against their own people. Much of the rest of the historical books of the Bible are the deeply discouraging account of what fallen and compromised kingship looks like. However, in David, Solomon, Josiah, and a handful of the other kings, we will see at least a hint of authentic kingship, according to God's own heart.

SAUL

An immediate confirmation of Samuel's reservations appears in the person of Saul, the man whom the prophet chooses to become the first king of Israel. On the one hand, Saul has characteristics that seem appropriate to kingly leadership: height and handsome looks, a warrior's spirit, and even a touch of the prophetic gift. But it soon enough becomes clear that Saul is a compromised character. One of the first indications is not so much a moral failing on Saul's part but the simple fact that he comes not from the tribe of Judah but from the tribe of Benjamin. We know from the prediction of Jacob in the book of Genesis that the leaders of Israel would come from Judah's stock: "The scepter shall not depart from Judah, nor the ruler's staff from between his feet, until tribute comes to him; and the obedience of the peoples is his" (Gen. 49:10). Were Samuel and the people so beguiled by Saul's pleasing appearance that they failed to see what God wanted for a ruler of Israel? Indeed, we shall see anon that when Samuel later seeks to anoint a successor to Saul, he is explicitly warned by the Lord *not* to choose on the basis of impressive looks, for "the LORD looks on the heart" (1 Sam. 16:7).

In regard to the questionable actions that undermined Saul's claim to legitimate kingship, I would mention three in particular. First, at the very moment he was chosen, Saul was hiding himself "among the baggage," and it is the Lord himself who indicates this quasi-comical reluctance to assume responsibility (1 Sam. 10:22). Is the biblical author suggesting that Saul, from the beginning, was lacking in moral courage? Second, Saul performed an unlawful act of sacrifice, arrogating to himself a priestly prerogative. As Israel was preparing for battle against the Philistines, Samuel was supposed to perform the sacrificial offering, but he was delayed. Alarmed that his army was commencing to melt away, Saul therefore assumed Samuel's role, but just as he was making the oblation, Samuel arrived on the scene and upbraided him: "You have done foolishly; you have not kept the commandment of the LORD your God, which he commanded you. The LORD would have established your kingdom over Israel forever, but now your kingdom will not continue" (1 Sam. 13:13–14).

But the greatest offense that Saul committed was his failure to impose the ban on the Amalekites after he had won a decisive victory. The Lord had instructed Saul, "Now go and attack Ama-lek, and utterly destroy all that they have; do not spare them, but kill both man and woman, child and infant, ox and sheep, camel and donkey" (1 Sam. 15:3). But instead, Saul spared King Agag of the Amalekites, along with the best of the animals and other valuables of the conquered people, which prompted this divine word to Samuel: "I regret that I made Saul king, for he has turned back from following me, and has not carried out my commands" (1 Sam. 15:11). Flying into high dudgeon, Samuel confronted Saul and told him that the Lord had stripped the king of his kingship, whereupon he had Agag brought before him and "hewed Agag in pieces" (1 Sam. 15:33). We need not rehearse in detail what we have already clarified about the *herem*. Suffice it to say that Saul, on the biblical reading, was guilty of not properly exercising his kingly leadership in the measure that he did not utterly eradicate evil, but rather played with it, eliminating most of it, but allowing some to endure for his own benefit. He fought evil, but on his own terms and not according to God's will. Can we see Samuel's brutal act, hacking Agag to pieces, as a particularly vivid metaphor for the awful but necessary work of kingly leadership in regard to wickedness? One way to understand the cross of Jesus is to interpret it under the rubric of battle. On that terrible instrument of torture, Jesus did battle *mano a mano* with sin, death, and all of the dark powers. He did not toy with these forces, but rather he fought them all the way down, hacking Agag, as it were, to pieces. In that climactic act of his public ministry, Jesus showed himself the true king of Israel, living up to Pontius Pilate's ironic declaration, "Jesus of Nazareth, the King of the Jews" (John 19:19).

THE ANOINTING OF DAVID

Once it was clear that Saul was fatally compromised as king, Samuel, at the prompting of the Lord, made his way to Bethlehem, the city of Naomi, Ruth, and Boaz, in order to anoint a new ruler for Israel. He is told to go to the house of Jesse, Ruth's grandson, and to look for the king among his sons. When they are brought before him, Samuel notices Eliab, the eldest, and is deeply impressed by his looks. One would think that the prophet would have learned this lesson from the Saul debacle, but the Lord has to remind him, "Do not look on his appearance or on the height of his stature, because I have rejected him" (1 Sam. 16:7). After this, Jesse orders six more of his sons to present themselves to the prophet, but Samuel says that the Lord has chosen none of these. Puzzled, the prophet asks, "Are all your sons here?" Jesse responds that the youngest is out in the fields tending the sheep. Obviously, no one on the scene thought that this boy could be the one Samuel was seeking. But when David presents himself, Samuel knows that he is the one and he immediately anoints him before the eyes of all and, we are told, "The spirit of the LORD came mightily upon David from that day forward" (1 Sam. 16:13).

In accord with a standard biblical instinct, God works best with the lowly, the unlikely, the humble. The most overlooked of Jesse's sons is in fact the one. Moreover, this David emerges as the anointed one (the *Mashiach*) *par excellence*. From this moment on, David becomes the archetype of the messianic figure, which is why very much up to the time of Jesus, David-like qualities were associated with anyone claiming messianic status. How Jesus does and does not fit this expectation will be of enormous interest to the first Christians. Just as Israel was chosen not because of its antecedent merits, so David was seized by the spirit when he is an unproven child, indicating thereby another central biblical motif of the primacy of grace. The narrative of David's life will largely unfold as a story of his cooperation or noncooperation with this grace.

It is most significant that David's first real entry into the story of Israel is as a musician. Saul, we are told, troubled by an evil spirit, asked that someone skilled at playing the lyre should be brought to soothe the king. A courtier remarks that he knows a son of Jesse who is not only a gifted musician but also a man of

valor and prudent in speech. So Saul brings David into his court
and soon comes to love him. Though David will undoubtedly
prove himself to be a great warrior and man of affairs, he first
appears as a singer and player of music, and this aesthetic, "sweet
singer" quality will be ingredient in his manner of leadership
(2 Sam. 23:1).[2] Before he engages Goliath, he will utter a stirringly
poetic challenge; upon the deaths of Saul and Jonathan, he will
speak an achingly beautiful lament; and of course, he comes to be
associated with the most lyrical book of the Bible, the Psalms. So
many of the truly effective political leaders—Lincoln, Churchill,
Napoleon—governed as much by *pathos* as by force of arms or
legislative maneuvering, and this was certainly true of David. Not
to be overlooked, of course, is the fact that God's power is expressed
by means of his word in the creation of the world. God speaks and
things come into being, which signals that God's word is not so
much derivative and descriptive as antecedent and creative. So the
leader who is filled with the Spirit and who wields the divine word
will make things happen. We will remark that when David attends
to God's word, he succeeds, even in his military and political
endeavors. And when the definitive son of David appears, he will
effect change through the power of his word: "Little girl, get up!"
"Lazarus, come out!" "Son, your sins are forgiven;" "This is my
blood of the covenant" (see Mark 5:41, John 11:43, Mark 2:5,
Matt. 26:28).

DAVID AND GOLIATH

But certainly, in the biblical framework, an important dimension
of leadership is skill and courage in battle, and David's possession
of these qualities is presented as unambiguously as possible in his
first appearance on the national scene. We hear that the armies of
Israel and the Philistines are arrayed on facing hilltops. Coming
forth from the Philistine ranks is one Goliath of Gath, described

2. Robert Alter, *The Hebrew Bible: A Translation with Commentary*, vol. 2, *Prophets* (New York: W.W. Norton, 2019), 414.

as standing at a height of "six cubits and a span," which would put him at over eight feet tall. This giant offered to take on a champion from the Israelite army, the winner of this single combat determining the outcome of the war: "If he is able to fight with me and kill me, then we will be your servants; but if I prevail against him and kill him, then you shall be our servants and serve us" (1 Sam. 17:9). As if the giant's stature was not intimidating enough, we are told how impressively Goliath is accoutered for war, a description that can only be characterized as "Homeric" in its specificity: "He had a helmet of bronze on his head, and he was armed with a coat of mail; the weight of the coat was five thousand shekels of bronze. He had greaves of bronze on his legs and a javelin of bronze slung between his shoulders. The shaft of his spear was like a weaver's beam, and his spear's head weighed six hundred shekels of iron" (1 Sam. 17:5–7). And if we are not yet sufficiently impressed by his martial might, we hear that a servant carries Goliath's great shield before him.

Probably more than any other figure in the Scriptures, Goliath, armed and defended by the most sophisticated military technology of the time, symbolizes the power that worldly rulers can muster. He is an anticipation of, and avatar for, Alexander, Caesar, and Stalin. I cannot help but see a connection between this extraordinary array of coverings on the body of Goliath and that first covering of leaves that Adam and Eve used to hide their nakedness, for the former is, in a way, but the full flowering of the latter. Once we step into the world of sin, we must adopt an attitude of suspicion vis-à-vis our fellows, defending ourselves and remaining constantly prepared for battle.

All of Saul's army shrank from the challenge, and Goliath humiliated Israel with further taunts. At this juncture, young David, who had been carrying provisions from his father to his brothers at the front, became cognizant of the situation and eagerly inquired, "What shall be done for the man who kills this Philistine, and takes away the reproach from Israel? For who is this uncircumcised Philistine that he should defy the armies of the living God?" (1 Sam. 17:26). Significantly, these are the first words spoken by David in the Bible, and as is often the case in these scriptural narratives, the opening speech of a hero gives a strong indication of his character. Judging from his first lines, young David is ambitious, fearless, ready to act, and devoted to the Lord. This basic disposition will indeed remain more or less intact for the entire arc of David's life.

Indignant at the effrontery of the giant, David volunteers to take him on, and the young man is brought to the king. At first, Saul is incredulous: "You are not able to go against this Philistine to fight with him; for you are just a boy, and he has been a warrior from his youth." But David protests that, as a shepherd, he successfully fought off lions and bears, and adds, with considerable bravado, "this uncircumcised Philistine shall be like one of them" (1 Sam. 17:33–36). Persuaded, Saul endeavors to outfit the young man with the king's own armor, but David is unable to move under such weight and so encumbered. This is a key indication that this battle will be between worldly power and the higher power of God. Gathering a few stones from the dry creek bed, David goes out, simple sling in hand, to meet the armored titan. Shocked at David's youth and small stature, and certainly more than a little insulted that Israel would have chosen such a pathetic champion to confront him, Goliath cries, "Am I a dog, that you come to me with sticks? . . . Come to me, and I will give your flesh to the birds of the air and to the wild animals of the field." But David reveals the source of his power: "You come to me with sword and spear and javelin; but I come to you in the name of the LORD of hosts, the God of the armies of Israel, whom you have defied" (1 Sam. 17:43–45). And in short order, David slings a stone that embeds itself in the giant's forehead, and the prodigious warrior falls unconscious to the ground, at which point David decapitates Goliath with the Philistine's own sword. The clear implication of this memorable narrative is that the power of God is greater than even the most impressive military force mustered by human beings.

This motif, of course, is a commonplace in the Bible. Though the Scriptures certainly present a good deal of military conflict, and though Israel at times is fairly bloodthirsty, it is remarkable how often the incapacity of Israel is emphasized and the power of God working through its armies is brought to the fore. One thinks, for example, of the paltry band of three hundred soldiers that manages, under Gideon, to win the day; or of the battle described in the tenth chapter of Joshua, during which the stones hurled by God killed more than were killed by the sword; and perhaps most famously, of the conquest of Jericho which, as we saw, was accomplished not by arms but by a kind of liturgical enactment. Thus, apart from the active presence of God, the victory of an adolescent boy, armed only with a slingshot, over an armored giant, is unthinkable.

And all of this points toward the battle that is the culminating event in the history of salvation, the contest that took place on a cross erected on a squalid hill near a quarry outside the walls of Jerusalem. Arrayed against Jesus was the full might of both the Jewish and Roman establishment. The deeply unjust decisions of both the Sanhedrin and Pontius Pilate were backed up by the Roman soldiers stationed in the Antonia Fortress adjacent to the temple, and a coterie of armored Romans conducted Jesus to the instrument of torture that symbolized Rome's intimidation of its enemies. The condemned man was stripped naked and then nailed to the cross, a naked David going out against fully accoutered Goliath. But the power wielded by the crucified Jesus was apparent in his words, "Father, forgive them; for they do not know what they are doing" (Luke 23:34). For the divine forgiveness is greater than anything that is in the world; cruelty, hatred, violence, injustice, and plain stupidity are swallowed up in the mercy of the God of Israel. What the first Christians understood in the wake of the Resurrection of Jesus from the dead is that David had definitively defeated Goliath, that God's love is more powerful than all of the negativity of the sinful world. Paul's ecstatic "I am convinced that neither death, nor life, nor angels, nor rulers, nor things present, nor things to come, nor powers, nor height, nor depth, nor anything else in all creation, will be able to separate us from the love of God" is a consequence of this victory (Rom. 8:38–39). Paul knows this because the sinful world killed God, and God returned in forgiving love: the *shalom* (peace) of the risen Christ (see John 20:19, 21). Jesus indeed came out against Goliath, not with the weapons of the world but "in the name of the LORD of hosts" (1 Sam. 17:45).

SAUL PURSUES DAVID

The next several chapters of 1 Samuel have to do with the internecine war between David and Saul, as the reputation and power of the former increase and those of the latter decrease. Though David began as a servant of Saul, the king comes rather quickly to see David as a rival and seeks to wipe him out. We find here a motif that is often presented in the Bible—namely, the undermining of the mission of Israel through internal strife. To be sure, the holy people is frequently threatened by external forces, but perhaps the most pernicious menace to its integrity and efficacy is civil war.

Trouble commenced in this case when the jealousy of Saul was aroused against the handsome and successful David. When the young man was coming home from a successful sally against the Philistines, "the women sang to one another as they made merry, 'Saul has killed his thousands, and David his ten thousands'" (1 Sam. 18:7). When Saul heard of this, he was livid and sought, from that moment on, to eliminate David. At first, his methods were direct enough. We are told that an evil spirit came upon the king while David was playing the lyre for him, and Saul threw a spear at the singer, hoping to "pin David to the wall" (1 Sam. 18:11). When this proved unsuccessful, Saul adopted a method subtler and more indirect. He promised David that he could have the king's daughter Michal as his wife, but only if he proved sufficiently valiant against the Philistines—hoping that his young rival would be killed in battle. And to make this outcome more certain, he specified the kind of valor he was expecting of David: "The king desires no marriage present except a hundred foreskins of the Philistines, that he may be avenged on the king's enemies" (1 Sam. 18:25). But David turned the tables on the murderous Saul, killing a hundred Philistines and, gruesomely enough, counting out their bloody foreskins in the presence of the king, thereby winning Michal for himself. It cannot, of course, be accidental that, many years later, when David himself wanted to get rid of a rival, he adopted the very method employed by Saul, using Israel's enemies to kill Uriah the Hittite. How often we have seen in our time that the victims of a given sin often become the perpetrator of that same sin upon others.

But the full devastating effects of the civil war between the forces of Saul and those of David are laid out in the remainder of 1 Samuel. Certainly for months, and possibly for years (the chronology is not entirely clear), Saul pursues David, and David is forced to flee from pillar to post. The most terrible moment in this process is Saul's wanton slaughter of the priests at Nob. David had come to Ahimelech and his company of priests, seeking refuge and refreshment for his men. Though all he had was the bread sacred to the Lord, the so-called bread of the presence, Ahimelech agreed to share it with David's band. Subsequently, the high priest gave David the sword of Goliath, which had been sent there for safekeeping, and David made good his escape. Infuriated by this collaboration with his enemy, Saul ordered the priests of Nob, and indeed all of the inhabitants of the city, put to the sword. So awful, in short, was this internecine war that it devastated even the liturgical life of Israel. Kings and priests, instead of embodying the fullness and integrity of Israel, the chosen nation of the Lord, were now at each other's throats. The failure of Adam in the garden was once more playing itself out.

An intriguing feature of this section of the narrative is that David refuses, on numerous occasions, to dispatch Saul when he has the chance. Once, Saul came to relieve himself in a cave where David and his men were hiding, and the rebel could have done in his nemesis with ease. Another time, David and a few companions managed to sneak into Saul's camp while the king and his entourage were asleep. Though Abner, his top military man, offered to kill the slumbering Saul with one spear thrust, David again refused. His rationale, consistent with his harsh response to the Amalekite who later confessed to killing Saul, was that the anointed of the Lord should not be harmed, despite his moral turpitude. At this stage of his life, David was still operating very much under the aegis of God, obedient to his commands and decisions, and willing to accept advancement when God saw fit.

Though David remains, throughout this lengthy episode, remarkably under control and clear in his moral motivation, there is one lapse worthy of consideration. Worn out by the constant harassing he had been receiving from Saul, David reaches a point of near despair: "I shall now perish one day by the hand of Saul; there is nothing better for me than to escape to the land of the Philistines" (1 Sam. 27:1). Subsequently, he moves into Philistine territory, taking up residence in the town of Ziklag, and when the time comes for the Philistines to confront Saul, David joins the enemy! Achish, a Philistine king, says to him, "You know, of course, that you and your men are to go out with me in the army," and David responds, "Very well, then you shall know what your servant can do" (1 Sam. 28:1–2). As Robert Alter indicates, this is analogous to Winston Churchill "spending 1914–1918 in Berlin, currying the favor of the Kaiser."[3] That the young warrior who collected one hundred Philistine foreskins, the slayer of Goliath, the commander of Saul's army pitted for years against Philistia, would blithely become an ally of the enemy is simply astounding. The

3. Robert Alter, *The Hebrew Bible*, 2:291n2.

insertion of this story within the grand narrative is also a powerful indication of the historicity of David, for what mythmaker would include such a puzzling and potentially scandalizing story unless it was part of the well-attested historical record.

The episode is enlightening from a spiritual and moral stand-point as well. The relentlessness of internecine warfare among the followers of the Lord can lead in some to despair and, in others, even to a conversion to the side of the enemy. The Church of Jesus is meant to be the new Israel, an extension of God's holy people. When it is unified, it achieves its ends readily, but when it is divided against itself, it founders, and some of its members even fall into opposition to the Church, crossing, as it were, enemy lines. Saul's harassment of David produced in his former protégé a sort of madness, and the same dynamic obtains up and down the ages, as one faction in the Church persecutes and attacks another.

Just in advance of the decisive battle between the Philistines and Israel, we have the curious episode of the "witch" or necro-mancer of Endor. In accord with Israel's strict monotheism and in line with its suspicion of the religious practices of its neighboring peoples, Saul had issued an edict against all forms of communica-tion with the dead. However, finding himself mortally threatened by the advance of Philistia and incapable of receiving a divine communication through the ordinary means, Saul has recourse to an apparently well-known medium. Disguising himself as well as he can, the king inquires of the woman, "Consult a spirit for me, and bring up for me the one whom I name to you." Aware of the king's prohibition against this sort of enterprise, the woman balks: "Why then are you laying a snare for my life to bring about my death?" But Saul reassures her, and when the necromancer asks whom he wants her to awaken, he says, "Bring up Samuel for me" (1 Sam. 28:8–11). We are not told the means she used to effect this summoning, but the shade of Samuel did indeed present itself, at which point, the woman screamed in terror, not so much at the specter of Samuel, but because she knew at that moment that it was Saul who had importuned her.

The speech of Samuel to Saul is devastating. As was true in life, the ghostly Samuel reacts to Saul with anger: "Why have you disturbed me by bringing me up?" When Saul explains his desperate situation, Samuel shows no sympathy: "Why then do you ask me, since the LORD has turned from you and become your enemy? The LORD has done to you just as he spoke by me; for the LORD has torn the kingdom out of your hand, and given it to your neighbor, David. Because you did not obey the voice of the LORD, . . . therefore the Lord has done this thing to you today" (1 Sam. 28:15–18). The tone and substance remind us of God's revelation to the boy Samuel regarding Eli and his sons. The clear implication, in accord with the constantly reiterated logic of the Bible, is that bad moral choices have bad practical consequences. A disruption at the center of one's life tends to radiate out and produce destructive reverberations.

Saul's spiritual decline reaches its nadir on Mt. Gilboa, where the decisive battle with Philistia is finally joined. Having overwhelmed the Israelite army, the enemy closes in on the king and his sons. With devastating understatement, the author says, "The Philistines killed Jonathan and Abinadab and Malchishua, the sons of Saul" (1 Sam. 31:2). Just like that, the one so dear to the heart of David is wiped out. Finally, they come for Saul. Badly wounded by arrows, the king turns to his armor-bearer and begs him to dispatch him with a thrust of his sword. But the servant balks, and thus Saul falls on his own sword, adding suicide to the long list of his offenses against God. The downward spiral that commenced with his disobedience ends with self-slaughter, and those two phenomena are related, for the latter is but the full expression of the former.

But the Bible never leaves us in despair, for the story it tells us is ultimately a story of grace and redemption. Israel was indeed defeated and its king and his sons dead, but from these ashes rose David, the greatest of Israel's kings and the prototype of the Messiah to come. The biblical intuition is always to look, even in the bleakest desert, for green shoots, for God is continually working his purpose out.

2 Samuel

DAVID LAMENTS SAUL AND JONATHAN

1 Samuel follows the arc of David's life from his youthful adventures with Goliath, through his great successes as an Israelite commander, to his life-and-death struggle with Saul. When we left him at the end of 1 Samuel, he had gone over to serve the Philistines as a sort of vassal. As 2 Samuel opens, David is receiving the news of the demise of Jonathan, Saul, and the entire Israelite army on Mt. Gilboa. The young man, identified as an Amalekite, who had run from the battlefield with Saul's crown and armlet, breathlessly conveys the details of Saul's death, claiming that he, the young man, had actually killed the king, though we had just been told that Saul fell on his own sword. Is he showing off? Is he in fact a more reliable narrator than the author of 1 Samuel? It is impossible to tell, but it is not difficult to understand that David is less than impressed with the Amalekite.

"Were you not afraid to lift your hand to destroy the LORD's anointed?" (2 Sam. 1:14), says the one who had, on numerous occasions, spared Saul's life when he could easily have killed him. David then gives the order to put the Amalekite to death. That the Samuel literature clearly portrays the flaws of kings is undisputed, but at the same time, it demonstrates a deep reverence for the office and person of the anointed of Israel, anticipating the definitive anointed one who is to come.

At this point in the narrative, David delivers himself of the famous elegy we referred to above: the lament over Saul and Jonathan. Once again, it shows to great advantage David the singer, the poet who led his people as much by rhetoric and imagery as by arms and political machination. The song begins, "Your glory, O Israel, lies slain upon your high places! How the mighty have fallen!" (2 Sam. 1:19). The term "high places" carries a range of meanings. First, on the practical level, the heights were the place to which Israel typically fled from the Philistines, whose preferred weapon of war was the chariot, which maneuvered most effectively on level ground. How tragic, David is saying, that even there, on the unlikeliest turf, Israel was conquered. But "high places" also calls strongly to mind the locales where the pagan tribes typically erected their places of worship. So David might also be drawing a connection between Saul's abandonment of the ways of the Lord, most fully expressed in his dealings with the witch of Endor, and the disaster that befell the nation.

He goes on: "Tell it not in Gath, proclaim it not in the streets of Ashkelon; or the daughters of the Philistines will rejoice" (2 Sam. 1:20). In other words, he cannot bear the prospect of a victory song sounding in the cities of the enemy. And could we miss the awful parallel between these humiliating chants and the cries of the Israelite women that accompanied the rise of David: "Saul has killed his thousands, and David his ten thousands" (1 Sam. 18:7). The contrast is breaking the poet's heart. He then curses the ground upon which Saul and Jonathan fell: "You mountains of Gilboa, let there be no dew or rain upon you, nor bounteous fields" (2 Sam. 1:21). This echoes God's malediction of the earth that followed upon the original sin: "Cursed is the ground because of you; in toil you shall eat of it all the days of your life; thorns and thistles it shall bring forth for you" (Gen. 3:17–18). Union with God is consistently associated in the Bible with fruitfulness and life; hence, the conquest of Israel by a nation that worships falsely gives rise to barrenness. David continues to sing: "The shield of Saul, anointed with oil no more" (2 Sam. 1:21). In the ancient world, warriors would anoint their shields so as to make them both more beautiful and more resistant to sword and spear. Thus, David is lamenting the unlovely and battered shield of the fallen Saul. But the mention of the word "anointed" cannot help but call to mind the anointing that Saul received as king of Israel and that he effectively forsook through his disobedience. Thus, his un-anointed shield functions as a symbol of his own discredited kingship. After urging the women of Israel to weep over Saul, David turns his attention to his dear friend, the son of Saul: "Jonathan lies slain upon your high places. I am distressed for you, my brother Jonathan; greatly beloved were you to me; your love to me was wonderful, passing the love of women" (2 Sam. 1:25–26). As Robert Alter suggests, we need not read this as expressive of a homoerotic interest on David's part, for in the warrior culture of that time and place, "the bond between men could easily be stronger than the bond between men and women."[1] What is perhaps of greater interest is David's persistent connection to the house of Saul: he married Saul's daughter; he stubbornly refused to harm the king, even when Saul was actively pursuing him; and he had a special friendship with the son of Saul. When the definitive Messiah came, the one referred to as the son of David, he made central to his teaching the love of one's enemies. Might we see in David's attitude toward the house of Saul an anticipation of this radical moral stance?

DAVID BECOMES KING

Now, in the wake of the demise of Saul, a civil war broke out in Israel between the family of the former king and David, who had begun to consolidate power in the city of Hebron. In short order, Abner, the leader of the Saulide army, and Ishbaal, the son of the former king, were killed, and the tribes came to realize that David

---

1. Robert Alter, *The Hebrew Bible: A Translation with Commentary*, vol. 2, *Prophets* (New York: W.W. Norton, 2019), 311n26.

was their natural leader. The language that their leaders used when they came to see David in Hebron is telling indeed: "Look, we are your bone and flesh. . . . The LORD said to you: It is you who shall be shepherd of my people Israel, you who shall be ruler over Israel" (2 Sam. 5:1–2). Shepherd and ruler are conventional enough, but declaring themselves of the same bone and flesh as David is rather egregious, especially given that these are men of varying tribal heritages. They are evoking practically a "mystical body of David" imagery, whereby David is the one in whom they cohere and live. Again, it is difficult to miss the connection to the descendent of David who, a thousand years later, would be described in similar terms: "For just as the body is one and has many members, and all the members of the body, though many, are one body, so it is with Christ" (1 Cor. 12:12). What is clear is that just as Christ is infinitely more than a mere spiritual teacher, so David is more than a mere political potentate. He is the mystical heart and soul of the nation.

THE CAPITAL AT JERUSALEM

Eager to establish a capital at least somewhat midway between the northern and southern tribes, David conquers the Jebusite city of Jerusalem, mentioned only occasionally prior to this in the Bible. From this time forward, it would play an outsize role in the biblical narratives and as a master symbol in the biblical imagination, evocative of the gathering point of the tribes of Israel and eventually the tribes of the world. What gave it this attractive power was none other than the ark of the covenant, which David endeavored to bring immediately to his new capital. When last we heard of the ark, it had fallen into the hands of the Philistines, but then, through a series of divine interventions, it had made its way to Baal-Judah, a town in the hill country of Judea. David fetched the ark and proceeded to lead it into the city, dancing before it with abandon, all the while wearing the ephod of a priest. Prior to the fall, Adam walked in easy fellowship with God, moving as it were in rhythm with the Lord. After sin, he and his descendants fell into disharmony with the Creator, moving to the rhythm of their own songs. The dance of David before the ark, imitated by the movements and gestures of temple priests in Israel and subsequently by those of Christian priests to the present day, represents the re-harmonization of God and his people. The vocation given to human beings in the very beginning, the summons to offer right praise to God on behalf of all creation, is realized liturgically in the ecstatic moves of David, who shows himself to be both priest and king. After the festive parade, the king placed the ark in a tent that had been prepared for it. This dwelling place, so like the tabernacle in the desert, is the precursor of the great temple, which would be built, in time, by Solomon, the son of David. And the king then did what myriads of priests would do in the presence of the ark for the next several hundred years: "David offered burnt offerings and offerings of well-being before the LORD" (2 Sam. 6:17). Once again, sacrifice is central to Israel's relationship with the Lord, and the Christian cannot help but see in this oblation of David an anticipation of the definitive son of David who, just outside the walls of Jerusalem, would make the ultimate oblation before the God of Israel.

I should like to make one more observation before turning from the festive dance of David. As the Church Fathers loved to point out, there is a profound connection between the ark of the covenant, which carried within it signs of the divine presence, and Mary the Mother of God, who carried within her womb the divine presence itself. We can catch the parallel in the ark's location in the hill country of Judea, for Mary, just after the Annunciation, made her way in haste to the home of her cousin Elizabeth, located precisely in that same region. Also, just as David leaped for joy before the ark, so the unborn John the Baptist leapt for joy in his mother's womb in the presence of the true Ark. And just as David commented, "How can the ark of the LORD come into my care?" (2 Sam. 6:9), so Elizabeth remarked, "And why has this happened to me, that the mother of my Lord comes to me?" (Luke 1:43). We saw that the ark was sometimes carried into battle by the forces of Israel as a conduit of the divine power. The author of the book of Revelation directly associates the ark, resting in the heavenly temple, with the woman clothed with the sun, who engages in battle with the dragon and his angels (Rev. 11:19–12:1).

A TEMPLE FOR THE LORD

With the seventh chapter of 2 Samuel, we come to one of the most pivotal texts in the entire Scripture, one that came to haunt the minds of the children of Israel and that proved decisive in the interpretation of who Jesus is and what he accomplished. At the center of this chapter is the promise given to David through the prophet Nathan that the line of David would last perpetually. This promise serves as a sort of hinge, turning our attention back to Adam, the first but fallen king, and forward to Christ, the son of David whose throne would be established forever. At the outset of the chapter, we find David in a reflective frame of mind. Having established his capital and having conquered the enemies surrounding him, he muses on the contrast between his own dwelling place and that of the Lord: "See now, I am living in a house of cedar, but the ark of God stays in a tent" (2 Sam. 7:2). And so, with the encouragement of his personal prophet, Nathan, David commences to make plans for the building of a temple. But that night, Nathan receives an extraordinary communication from the God of Israel to the effect that God is not pleased with this plan; he had happily dwelt in a tent from the time he led the Israelites from Egypt, and he had something different in mind for David. Instead of David building a house for God, God would build a house for David: "Moreover the LORD declares to you that the LORD will make you a house. When your days are fulfilled and you lied down with your ancestors, I will raise up your offspring after you, who shall come forth from your body, and I will establish his kingdom. He shall build a house for

my name, and I will establish the throne of his kingdom forever"
(2 Sam. 7:11–13).

We notice a moral point of some moment—namely, that
sometimes even our best-intentioned plans are not identical to
God's plans for us. When he was dreaming of the temple, David
was, doubtless, thinking of giving glory to God; nevertheless, the
dream did not correspond to the will of God. Sin obviously stands
athwart God's purposes, but so sometimes do our own non-sinful
aspirations. We ought always to be on our guard whenever a
character in the Bible—Adam, the builders of the Tower of Babel,
Moses at Meribah, David in this story—endeavors to implement
his own projects without a prior consultation with the Lord.

But when we read this communication at the theological and
spiritual level, we see the marvelous economy of grace whereby
what God intends for us is always greater than even our own best
aspirations and hopes. David was convinced, understandably,
that he was conceiving something beautiful for God, but God
had something even more beautiful in mind for David. When
we place our desires in the context of God's desire, something
greater than we had imagined becomes possible. Might we see this
motif expressed with particular clarity in the narratives of Jesus'
multiplication of the loaves and fishes? (see Matt. 14, Mark 6,
Luke 9, John 6). And this greater gift is not only a son who will
build the temple—namely, Solomon—but also this mysterious
descendent whose reign will be without end. What should be
eminently clear is that we are not talking about an ordinary,
merely human successor of David, but rather of a figure who
is indeed of the seed of David but also of another, higher seed.
I have long been struck by the rather astonishing fact that this
text was given its final form most likely in the aftermath of the
Babylonian captivity, in the relatively peaceful years after some of
the Israelite exiles had drifted back to the Promised Land. I say
"astonishing," for by that time, the royal line of David, though it
had had an impressive enough run of nearly four hundred years,

had come rather definitively to an end. So how could the author/editor have included this confident word of the Lord that David's line would last forever? Along practically Kierkegaardian lines, he must have been indulging in a hope against hope, an expectation of the impossible, grounded in the confidence that the story God is telling is unfolding at a level deeper than the surface of history.

That at least certain Israelites kept the dream of 2 Samuel 7 alive is demonstrated in the most vivid way possible in the opening chapter of the Gospel of Luke. We are told that an angel of the Lord appeared to a young girl called Mary and said, "Do not be afraid, Mary, for you have found favor with God. And now, you will conceive in your womb and bear a son, and you will name him Jesus. He will be great, and will be called the Son of the Most High, and the Lord God will give to him the throne of his ancestor David. He will reign over the house of Jacob for ever, and of his kingdom there will be no end" (Luke 1:30–33). Once again, by the time these words were written down, the royal line of David had been extinguished for five hundred years. And yet, we hear in the words of a messenger from a higher dimension of existence the assurance that God had not forgotten his promise to David and that he had indeed arranged for a real descendent of the Israelite king to sit on a throne forever. The one whom the angel announced would, in time, function as both king and priest, reigning from the cross (as Pontius Pilate, with unintended irony, made clear) and offering on that same cross the final sacrifice of praise.

The next three chapters of 2 Samuel lay out the process by which David, having established his capital and having received an incomparable blessing from the Lord, consolidates his rule over the twelve tribes of Israel and indeed over some of the surrounding peoples as well. From a purely political standpoint, we witness a minor potentate from the ancient Middle East extending his power, but from the theological standpoint, we are meant to hear an echo of the command to Adam to extend his reign from Eden to the ends of the world. Israel, God's chosen nation, has a vocation to bring all the nations under the Lordship of God. David's "empire" at least hints at this, and more importantly, it foreshadows the extension of the spiritual kingdom of his definitive son quite literally to the ends of the world.

DAVID AND BATHSHEBA

With chapter 11, we come to a turning point. Having reached the pinnacle of his power, prestige, and spiritual strength, David commences a downward spiral, which will end with the rebellion of his own son against him and an ignominious retreat from his capital. And the decline begins with his curious refusal to fight, his renunciation of one of the principal obligations of his kingship. The opening words of chapter 11 are these: "In the spring of the year, the time when kings go out to battle, David sent Joab with his officers and all Israel with him; they ravaged the Ammonites, and besieged Rabbah. But David remained at Jerusalem" (2 Sam. 11:1). The David that we have come to know never shrank from a fight. Even as an adolescent, he took on the giant Goliath; he culled the foreskins of a hundred Philistines; he led the armies of Saul and then faced down the opposition of the king himself; he successfully outmaneuvered the family of Saul and won control of the tribes of Israel. David was nothing if not a battler. Yet, as chapter 11 gets underway, he stays in the safety of his palace and leaves the fighting to his commander Joab. We hear that the king rose from his couch late one afternoon. In Mediterranean cultures, it is, of course, customary to take a siesta in the afternoon, but one wonders how long David had been asleep if he was arising so late. From the vantage point of the roof of his palace, the king then spied a very beautiful woman who was bathing, presumably on the roof of her own residence. In short order, he discovered that she was Bathsheba, the wife of Uriah the Hittite, one of his valiant soldiers. Without hesitation, heedless of the danger and of his own moral responsibility, he sent for her, had intercourse with her, and impregnated her.

In all of his previous activities, David had invoked the help and counsel of the Lord, but in this episode, David instead pretends to act like God. From his protected height, he surveys his kingdom, sees what he wants, issues his commands, and gets it. Robert Alter has remarked on the brutality of the king's staccato orders and preemptory "sendings" throughout this scene.[2] Rather than listening to a higher voice, as had been his wont, he assumes the prerogatives of supreme authority for the sake of his private pleasure.

What follows is one of the most morally sordid scenes narrated in the Old Testament, and that the central character of this narrative is David, Israel's greatest king, the sweet singer of the house of Israel, makes the story that much more difficult to hear. Panicked at Bathsheba's revelation, David summons Uriah the Hittite to the city, hoping that the soldier might have sex with his wife and thereby cover up David's indiscretion. But in a supreme irony, the foot soldier, who is not even Israelite by birth, proves to be more patriotic and morally upright than the king himself. Ordered by David to go to his house and "wash his feet" (a euphemism for having sex), Uriah refuses: "The ark and Israel and Judah remain in booths, and my lord Joab and the servants of my lord are camping in the open field; shall I then go to my house, to eat and to drink, and to lie with my wife? As you live, and as your soul lives, I will not do such a thing" (2 Sam. 11:11). Frustrated, David shamelessly tries again. He calls Uriah to the palace and proceeds to get the man drunk, hoping that in this compromised condition, he might acquiesce to the king's scheming. But once again, Uriah resists, spending the night with some of David's servants.

Realizing that his pathetic attempts at subterfuge and manipulation have failed, the king cuts to the chase, writing a letter to Joab commanding that Uriah be placed in the thick

2. Robert Alter, *The Hebrew Bible*, 2:351n1.

of the fighting. Adding insult to injury, he sends the letter by the hand of Uriah himself, compelling the consummately loyal Israelite soldier to convey his own death sentence. When Uriah is indeed cut down in battle, David qualifies as both adulterer and murderer, a violator of two of the most solemn commandments given to Moses. Though I have probably belabored this point, it is worth emphasizing how remarkable it is that the author of this text is willing to disclose, with such brutal honesty, the moral failure of one of Israel's greatest heroes, a man who, just a few chapters earlier, was the beneficiary of perhaps the most extraordinary promise given to any figure from the Old Testament. That Israel guards a repugnance for any move in the direction of apotheosizing her leaders is made unmistakably apparent here.

When David receives word that Uriah is dead, he takes Bathsheba as his wife, and it appears as though all has worked out well for him. His kingly authority and power have permitted him to sin grievously and pay no price. But the typically biblical perspective on human power in relation to God is revealed in the tagline at the very end of chapter 11: "But the thing that David had done displeased the LORD" (2 Sam. 11:27). Legitimate political power is correlated to the moral law and finally to the divine law, and hence even the greatest of kings are subject to a superior judgment. Kingly will might be expressed with abandon, but it does not provide for its own justification. What follows in the rest of 2 Samuel is the concrete playing out of this principle, as David is forced to feel, again and again, the negative consequences of his sin. The judgment commences with the famous visit of Nathan to David.

NATHAN AND THE PARABLE OF THE LAMB

Standing in the tradition of Samuel and anticipating the moves of Isaiah, Jeremiah, Ezekiel, Elijah, and Hosea, Nathan, in the name of the Lord, confronts the king, speaking, as the cliché has it, truth to power. With supreme artfulness, Nathan presents his charge indirectly in the form of a parable. In a certain city, he tells the king, there was a poor man who had nothing but a little ewe lamb, which he loved dearly, like one of his own children. Meanwhile, in that same town, there was a rich man who had "very many flocks and herds" (2 Sam. 12:2). One day, a traveler arrived at the home of the rich man, and instead of taking one of the sheep from his ample flock, he stole the poor man's ewe lamb from him and served it to his guest. Outraged by the gross injustice of this scenario, David calls out, "As the LORD lives, the man who has done this deserves to die," to which Nathan responds, with devastating laconicism, "You are the man!" He then lays out the consequences of this sin, channeling the words of the Lord: "I anointed you king over Israel, and I rescued you from the hand of Saul; I gave you your master's house, and your master's wives into your bosom, and gave you the house of Israel and of Judah. . . . Why have you despised the word of the LORD, to do what is evil in his sight?" To his credit, David realizes in a flash that he had done to Uriah precisely what the rich man in Nathan's parable had done to the pauper, and he confesses, "I have sinned against the LORD" (2 Sam. 12:5–9, 13).

Almost immediately, Nathan pronounces the forgiveness of God: "Now the LORD has put away your sin; you shall not die." But then he lays out a first terrible consequence of his offense: "Because by this deed you have utterly scorned the LORD, the child that is born to you shall die" (2 Sam. 12:13–14). I can testify that the standard reading of this passage in the years that I was coming of age was that God offers forgiveness no matter the gravity of our sin. This is indeed a lesson legitimately gleaned from the narrative, but practically no sermon or instruction on the matter that I received as a young man drew any attention to the negative side of the ledger—that is to say, to the "bad karma" that inevitably followed from David's crimes. Not only was the child of Bathsheba to die, but Nathan also indicates the sobering truth that "the sword shall never depart from your house, for you have despised me, and have taken the wife of Uriah the Hittite to be your wife" (2 Sam. 12:10).

THE GREAT STORY OF ISRAEL

Practically the remainder of 2 Samuel is the narrative of how that prediction came true.

TAMAR AND AMNON

The first sign of trouble is the incident involving two of David's children: Tamar and her half-brother Amnon. With the collusion of his crafty cousin, Amnon conspires to seduce the innocent Tamar. Pretending to be ill, he asks the king to send Tamar to nurse him. When she comes into his chamber with carefully prepared cakes, he petitions her to feed him. As she approaches, Amnon grasps her by the hand violently and says, "Come, lie with me, my sister" (2 Sam. 13:11). Knowing full well the penalty attached to such an incestuous crime and painfully aware of the shame that would come upon her if she acquiesces, Tamar resists strenuously. But overpowering her, Amnon has his way with his half-sister. Suddenly filled with loathing for the woman he has just raped, Amnon orders Tamar sent away, and the unfortunate girl, understanding that her life has just essentially come to an end, places ashes on her head, tears her long robe, and cries bitterly as she exits the place and the biblical narrative. With typically understated literary skill and very much in line with our sensibilities today in regard to such matters, the author of this text has allowed us to feel just how horrific this violation was. Taking full advantage of the power differential between them, Amnon has devastated Tamar physically, psychologically, morally, and spiritually. The sword has visited the house of David.

THE REBELLION OF ABSALOM

Hearing of this, Tamar's brother Absalom takes her in and cultivates an intense hatred for the man who has perpetrated the crime. When David learns of the rape, he is, we are told, "very angry," but he refuses to punish Amnon, who is his firstborn (2 Sam. 13:21). We see here a motif that is common in the Bible—namely, the refusal on the part of someone in authority to take appropriate action against evil. We encountered this, we recall, in the episode concerning Eli and his wicked sons, whereby the father's negligence led to a national disaster. Much the same thing unfolds in this context, for David's inaction sets in motion a series of events that bring about, in the long run, rebellion and civil war. Infuriated that David did nothing to Amnon, Absalom takes matters into his own hands. With the full knowledge of his father, he invites all of the sons of David to a festive gathering. He then instructs his servants, "Watch when Amnon's heart is merry with wine, and when I say to you, 'Strike Amnon,' then kill him" (2 Sam. 13:28). With ruthless dispatch, they then carry out the command, and David's remaining sons flee the scene in terror. Fearful for his own life, Absalom subsequently takes flight to the land of Geshur, the home of his mother's family, but David, rather than taking action against his murderous offspring, stays at home and pines for him. So one son had committed rape and another son murder, but David does essentially nothing.

After some time, David sends Joab, his military chief, to fetch Absalom and bring him back to Jerusalem. Showing a touch of backbone, David instructs his son not to come into the king's presence. Nevertheless, Absalom receives no further punishment, and he soon becomes a swaggering presence in the capital. With almost prurient interest, the author of 2 Samuel describes the remarkable attractiveness of David's son: "Now in all Israel there was no one to be praised so much for his beauty as Absalom; from the sole of his foot to the crown of his head there was no blemish in him." But his most stunning feature, we are informed, is his hair: "When he cut the hair of his head (for at the end of every year he used to cut it; when it was heavy on him, he cut it), he weighed the hair of his head, two hundred shekels by the king's weight" (2 Sam. 14:25–26). What is most impressive here is not only the sheer bulk of the young man's hair—roughly five pounds in our terms—but the weird fact that he bothered to weigh his hair at all! It is impossible to miss the narcissism. After two years, David relents and allows Absalom to come into his presence.

His son prostrates himself; David embraces him; and all seems forgiven. Yet a rape and a murder by two separate sons of his remains unaddressed.

Emboldened, Absalom commences to behave like Sonny Corleone, procuring "a chariot and horses, and fifty men to run ahead of him," and ingratiating himself to everyone who comes to the capital to do business with his father (2 Sam. 15:1). His motivation is obvious: to build up a sort of private army and to cultivate wide popular support so as to undertake a seizure of power from his feckless father. One would presume that any canny political observer would have understood what Absalom was up to and that one of the most perceptive and agile operatives in Israelite history—namely, David himself—would have grasped the threat that his son posed to his authority. And yet, the king is either blind or indifferent, or perhaps both. Once he knows that he has the requisite support, and sure that his father lacks the will to resist, Absalom makes his move. Gathering two hundred supporters in Hebron, the city where his father first consolidated his power, and having sent messengers throughout the country to announce the news, Absalom declares himself king. Almost immediately, David flees his capital. This is the same man, we recall, who had battled successfully all his life, often against fearsome odds. But at the mere suggestion of a rebellion, he caves in and commences a pathetic retreat from Jerusalem, up and over the Mount of Olives to the east. The sword, this time wielded by his own beloved son, has once again visited his house.

Though he meets and interacts with a number of people on his slow withdrawal over the mountain, the most famous and wrenching of his encounters is with a member of the house of Saul named Shimei. Seething with anger at David's supplanting of Saul and his family, Shimei confronts the humiliated king: "Out! Out! Murderer! Scoundrel! The LORD has avenged on all of you the blood of the house of Saul, in whose place you have reigned; and the LORD has given the kingdom into the hand of your son

Absalom. See, disaster has overtaken you; for you are a man of blood" (2 Sam. 16:7–8). Though Shimei is focused on David's supposed outrages against Saul and his family, he seems, perhaps despite himself, to be drawing attention to what were indisputably crimes of the king. We know—and David has admitted it—that he is indeed a murderer and a scoundrel because of what he did in the Bathsheba affair. The king effectively acknowledges this, admitting, when one of his aides offered to lop off the head of Shimei, "My own son seeks my life; how much more now may this Benjaminite! Let him alone, and let him curse; for the LORD has bidden him" (2 Sam. 16:11). And thus, as David and his men make their weary way forward, Shimei shouts, curses, and throws dirt at them. This tragic-comic scene is an interesting exemplification of the principle I laid out at the beginning of my analysis of the Samuel books—namely, that God works typically through secondary causes and through the ordinary events of life, which could easily enough be given a purely secular interpretation. Thus, Shimei is an angry Saulide who is excoriating David for what he takes to be the king's cruelty and violence; and he is also an instrument of God's judgment. And these two truths exist noncompetitively side by side.

David's humiliation reaches its nadir when Absalom, having seized the city and the royal palace, orders that a tent be constructed on the roof, that very place whence David had spied Bathsheba many years before. Then he "went in to his father's concubines in the sight of all Israel" (2 Sam. 16:22). Having sex in this grossly public way with all the denizens of his father's harem would have been appreciated by everyone in the city as the supreme insult to David—and it confirmed a prediction contained within Nathan's curse of the murderer of Uriah: "I will take your wives before your eyes, and give them to your neighbor, and he shall lie with your wives in the sight of this very sun. For you did it secretly; but I will do this thing before all Israel, and before the sun" (2 Sam. 12:11–12). Though this is certainly for David the most personally humiliating moment, the king's greatest suffering is still to come.

Having mustered the soldiers still supporting him and having arranged them into groups of hundreds and thousands, David surrenders command to three of his generals and then retires to the city gate. His last instruction to the troops is to "deal gently" with Absalom, if they are to come upon him (2 Sam. 18:5). The battle between David's troops and those of his rebellious son takes place in the forest of Ephraim, and the fighting is brutal, twenty thousand men falling on both sides. But we are told (and here we are reminded of the wilderness campaign in the American Civil War) that the "forest claimed more victims that day than the sword" (2 Sam. 18:8). In the midst of this slaughter and the fog of war, some of David's soldiers come upon Absalom himself. Riding on a mule, Absalom passes under a great oak tree, and the young man's impressive locks become entangled in the overhanging branches so that he is suspended "between heaven and earth" (2 Sam. 18:9). In this hopelessly vulnerable position, he is done to death by three thrusts of Joab's spear and follow-up blows by ten of Joab's armor-bearers. Upon the death of their leader, the rebels melt away, and David's troops carry the day.

A supreme irony, of course, is that Absalom was done in by the very hair that he had carefully cultivated, weighed, and obviously cherished. The tragic-comic manner of his death is an apt symbol of the self-regard that seemed to have been the dominant mark of his character. Though the defeat of Absalom's rebellion is undoubtedly a welcome development for David, the death of Absalom himself is devastating. When messengers come running from the battlefield to inform David of the favorable outcome, the king seems uninterested, even distracted. The one thing he wants to know is the fate of his son. When he is told the awful news, David falls into an inconsolable state, repairing to a chamber over the city gate and weeping loudly, crying out, "O my son Absalom, my son, my son Absalom! Would that I had died instead of you,

O Absalom, my son, my son!" (2 Sam. 18:33). Is there any more emotionally affecting scene in the entire Old Testament? Once again, we are meant to take in not simply the wrenching experience of a father losing a son but also the further confirmation of the awful prediction of Nathan that, due to David's great sins, the sword would never leave his house. God is allowing the king to drink the cursed chalice to the dregs, to feel every possible consequence of his misbehavior. From the sin against Bathsheba and Uriah, the deaths of three of David's children have followed, either directly or indirectly, and his kingdom is, for a time, torn away from him.

THE CENSUS

There is one more story from 2 Samuel that I should like to consider, and it is conveyed in the twenty-fourth and final chapter of the book. It is a peculiar narrative in many ways, and it is rife with theological questions and conundrums. It has to do with David's taking a census of the entire nation. The confusion begins right away, for we are told that God's anger is stirred up (though we are not told why) and that the Lord "incited" David to count the people as a punishment (2 Sam. 24:1). The first question is why enumerating the people would count as punishment. We might venture an answer along these lines: the more carefully a people is counted, the more effectively they can be controlled, taxed, drafted into war, etc. We might see the census, therefore, as an act of administrative and political aggression, much like the census commanded by Caesar Augustus in the first century and described in Luke's Gospel (see Luke 2:1–3). But the real puzzle is why God would stir up David to do something wicked. In order to shed some light on this matter, it might be wise to consult the parallel text in 1 Chronicles, which states that Satan was the one who inspired David to take this evil course (1 Chron. 21:1). Perhaps then, in accord with the customary theological protocol, we could say that the devil directly compels David to wickedness but that God, for his own providential purposes, allows this evil to happen.

At any rate, David sponsors a census of the entire nation, from "Dan to Beer-sheba," and the faithful Joab is given the task of coordinating the effort. Knowing the full implications of the act, Joab initially balks: "May the LORD your God increase the number of the people a hundredfold, while the eyes of my lord the king can still see it! But why does my lord the king want to do this?" (2 Sam. 24:2–3). David's chief warrior provides here an intriguing theological perspective on why the census is such a bad idea. God promised through Abraham and his successors that he would raise up a strong and holy people, that he would, in a word, care adequately for his specially chosen nation. Is David's obsessive counting of the people then not a sign of his mistrust in the Lord and an overweening trust in his own administrative authority? In other words, is the king in this context not attempting to control and manipulate matters just as surely as he did in the Bathsheba-Uriah episode?

However, in time, Joab gives in and conducts the survey, taking over nine months to travel through the land. He dutifully reports the findings to David, but the king is immediately struck in conscience and cries out, "I have sinned greatly in what I have done. But now, O LORD, I pray you, take away the guilt of your servant; for I have done very foolishly" (2 Sam. 24:10). Again, we might be a bit puzzled by this reaction, which seems comparable to that which followed upon David confessing adultery and murder, but the Lord apparently sees nothing anomalous, for he invites the king to choose among three rather awful penances: three years of famine, three months fleeing before David's enemies, or three days of pestilence in the land. This is the only time, by the way, in the entire Scripture that a human being is given the prerogative of choosing the manner of his punishment. Typically, this is a function of the sovereign will of God; therefore, might we see this proposal as still another sign of God's predilection for David?

Preferring to fall into the hands of God rather than into the hands of men, David chooses pestilence, and the Lord follows suit, resulting, we are told, in the deaths of seventy thousand. Is there irony in the fact that this figure comes to just over half the number of the 130,000 fighting men that had been counted in the census? Is the author, as it were, mocking David's attempt to control and manage his situation, indicating clearly that God can eliminate, in three days, most of what the king had built up over many years? But still, the stubborn question remains—and it comes up again and again in the biblical texts: How could an omnibenevolent God permit such a seemingly indiscriminate slaughter, precisely of people who had nothing to do with the sin that is being addressed? St. Jerome himself commented on this episode, placing God's action in a capacious context: "Ask [God] why, when Esau and Jacob were still in the womb, he said, 'Jacob have I loved, but Esau have I hated.' . . . And why, when David sinned by numbering the people, so many thousands lost their lives. . . . [You] condescend to remain ignorant of that into which you inquire. Leave to God his power over what is his own.'"[3] The issue is not simply the number of the slain but what at least appears to be the stark unfairness of God's action. Though this matter will be addressed fully only in the book of Job, we are obliged to say, even at this point in the biblical narrative, that everything that transpires—both the good and the bad from our perspective—is ingredient in God's ultimately benevolent design. Flannery O'Connor rather blandly reminded us that, for people of faith, physical death is not the worst of fates.[4] Therefore, whatever God effects or allows within this world—including the deaths of tens of thousands—contributes to a purpose that we cannot see with clarity. It is, I know, exceptionally hard to say this, but to say otherwise is to imply that God should not be God.

3. Jerome, *Letters* 133.9, in *St. Jerome: Letters and Select Works*, ed. Philip Schaff and Henry Wace, trans. W.H. Fremantle, G. Lewis, and W.G. Martley, vol. 6, A Select Library of the Nicene and Post-Nicene Fathers of the Christian Church, Second Series (New York: Christian Literature Company, 1893), 278.

4. Flannery O'Connor, "An Interview with Flannery O'Connor" in *Conversations with Flannery O'Connor* (Jackson: University Press of Mississippi, 1987), 58.

The tale of the census-pestilence comes to its climax with the avenging angel of the Lord—so reminiscent of the angel of the Passover—stretching out his "hand towards Jerusalem to destroy it" (2 Sam. 24:16). Because of David's sin, his great capital, established for the express purpose of uniting the tribes around the right worship of God, is now in danger of annihilation. Giving voice to one of the most emotionally affecting prayers in the entire Bible, David cries out, "I alone have sinned, and I alone have done wickedly; but these sheep, what have they done? Let your hand, I pray, be against me and against my father's house." In answer to this prayer, God gives a peculiar answer. Through the prophet Gad, the Lord instructs David to "erect an altar to the LORD on the threshing floor of Araunah the Jebusite" (2 Sam. 24:17–18). So the king buys that ground, builds an altar, and there makes sacrifice to God, and the Lord answers his supplication and the "plague was averted from Israel" (2 Sam. 24:25).

There are a number of details that warrant commentary here. First, the presence of a Jebusite in the city that David had conquered shows, first, the clemency of the king, since he obviously did not simply slaughter the inhabitants of the vanquished town. More importantly, the "foreigner" draws attention to the consistent biblical motif of the international purpose of God's dealings with Israel. We are meant to see that whatever happens on this newly purchased site will have implications for nations beyond Israel. Second, the identification of this ground as a "threshing floor" is of considerable moment. Mentioned frequently in biblical texts, threshing floors were places where the edible portion of grain was separated from husky chaff. Using a kind of fork or rake (it's called a "winnowing fork" in the Gospel of Luke [see Luke 3:17]), the thresher would toss the grain into the air on a windy day, thereby permitting the wheat to fall to the ground and the chaff to be blown away. A threshing floor was, therefore, a place of separation, demarcation, isolation of good from bad—motifs of obvious importance to a people shaped by the books of Leviticus and Deuteronomy. Finally, the erection of an altar, a place of sacrifice, is theologically crucial. This threshing floor of Araunah will come, in time, to be the locale of the Jerusalem temple, the place where, for a thousand years, sacrifice would be offered to the God of Israel—that is to say, ritual acts that effectively separated the chaff of sin from the people, rendering them righteous. The entire purpose of that place and those acts would be to hold off the pestilence of sin, which threatens to destroy the people Israel.

How wonderful that the books of Samuel, which commenced with the story of a simple woman begging God to give her a child, should end with the buying of the land on which the begging prayers of the entire people would go up to God.

1 Kings

There is a rather hodgepodge or miscellaneous quality to the books of Kings (which, like the books of Samuel, were originally one text), but we might identify two master themes. The first is the play between kings and prophets, and the second is the centrality of the temple. As the title indicates, this literature has a great deal to do with kings—David and his immediate successor and then the kings of Israel and Judah, who emerge as rivals to one another after the splitting of David's kingdom. But these political rulers, so often corrupt, are consistently presented in tensive relationship with the representatives that God sends to speak his word. The paradigmatic instance of this relationship is the narrative at the center of 1 Kings concerning Ahab the king and Elijah the prophet. The second key theme is the temple, the building and decoration of which is obsessively laid out toward the beginning of 1 Kings and the heartbreaking destruction of which is baldly laid out at the end of 2 Kings. How and where God is to be rightly worshipped, a preoccupation of the Bible from the very beginning, clearly engages the attention of the author of Kings—as does the vexed problem of why the sovereign Lord of Israel would permit the annihilation of the very place that he had so carefully and over such a long period of time cultivated.

THE DEATH OF DAVID

1 Kings opens with a section that might have belonged originally to 2 Samuel, for it deals with the final period of David's life. More than in regard to any other figure in the Old Testament, we have an account of the entire arc of David's life, from the time of his youth, through myriad accomplishments and trials, to the bitter end of his days as a decrepit old man. When we first encounter him on the opening page of 1 Kings, he lies in his bed, freezing cold, though he is covered in blankets. We are given the memorable detail that a beautiful girl by the name of Abishag the Shunammite is sent to keep him warm, though they do not engage in sexual intercourse. The great warrior, in a word, has become helpless, vulnerable, cold, and impotent.

As happens almost invariably in monarchical polities, the imminent death of a king produces enormous tension. In this case, one of David's sons, Adonijah, had commenced to organize support for himself throughout the country, which roused Nathan the prophet to take action on behalf of Bathsheba and her son Solomon. Though we are not told of this directly in the narrative, David had evidently promised that Solomon, his second son with Bathsheba, would succeed him, and so Bathsheba, with the collusion of Nathan, laid out the case to the aged king. Acquiescing without argument, David arranged for Solomon to be named a sort of coadjutor king, even as David still lived, and thus in Gihon, not far from the capital, Solomon was formally declared ruler. Well aware of the *Realpolitik* that governed such situations, Adonijah's followers fled in fear, and Adonijah himself "went to grasp the horns of the altar," effectively seeking sanctuary from any punishment his kingly brother would see fit to visit upon him (1 Kings 1:50). For the moment, Solomon allowed his rival to live.

David's death is recounted in a somewhat disedifying manner. The old man drew Solomon close and gave his last instructions. The young man was indeed to obey the commandments of the Lord, but he was also to carry out some brutal assignments—namely, to kill Joab, whom David cannily surmises to be a potential rival to Solomon, and to murder Shimei, the man who had cursed David on his journey up the Mount of Olives after Absalom's rebellion. In point of fact, the very last words we hear from the great King David in the Bible are these, in regard to Shimei: "Therefore do not hold him guiltless, for you are a wise man; you will know what you ought to do to him, and you must bring his gray head down with blood to Sheol" (1 Kings 2:9). How odd that the sweet singer of Israel, the composer of the magnificent lament over Jonathan and Saul, the eloquent challenger to Goliath, the one traditionally associated with the writing of the Psalms, should go out with such a bluntly stated, indeed murderous, command on his lips. Once again, the frankness of the Bible in regard to even its greatest heroes is on full display.

KING SOLOMON AND THE GIFT OF WISDOM

Following the death of his father, Solomon quickly consolidated his power, indeed rapidly putting to death the two men that David had designated, and "so the kingdom was established in the hand of Solomon" (1 Kings 2:46). Once again, we might focus on the desperate Michael Corleone dimension of this story, but we must always keep in mind that the establishment of a king was tantamount to a recovery of the Adamic function. An Israel without stable kingly leadership would be unable to fulfill its missionary mission vis-à-vis the rest of the world.

And the Adamic quality of the new king comes to expression in the very next story, the famous narrative of Solomon's request of wisdom, the same faculty that Adam demonstrated in the naming of the animals in Eden. While he is in Gibeon to offer sacrifice, the Lord appears to Solomon in a dream and says, "Ask what I should give you" (1 Kings 3:5). In the first chapter of the Gospel of John, we hear that two disciples of John the Baptist follow after Jesus. The Lord turns on them and inquires, "What are you looking for?" (John 1:38). There is a story told of Thomas Aquinas in the latter years of his life. Having laid the text of the Eucharistic treatise from the third part of the *Summa theologiae* at the foot of the cross, Thomas heard a voice saying, "You have written well of me, Thomas, what would you have as a reward?" Solomon, the disciples of the Baptist, and Thomas Aquinas all faced a moment of truth, a time to articulate what was of prime value to them. God himself was asking, frankly and directly, what they wanted with all their heart. Thomas responded, "Nothing but you, Lord," and the disciples of John replied with another question, "Where are you staying?" (John 1:38). They were asking essentially for the same thing: not a good to satisfy some superficial desire, not for wealth or power or prestige or pleasure, but for Christ himself.

Solomon's answer to the Lord is of the same type: "Give your servant therefore an understanding mind to govern your people, able to discern between good and evil; for who can govern this your great people?" (1 Kings 3:9). As God himself specifies in his response to Solomon, the king, to his credit, did not seek the superficial goods that would satisfy the ego—"Because you have asked this, and have not asked for yourself long life or riches, or for the life of your enemies . . . I now do according to your word" (1 Kings 3:11–12). Rather, he had petitioned for a participation in the mind of God, an opportunity to see the world from God's perspective and to engage it with God's intentionality. The spiritual point in all of these stories is clear. When we place God and God's purposes at the center of our lives, we can live happily with either wealth or poverty, with either fame or obscurity, with either power or weakness. And when we place some worldly good at the center, that very value will in time destroy us, for we will not have the wisdom to manage it properly. That God grants to Solomon riches and honor as well as the wisdom that the king directly petitioned is a sign of this right ordering; endowed with God's perspective, he will know, presumably, how to use his wealth and prestige for God's purposes. The first indication that the gift has been truly given and received is that Solomon, upon waking from the dream, "offered up burnt offerings and offerings of well-being" (1 Kings 3:15). Authentic wisdom conduces invariably toward right worship, and the establishment of right worship is the prime responsibility of the new Adam.

Of course, the famous story of the "Solomonic" judgment that the king makes in regard to the two prostitutes, each claiming to be mother of the same child, is designed to show the wisdom with which God had endowed the king. What is perhaps most remarkable about that narrative is that Solomon's harsh decision to sever the disputed baby in two was meant to discern the love of the true mother. So concerned was she with the baby and not her own vindication that she was willing to let him go in order to save him. In a word, the wisdom of the king did not simply uncover the truth of the matter but also discovered and awakened love, which is precisely the mark of God's wisdom.

THE TEMPLE IN JERUSALEM

With the fourth through tenth chapters of 1 Kings, we come, in a sense, to the high point of the entire Old Testament narrative, for in this section we see Solomon reigning over a united Israel as well as commanding a number of neighboring nations in an imperial manner, having become the king that Israel had been longing for since the fall of Adam. Moreover, in these chapters, we find the stirring description of the building of the Jerusalem temple in all of its splendor, which brought to fulfillment Israel's vocation to be a priestly people. Finally, we see potentates coming to Jerusalem to bask in Solomon's glory and to benefit from his wisdom, thus realizing Israel's destiny to be a magnet to the nations of the world. From both a material and spiritual standpoint, things never get better for ancient Israel, and thus this Solomonic splendor also serves as a kind of fulcrum on which the rising and falling of Israel can be measured.

From a Christian standpoint, Solomon, the son of David and Israel's most successful king, is an obvious type of Christ Jesus, the king *par excellence* destined to rule spiritually over all the nations. And thus, how could we overlook the curious detail recounted in chapter 4 that "Solomon had twelve officials over all Israel, who provided food for the king and his household" (1 Kings 4:7). Representing, of course, the twelve tribes of Israel, they are carefully named, just as their successors, the twelve Apostles of Jesus, are also specified by name in the Gospels. We hear that "Judah and Israel were as numerous as the sand by the sea," thus fulfilling the prophecy made to Abraham and that "Solomon was sovereign over all the kingdoms from the Euphrates to the land of the Philistines, even to the border of Egypt" (1 Kings 4:20–21). This kind of sovereignty would be surpassed in the biblical witness only by the one declared "King of the Jews" and "*Kyrios*," and who said of himself, "something greater than Solomon is here " (Matt. 12:42; Luke 11:31). Moreover, the intelligence of Solomon "surpassed the wisdom of all the people of the east, and all the wisdom of Egypt," and was evidenced in the "three thousand proverbs" that he composed, the one thousand and five songs that he wrote, and in his disquisitions on "animals, and birds, and reptiles, and fish" (1 Kings 4:30–33). The king was an astonishing amalgam of poet and scientist. Here again, of course, the Christian is put in mind of Christ, who was not only a great connoisseur of the Logos, but the Logos himself in person. Thus, we are meant to see in the glory and power and intellectual capaciousness of Solomon a this-worldly reflection, an iconic representation, of the splendor of Christ.

With chapter 5, we come to the description of the construction of the temple. Anticipated by the tabernacle in the desert and dreamed of by David, it is now brought to fulfillment, as the Lord had indicated, by the son of David. We hear first that Solomon enjoyed the support of Hiram, the king of Tyre, who had been an ally to David, and who agreed to send massive amounts of cedar wood, for which his country was famous. Both the servants of Hiram and the servants of Solomon worked together on the project of preparing and transporting the timber, signaling the inauguration of a reign of peace. Moreover, the international nature of the work spoke of the universal purpose of the building that they were endeavoring to erect: "So Solomon's builders and Hiram's builders and the Gebalites did the stonecutting and prepared the timber and the stone to build the house" (1 Kings 5:18).

The structure itself, around which there has been endless fascination over the centuries, is described in chapter 6: "In the four hundred eightieth year after the Israelites came out of the land of Egypt . . . [Solomon] began to build the house of the LORD" (1 Kings 6:1). The passage of time referenced is almost certainly a symbolic number, the result of multiplying two sacred figures—namely, forty and twelve—for as Alter indicates, the real amount of time would be roughly half of that.[1] What is hinted at in the symbolic number, of course, is that the temple represents a *Kairos* or a fullness of time. We are told that the structure was "sixty cubits long, twenty cubits wide, and thirty cubits high" (1 Kings 6:2). Though this involves a fair amount of guesswork, since the exact meaning of these measures is unclear, we can speculate that the temple itself was actually quite compact, its length being less than 120 feet—which is to say, about a third of the size of a typical Gothic cathedral. What matters, of course, is not the sheer size of the place but its proportionality. The harmonic relationships of height, length, and breadth in the temple—which gave rise in turn to a complex series of further harmonies and mathematical relationships—were meant to symbolize the reharmonizing of humanity and indeed all of creation with God. Adam's effortless walking with the Lord, which was compromised by sin, is reestablished through the right praise offered within the pleasingly ordered space of the temple.

Like the tabernacle of Moses in the desert, Solomon's temple had three major divisions: an outer court, an inner sanctuary, and the Holy of Holies, which was the receptacle of the ark of the

1. Robert Alter, *The Hebrew Bible: A Translation with Commentary*, vol. 2, *Prophets* (New York: W.W. Norton, 2019), 457n1.

covenant. The liturgical movement from one to another suggested the transformation of the worshiper from death to life, from sin to salvation. The association with the Garden of Eden is made even clearer when we learn that the decorations of the temple included cherubim, palm trees, open flowers, etc. As we have seen from the very beginning of the Bible, salvation is never construed by the biblical authors as having uniquely to do with human beings. Rather, human beings were meant to be the priests through whom a unified creation gives praise to the Creator. That very dynamic of cosmic unity accomplished through praise is on display in the plants, animals, and angels subsisting within the ordered harmonies of the temple's architecture. It is, of course, no accident whatsoever that so many of the great sacred edifices of Christianity, from Roman basilicas to Romanesque churches, to Gothic cathedrals and neoclassical chapels, found their inspiration in the temple of Solomon. In Notre Dame and Chartres Cathedrals, to give just two examples, one can find the same harmonic proportions and the presence of plants, animals, angels, fantastic creatures, planets, and stars in the decoration. One is meant to be changed by such places, harmonized and brought into right relationship with God and his creation, precisely through the right praise that unfolds therein.

Finally, we are informed that it required seven years to complete the building of the temple. Though this might reflect the historical truth, it is more likely a number meant to convey a theological point, for seven represents, of course, the sabbath day, the day of rest after the effort of creation—the day, therefore, of worship. Moreover, seven is consistently associated in ancient Israel with the cutting of covenants, and the temple is the place *par excellence* where the covenant between God and his people is enacted and concretized.

Chapter 7 of 1 Kings will detail many more of the features of the temple and its environs, but it commences in a curious way with the description of Solomon's construction of his own palace, so that this account effectively interrupts the narrative of the temple's coming to be. We are told that the erection of his personal home took thirteen years, nearly twice what it required to build the temple, and that it is almost twice the size of that great place of worship: a hundred cubits long, fifty cubits wide, and thirty cubits high. There appear to have been, in fact, a number of buildings making up a sort of palace complex, for there is reference to "the House of the Forest of the Lebanon," as well as to "the Hall of Pillars" and "the Hall of the Throne" (1 Kings 7:2, 6–7). And for good measure, he also constructed, we learn, a separate house for the Pharaoh's daughter whom he had taken as his wife. Now, the fact that Solomon commenced the construction of his private residence after the major work on the temple had been completed can be given a spiritually positive reading to the effect that the king clearly prioritized the house of the Lord over his own house, the sacred over the secular. However, the rather substantial difference in size between the two edifices, unmistakably emphasized by the author of 1 Kings, certainly could be construed as a foreshadowing of Solomon's spiritual decline, his tendency, increasingly evident over time, to privilege his own comfort and power over the demands of God.

After the relatively brief description of the construction of the king's home, the narrator returns to the work on the temple, commencing with the fashioning and placing of stately pillars at the vestibule of the holy place. He then moves on to a description of the "molten sea," which is to say a capacious vessel of water that stood five cubits in height and that was situated at the entrance of the temple (1 Kings 7:23). The great bowl is supported by twelve metal oxen, three facing in each of the cardinal directions, their hindquarters toward the inside. The reference to this receptacle as a "sea" is meant to capture its cosmic significance, perhaps as a kind of symbol of the oceans and rivers of the world, but it has a practical and liturgical purpose—namely, to aid in the purification of the hands and feet of both worshippers and priests.

We are furthermore told of the ten lampstands or menorahs that serve to illumine the interior of the inner sanctum, as well as "the golden table for the bread of the Presence" (1 Kings 7:48). These loaves of "show-bread" were probably pita-like and were stacked in two piles of six and changed every sabbath. In a sense, they functioned as offerings to God by the people Israel, but, as the name suggests, they were also, due to their proximity to the Holy of Holies, imbued with the "presence" of God. How could a Christian, especially a Catholic Christian, possibly overlook the link between these loaves of bread, stored in the temple and radiant with God's presence, and the Eucharistic species, stored in the tabernacle and functioning as the physical sign of the Real Presence of Christ?

The beautiful and liturgically exuberant eighth chapter of 1 Kings is the climax of the narrative of the temple. Having completed his astonishing work, the king calls together all of the leaders of the nation to celebrate the dedication of the edifice and the transfer thereto of the ark of the covenant, which his father, many years before, had brought to Jerusalem. In the presence of this throng, Solomon then delivers himself of one of the most extraordinary prayers preserved in the Bible, one that not only expresses the solemnity and joy of the moment but also contains an extremely subtle theology of God. The opening words of the oration are worthy of careful attention: "O LORD, God of Israel, there is no God like you in heaven above or on earth beneath" (1 Kings 8:23). Like many in the Israel of that time, Solomon holds, it seems, not to a strict monotheism but to a kind of sophisticated henotheism—that is to say, the belief in the superiority of one's particular God over other divine entities in the pantheon. But we should attend to the nature of the superiority that Solomon is claiming for the God of Israel. He is maintaining not so much that his God is the greatest in the category of "divine realities," but that no other god is even like his God. The divine power that Solomon evokes is not supreme among gods but utterly unique, unlike anything, even of the highest ontological quality, in either heaven or earth. As the prophet Isaiah will insist, almost obsessively, in text after text in the middle chapters of his book, God is, properly speaking, incomparable: "I am the LORD, and there is no other; besides me there is no god" (Isa. 45:5), and "There is no other god besides me, a righteous God and a Savior; there is no one besides me" (Isa. 45:21); "For I am God, and there is no other" (Isa. 46:9); "To whom will you liken me and make me equal, and compare me, as though we were alike?" (Isa. 46:5).

We must recall, at this point, the observations made in regard to the opening verses of the Bible. Precisely as *Creator* of the finite world, God cannot be construed as one of the beings within that realm or as belonging to any categories suited to the description of things in it. *Ipsum esse* rather than *ens summum*, the Creator God is, strictly speaking, incomparable to any worldly object or state of affairs. He is other to the universe he has made but in a non-contrastive manner. If he were "other" in a conventional way—as, say, the planet Jupiter is other than the earth—then he could be compared and contrasted easily enough with similar objects within the same metaphysical framework. By the same token, if he were identical to the world or to nature—according to, say, the Spinozan or pantheist conception—he would be easily controlled and understood. But, as we saw, God is neither graspable nor avoidable; he is both *intimior intimo meo et superior summo meo*, precisely because of the unconditioned quality of his existence.

This rather abstract philosophical language is given a parallel imagistic expression in Solomon's great prayer. As the temple fills with the smoke of God's presence, an indication simultaneously of both God's visibility and invisibility, Solomon asks rhetorically, "But will God indeed dwell on the earth? Even heaven and the highest heaven cannot contain you, much less this house that I have built!" And he petitions, "Hear the plea of your servant and of your people Israel when they pray toward this place; O hear in heaven your dwelling place; heed and forgive," and "When your people Israel, having sinned against you, are defeated before an enemy but turn again to you, confess your name, pray, and plead with you in this house, then hear in heaven" (1 Kings 8:27, 30, 33). This temple is undoubtedly God's dwelling on earth, his home in a practically literal sense, the place where God delights to dwell. But at the same time, Solomon is perfectly cognizant of the fact that the Creator of the universe is not a local deity whose presence can be specified and circumscribed. Even as God is approachable in the building where he has deigned to reside, he remains uncontainable. The language being employed here is paradoxical and not contradictory since that which transcends time can be present to every moment of time, and that which transcends space can be present to every particular space. "Over" time and "over" space, God can be in time and in space noncompetitively. We recall in this context the symbolism of the burning bush: as the true God comes close to what he has made, he does not destroy it, forcing it to give way; rather, he elevates it and makes it more beautiful, more authentically itself.

Especially with these theological clarifications in mind, the Christian sees in this dedication of the temple a foreshadowing of the one who said, in reference to himself, "something greater than the temple is here" (Matt. 12:6). One of the most startling claims that Jesus made about himself is that the people of Israel should come to him for those goods that they formerly sought in the temple: forgiveness, teaching, and healing. And he confirmed this identification when, after purifying the temple of the money changers, and after having been challenged to give a sign to justify his action, he blithely commented, "Destroy this temple, and in three days I will raise it up" (John 2:19). The bystanders remark on the absurdity of this claim, reminding him that the construction of this Herodian version of the sacred place had taken forty-six years. The author of the Gospel provides the indispensable gloss: "But he was speaking of the temple of his body" (John 2:21). In a word, Jesus himself is the very particular "place" where the God of Israel, who cannot be contained by the entire universe, deigned in a unique and unrepeatable way to dwell. The coming together in him of divinity and humanity, in such a way that neither is compromised by its proximity to the other (without mixing, mingling, or confusion, as the Council of Chalcedon puts it), is made possible, once again, by the noncompetitive otherness of the unconditioned reality.[2] As we shall see, the temple of Solomon, presented to us in all of its splendor, will, in relatively short order, be destroyed, just as the temple on the same site known to Jesus and his followers would be obliterated just forty years after the time of Christ. But the temple of Jesus' Body, the Church, will endure forever. And thus, we can appreciate these earthly incarnations of the temple as beautiful but ultimately fragile anticipations of the true and heavenly temple.

A particularly vivid example of the biblical tendency to plant the seeds of destruction even in the soil of the greatest accomplishment is the Lord's answer to the great prayer of Solomon, which can be found in the ninth chapter of 1 Kings. God tells the king that he has heard Solomon's prayer and stands ready to respond favorably, as long as the people walk in the Lord's ways. But if they do not (and it is practically guaranteed that they will not, if the biblical narrative to this point is any indication), then, he says, "I will cut Israel off from the land that I have given them; and the house that I have consecrated for my name I will cast out of my sight; and Israel will become a proverb and a taunt among all peoples. This house will become a heap of ruins; everyone passing by it will be astonished" (1 Kings 9:7–8). Mind you, this dire warning comes just a handful of lines after the triumphant description of the building of the temple, and just a handful of chapters later, at the end of 2 Kings, it will all come true. Even as the text says yes, it insists upon saying no, lest we are tempted to cling to any worldly symbol of God, no matter how impressive.

2. Council of Chalcedon, "Definition of the Two Natures of Christ," in Heinrich Denzinger et al., *Compendium of Creeds, Definitions, and Declarations on Matters of Faith and Morals*, 43rd ed. (San Francisco: Ignatius, 2012), no. 302.

THE QUEEN OF SHEBA

The tenth chapter of our text, which treats of the visit to Solomon of the queen of Sheba, is, in a similar way, both triumphant and admonitory. Once he has consolidated his power within Israel and built his palace and temple, Solomon emerges as a figure of enormous attractiveness to the surrounding nations. We are told that his fame is so great that it has spread to the land of Sheba (most likely somewhere in the vicinity of present-day Yemen, quite a ways from Israel, along the southern shore of the Red Sea). Accordingly, the queen of that land endeavors to travel north to see for herself if Solomon were as wise as advertised. She arrives in Jerusalem, we hear, "to test him with hard questions" (1 Kings 10:1). But when she poses her puzzles and riddles to Solomon, he solves them all effortlessly and dazzles her further with the splendor of his palace, possessions, and retinue until "there was no more spirit in her." Frustrated, but delighted in her frustration, she says, "The report was true that I heard in my own land of your accomplishments and of your wisdom, but I did not believe the reports until I came and my own eyes had seen it. . . . Blessed be the LORD your God, who has delighted in you and set you on the throne of Israel!" (1 Kings 10:5–9). This charming scene once again signals the finally international purpose of the revelation given to Israel. In the second chapter of his book, the prophet Isaiah imagines all of the tribes of Israel, and indeed all the nations, going up to Jerusalem to worship the true God. The queen of Sheba is an anticipation of this general pilgrimage.

We are then given an account of Solomon's astonishing wealth: "The weight of gold that came to Solomon in one year was six hundred sixty-six talents of gold," so that he was able to make "three hundred shields of beaten gold" and "all [his] drinking vessels were of gold" (1 Kings 10:14, 17, 21). Moreover, he gathers an enormous number of horses and chariots, more specifically, "fourteen hundred chariots" and "twelve thousand horses" (1 Kings 10:26). And as chapter 11 commences, we learn that he also has a staggering number of women at his disposal: "seven hundred princesses and three hundred concubines" (1 Kings 11:3). Especially in the context of the ancient Middle East, all of this was considered impressive indeed. But then we recall what the book of Deuteronomy had said regarding the containment of the arrogance of kings. John Bergsma and Brant Pitre point out that in chapter 17 of that text, we find explicitly condemned all three of the ways in which Solomon had aggrandized himself: "Even so, he must not acquire many horses for himself. . . . And he must not acquire many wives for himself, or else his heart will turn away; also silver and gold he must not acquire in great quantity for himself" (Deut. 17:16–17).[3]

What is being not so subtly forecast here is the downfall of Solomon, which will result in the division of the nation into two. Once more, reading these texts through Christian lenses, we see that we are meant finally to focus not on Solomon in all of his worldly glory, but rather on the true King who reminded us that even the lilies of the field are clothed more gloriously than Solomon and who said, in reference to himself, "something greater than Solomon is here" (Matt. 12:42; Luke 11:31). We look at Solomon, to be sure, but then we look, as it were, through him to a truer king.

THE DOWNFALL OF SOLOMON

The corruption of the king becomes unmistakably apparent in chapter 11, situated more or less at the midpoint of 1 Kings. The opening line of the chapter gives away the game: "King Solomon loved many foreign women along with the daughter of Pharaoh: Moabite, Ammonite, Edomite, Sidonian, and Hittite women, from the nations concerning which the LORD had said to the Israelites, 'You shall not enter into marriage with them, neither shall they with you; for they will surely incline your heart to follow their gods'" (1 Kings 11:1–2). What should be eminently clear from this

---

3. John Bergsma and Brant Pitre, *A Catholic Introduction to the Bible*, vol. 1, *The Old Testament* (San Francisco: Ignatius, 2018), 392–393.

statement is that the Lord's prohibition has nothing to do with blind prejudice against non-Israelite tribes, still less against women as such. Rather, in line with one of the most fundamental themes of the Bible, it is a warning against the worship of false gods, or bad praise. Solomon's glory was precisely his construction of a place of right praise and his leadership of the nation in the direction of that praise. And so his downfall will be connected to the suspension of orthodoxy. Despite his vaunted wisdom, Solomon's mind and heart were turned to "Astarte the goddess of the Sidonians, and Milcom the abomination of the Ammonites," and he even endeavored to build a "high place for Chemosh the abomination of Moab, and for Molech the abomination of the Ammonites, on the mountain east of Jerusalem" (1 Kings 11:5–7). How could anyone miss that all of this constituted a pathetic parody of the construction of the temple? And that the gods in question here were typically honored through human sacrifice shows the depths of Solomon's moral depravity. On the biblical reading, morality is downstream of liturgy, so the worship of false gods conduces ineluctably toward wicked ethical behavior.

And still another consequence of false worship is political and social disintegration. David and Solomon, despite their sins and limitations, both labored to bring the tribes of Israel together around the ark of the covenant. Once false worship held sway in the nation, that unity, however tenuous, commenced rapidly to fall apart. The Lord, we are told, raises up a number of external enemies to Israel. But then, a devastating internal division takes hold, led by Jeroboam, an erstwhile supporter of Solomon, who consolidates power in the north, gathering ten of the twelve tribes under his leadership. This political development is given a devastating theological interpretation by the prophet Ahijah, who gives God's own justification for the division: "This is because [Solomon] has forsaken me, worshiped Astarte the goddess of the Sidonians, Chemosh the god of Moab, and Milcom the god of the Ammonites, and has not walked in my ways" (1 Kings 11:33).

But out of loyalty to David, God determines to leave one tribe with Solomon, along with his own tribe of Judah. With that, we have the awful rending of the nation, which would never really be healed. In time, the Assyrians would carry off the northern tribes into exile, and a century or so later, the Babylonians would carry off the leadership of the southern tribes, both invaders effectively scattering the people whom Moses had liberated, Joshua had cared for, and David and Solomon had united in an empire. When Jesus comes upon the scene and announces, first and foremost, the coming of God's kingdom, he was taken to mean, among other things, that the tribes of Israel, scattered for so long, were at last coming together.[4] His choice of twelve Apostles was, of course, symbolically charged, for it signaled the uniting of the northern and southern tribes into one great nation again. The one often called the son of David would indeed be a new Solomon who would knit back together what the old Solomon had rent apart.

THE PROPHET ELIJAH

What follows the dissolution of the kingdom and the death of King Solomon is a long and dreary civil war between the kings of the north and those of the south and even more dispiriting internal struggles between claimants to the two thrones. As often happens in the course of the biblical narrative, the reader is tempted to wonder how in the world this people is fulfilling its mission to embody the compassionate and just ways of the Lord. Commencing with chapter 17 of 1 Kings, we find a cycle of stories dealing with the man who would become the paradigmatic Israelite prophet—namely, Elijah the Tishbite. His sudden arrival is somewhat analogous to the emergence of the prophet Samuel at another low point in Israelite history, as well as the appearance of Nathan at the time of the Bathsheba incident. When the kings have made a colossal mess of things, the prophets tend to rise up as a corrective.

4. N.T. Wright, *Jesus and the Victory of God* (Minneapolis: Fortress, 1996), 198–243.

Though they cover only a handful of chapters in 1 Kings, the stories dealing with Elijah are packed with spiritual power and theological significance, and they have haunted the minds of believers up and down the centuries. We are told, first, that Elijah confronts Ahab, the king of Israel, who had gone over with enthusiasm to the worship of false gods, saying that there would be drought in the land because of the king's sin: "There shall be neither dew nor rain these years, except by my word" (1 Kings 17:1). This, of course, is the familiar biblical trope of garden and desert, the former produced by fidelity to the Lord and the latter by infidelity. During the drought, when he is in danger of starvation, Elijah is instructed to go to the land of Zarephath—which is to say, outside of the confines of Israel—to a poor widow in order to find sustenance. It would be difficult to imagine a less promising candidate for savior than a penniless widow from a land traditionally hostile to Israel, but Elijah follows the prompting of the Lord.

ELIJAH AND THE WIDOW OF ZAREPHATH

When he arrives in town and finds the widow, he asks her for some bread and water, but she calmly tells him that she has precisely enough to prepare one more meal for herself and her son before the two of them die. At this, Elijah says, with impossible chutzpah, "Do not be afraid; go and do as you have said; but first make me a little cake of it and bring it to me, and afterwards make something for yourself and your son" (1 Kings 17:13). The woman has just informed him that she had enough for one more meal, and yet he asks her to serve him first. His coming to her for help was more than a little ludicrous; and now, though it seemed the height of folly, she proceeds to do what he requested. And she discovers that "the jar of meal was not emptied, neither did the jug of oil fail, according to the word of the LORD that he spoke by Elijah" (1 Kings 17:16). What sense can we make of this rather fantastic tale? We might appreciate it as a vivid exemplification of what St. John Paul II called "the law of the gift"—namely, that one's being increases in the measure that one gives it away.[5] By a fundamental but ultimately self-destructive instinct, we cling, even tenaciously, to the goods of the world, which we are convinced are necessary for our survival. But this very act of clinging causes those goods to disintegrate, as it were, in our hands. We might be put in mind of the prodigal son, who endeavored to seize, even before his father's death, the inheritance that was due to him, but who found his wealth quickly evanescing (Luke 15:11–32). Now, why should this be the case? The truth of the principle follows from the nature of God as self-emptying love. Just as the Father gives himself utterly to the Son, indeed *is* the Father only in the measure that he engages in such giving; and just as the Father and Son give themselves to the Holy Spirit, and indeed *are* Father and Son precisely in that measure,[6] so human beings truly *have* what God gives them—which is nothing other than everything that they have—inasmuch as they make of those possessions a gift. What they receive as a gift, they must give as a gift, for it will remain what it really is only as it is given away. It will be *had*, as it were, only on the fly, as it passes from God to one's neighbor. And once it is surrendered in the proper spirit, it is automatically replaced, hence increasing as it is given away. The miracle of the widow of Zarephath is repeated, in even more dramatic form, in the miracle of the loaves and fishes, which is one of the rare scenes described in all four of the canonical Gospels. The original five loaves and two fish, once handed over to Jesus and for his purposes, are multiplied unto the feeding of a multitude.

ELIJAH AND THE PRIESTS OF BAAL

Following this scene comes one of the most memorable narratives in the Old Testament: Elijah's challenge to the priests of Baal. Confronting Ahab once more, Elijah calls the king out, compelling

5. John Paul II, *Love and Responsibility*, trans. H.T. Willetts (San Francisco: Ignatius, 1993), 126.

6. Hans Urs von Balthasar, *Theo-Drama: Theological Dramatic Theory*, vol. 4, *The Action* (San Francisco: Ignatius, 1994), 319–331.

him to defend the false gods that he serves: "Now therefore have all Israel assemble for me at Mount Carmel, with the four hundred fifty prophets of Baal." In front of a large crowd, Elijah demands a decision: "How long will you go limping with two different opinions? If the LORD is God, follow him; but if Baal, then follow him" (1 Kings 18:19–21). There are shades here, of course, of Joshua's admirable either/or challenge to Israel upon entering the Promised Land. Since the true God is the unconditioned reality, and since there can be only one reality in whom essence and existence coincide, God can broach no opposition. There simply cannot be two or more ultimate concerns; whatever is other than God is less than God and unworthy of worship. Thus, the Elijah question remains pertinent in every age and every person: you have to decide whether it is God that you worship or some instantiation of Baal.

The great Israelite prophet proposes a test. The priests of Baal are to erect an altar to their god and place a slaughtered bull upon it, and Elijah will erect an altar to the Lord, also with a slaughtered animal on it. They will be given every opportunity to call upon their deities and then Elijah will call upon the Lord and everyone will see which transcendent power (if any) responds. So the priests of Baal called upon their lord from "morning until noon, crying, 'O Baal, answer us!'" But, we are told, "there was no voice, and no answer." At which point, Elijah commenced to mock them: "Cry aloud! Surely he is a god; either he is meditating, or he has wandered away, or he is on a journey, or perhaps he is asleep and must be awakened." In their desperation, the priests of Baal then "cut themselves with swords and lances until the blood gushed out over them" (1 Kings 18:26–28).

Might we imagine the altar around which the devotees of Baal dance as an evocation of all of those false forms of ultimacy that we worship to our detriment and ultimately to our spiritual destruction? In the place of the true God, we worship (give highest value) to wealth, power, privilege, honor, pleasure, country, political party, charismatic leaders, etc. Since we are designed to give praise to the Creator alone, our gestures toward Baal will, of course, be fruitless. No fire will fall. Moreover, our efforts in this direction will harm us spiritually, just as surely as the flailings of the priests of Baal harmed them physically. When something other than God is put in the place of God and worship of that substitute commences, the worshiper might experience a brief rush from his passionate proximity to that finite good. But the rush will inevitably wear off, and a deeper thirst will set in. This in turn will compel the worshiper to devote himself with even more energy, to hop even more manically around the altar, which will conduce toward a rush, though smaller this time. In short order, the false worshiper is caught in a desperate addictive pattern and will indeed come to harm herself, as anyone who has ever been in the grip of an addiction can testify.

After the abject failure of the followers of Baal, Elijah confidently moves to center stage and invites the people to come close. He prepares the sacrifice, digs a trench around the altar, and orders his followers to cover the altar and offering with water. Then, he invokes the God of Israel: "O LORD, God of Abraham, Isaac, and Israel, let it be known this day that you are God in Israel, that I am your servant, and that I have done all these things at your bidding." With that, the fire comes down, consuming sacrifice, altar, stones, and dust, even licking up all the water in the trenches. Seeing this display, the people fall on their faces and confess their faith: "The LORD indeed is God; the LORD indeed is God" (1 Kings 18:36–39). It is crucially important to understand that this narrative represents much more than a jingoistic affirmation of one "religion" over another. If that were all that was at stake, we would be justified in dismissing this story as so much chauvinism or parochialism. In point of fact, it is affirming the master-theme of the Bible—namely, that right praise, worship directed to the unconditioned reality alone, will satisfy the longing of the human heart. The fire will come down, only the measure that our minds and wills, passions and energies, are directed aright.

The scene ends on a brutal note. Elijah calls out, "Seize the prophets of Baal; do not let one of them escape" (1 Kings 18:40). Bringing them down to the river, Elijah then, we are told, kills every last one of them. This is reminiscent, to be sure, of Samuel's cutting Agag to pieces and of Joshua putting the ban on entire cities, and we might, therefore, apply the same hermeneutic here as we did in regard to those episodes. We should construe this not as a license to murder our ideological opponents, but rather as an encouragement to destroy every last vestige of false worship in us. At any rate, as we have come to expect in these biblical narratives, any positive spiritual action tends to awaken an equal and opposite reaction. Hearing of the dramatic events on the mountain, King Ahab and Queen Jezebel are incensed and send their forces to capture the victorious prophet. So Elijah flees for his life, going a day's journey into the wilderness. Worn out from the physical exertion and likely from severe emotional distress, Elijah sits under a broom tree and begs for death. But the Lord sends an angel who tells him to eat and to drink. When, after doing so, he lies down again, the angel pokes him once more and says, "Get up and eat, otherwise the journey will be too much for you" (1 Kings 19:7). At the limit of his strength, Elijah eats and drinks from a spiritual source, which enables him to make the long journey to "Horeb the mount of God" (1 Kings 19:8)—which is to say, to one of the most sacred locales, the privileged place of encounter between God and his people Israel. How can we not see in this extended scene a recapitulation of the journey of Israel from the place of false worship, through the pain and deprivation of the desert, to the holy mountain, sustained on the way by bread (manna) from heaven? Putting to death forms of idolatry will always cost severely, prompting opposition from without and from within. But the struggle and the passage to right praise (Mt. Horeb) are made possible by nourishment that comes not from the world but from God.

After the long journey, Elijah finally comes to the mountain of the Lord, where he hears God's somewhat puzzling question: "What are you doing here, Elijah?" In response, the prophet draws attention to his "zealousness," for the Lord insists that he is the only Israelite left who truly honors the covenant (1 Kings 19:9–10). One wonders whether this is just bravado, somewhat in keeping with Elijah's wanton killing of the priests of Baal. In any case, the Lord instructs the prophet to "stand on the mountain before the LORD, for the LORD is about to pass by" (1 Kings 19:11). It would be impossible, of course, to miss the reference to Moses, who was similarly invited, on the holy mountain, to watch as the God of Israel passed by. What follows is a recapitulation of the many extraordinary ways that the Lord had manifested himself to the children of Israel, especially during the Exodus: wind, the breaking of rocks, earthquake, and fire. But God, we are told, is not in these powerful signs, but rather in the "sound of sheer silence" (1 Kings 19:12). To be sure, the source of all finite existence can show himself through vivid events within the created order, but he can also signal his deeply mysterious manner of existing, precisely by eschewing any dramatic form of communication. We might see a hint here of the so-called kataphatic and apophatic styles of divine self-revelation. However, it might be the case that God senses that Elijah, given his penchant for the over-the-top gesture, requires something quieter.

Wrapping his face in the mantle of his cloak, Elijah presents himself before the Lord, and once again he repeats, practically word for word, the somewhat blustery and self-important speech he has just made, protesting that he alone remained among the adorers of the God of Israel. God's answer is swift and more than a tad brutal. After telling Elijah to anoint a successor to the king of Israel, the Lord also instructs the prophet to choose his own replacement: "You shall anoint Elisha son of Shaphat of Abel-meholah as prophet in your place" (1 Kings 19:16). One might be forgiven for interpreting this command as a barely cloaked "you're fired." Moreover, to the man who twice had insisted that he was the only one left in Israel to worship the Lord, God dryly comments, "Yet I will leave seven thousand in Israel, all the knees that have not bowed to Baal, and every mouth that has not kissed him" (1 Kings 19:18). I cannot help but read this part of the Elijah story as a knowing commentary on the typical excesses of the religious personality. Though he was undoubtedly a man of enormous spiritual perceptiveness and courage, Elijah was also something of a fanatic, prone to just the kind of religiously motivated violence that has bedeviled humanity throughout the ages.

THE PROPHET ELISHA

The calling of Elisha is a beautiful story, reminiscent of the accounts of Jesus' summoning of his first disciples. We are told that Elijah comes upon Elisha as the latter is plowing a field with "twelve yoke of oxen" (1 Kings 19:19). This detail is meant to signal that Elisha is quite a prosperous man, something along the lines of saying, in our context, that he is driving a sports car and wearing a Rolex watch. To be sure, as Alter points out, the number twelve also indicates the twelve tribes of a united Israel. Without a moment's hesitation and without in any way seeking Elisha's permission, Elijah "threw his mantle over him" (1 Kings 19:19). And immediately, despite his wealth and commitments both professional and personal, Elisha leaves everything and follows his new master. As I say, this immediacy calls vividly to mind the reaction of Peter, James, John, Matthew, Saul, and others when Jesus called them to discipleship. Sometimes conversion is a lengthy and psychologically tortuous process; but other times grace seems simply to overwhelm any resistance. We are given the wonderful detail that, upon deciding to follow Elijah, Elisha "took the yoke of oxen, and slaughtered them; using the equipment from the oxen, he boiled their flesh, and gave it to the people, and they ate" (1 Kings 19:21). Like the Apostles who left everything to follow Jesus, and like some of St. Francis' disciples who literally handed their wealth to the poor, Elisha turns radically and dramatically away from his old life. Some within the family of God are meant to use the goods of the world under the aegis of God's law for the sake of certain values both material and spiritual. But others are meant to eschew worldly goods utterly and to belong completely to God. Within the Christian context, we speak of the evangelical counsels of poverty, chastity, and obedience—which certain members of the Body of Christ are called to live out radically as a startling witness. Elisha seems an Old Testament anticipation of this style of life.

2 Kings

The second half of this great book of Kings deals primarily with the political split between north and south that occurred upon the death of Solomon and the string of most inadequate, squabbling potentates that reigned ingloriously on both sides of the divide. It is, to be perfectly frank, a rather dispiriting tale. But what is perhaps most striking, and most unnerving, about 2 Kings is the way it ends. After the detailed account of the glories of Solomon's kingship and the splendors of the temple in 1 Kings, we find, at the conclusion of the grand narrative, the utter demolition of Solomon's kingdom and the destruction of his temple. As we shall see, the author allows us just a glimmer of hope as the tale comes to its conclusion, but the main thrust of the narrative seems to undercut any confidence we might have that Israel is the specially chosen people of God and that its political unity and right worship are meant to be the magnet to attract the nations. Unless, of course, this nation and that temple are not the final story, but rather foreshadowings of God's ultimate intention.

ELIJAH IS TAKEN UP TO HEAVEN

With the second chapter of 2 Kings, we pick up the narrative of Elijah and Elisha. The opening line of the chapter is rather startling, for it introduces, in a subordinate clause no less, a spiritual dimension that had been almost entirely absent from the Old Testament to this point: "Now when the LORD was about to take Elijah up to heaven by a whirlwind" (2 Kings 2:1). That God deals with his people in this world in a healing, punishing, instructing, and liberating way has been taken for granted from Genesis on. But that God holds out to his people a fulfillment beyond this world, a life "in heaven," is almost totally absent. To be sure, as we've seen, shadowy *Sheol*, a pathetic simulacrum of real life, was imagined, but not as a transcendent, supra-terrestrial form of existence. The one exception might be the mysterious text in Genesis regarding Enoch: "Enoch walked with God; then he was no more, because God took him" (Gen. 5:24). Otherwise, the biblical authors seem unanimous that our dealings with God are restricted to this life alone. From a Christian perspective, of course, this almost tossed off text has a powerful resonance, for it anticipates what might be called resurrected life, the life of the world to come, the manner of being made plain to us in the bodily resurrection of Jesus from the dead—namely, one that shares qualities of this dimension and of a higher dimension.

In many Christian accounts of the transition from this life to the higher life, comparisons with the Exodus are customary: transiting from the land of transitoriness and sin into the Promised Land. So here, Elijah and Elisha make their way through the towns of Gilgal, Bethel, and Jericho and come at last to the shores of the Jordan, recapitulating the journey of the ancient exiles from Egypt. Echoing the gestures of both Moses and Joshua, Elijah then takes his mantle and strikes the waters of the river, causing them to divide in two and permitting the two prophets to cross on dry land. Once again, we are commencing to glimpse the transition of which the Exodus was but an iconic anticipation.

Just before making his transit, Elijah asks his protégé, "Tell me what I may do for you, before I am taken from you," and Elisha responds, "Please let me inherit a double share of your spirit" (2 Kings 2:9). I cannot help but conclude that Elisha, having taken in the extraordinary struggles of Elijah, most notably against the army of the priests of Baal and the fury of Jezebel, understands just how trying the life of a prophet is. In point of fact, Elisha does receive an extraordinary share of Elijah's spirit, for the narratives that follow in 2 Kings make plain that he could perform miracles beyond the capacity of his master. As the two prophets continued walking and conversing, "a chariot of fire and horses of fire separated the two of them, and Elijah ascended in a whirlwind into heaven" (2 Kings 2:11). We notice, first, the familiar biblical theme of separation, in this case one man leaving the world and the other staying behind, one man moving into the properly heavenly realm and the other remaining within the realm of nature and history. That this kind of separation was deemed unlikely is made clear in the odd addendum to the story, according to which a company of prophets pressed Elisha to allow them to send a search and rescue team to find Elijah, for "it may be that the spirit of the LORD has caught him up and thrown him down some mountain or into some valley" (2 Kings 2:16). It is as though they cannot imagine the possibility of a "flight" that is anything other than a journey within nature.

Upon Elijah's departure, Elisha picked up the mantle that his master had left behind and proceeded immediately to use it to divide the river Jordan, proving thereby that the Lord had transferred Elijah's spirit to him. But as is so typical of the Bible, even as a divine prerogative is affirmed, a caution is raised. Can it be accidental that, just after this extraordinarily dramatic account of Elisha's succession unfolds, we find a curious, tragic-comic story that fills the reader with doubts regarding the prophet's goodness and psychological stability? We are told that, on his way to Bethel, Elisha encountered a group of young boys who taunted him on account of his bald pate: "Go away, baldhead! Go away, baldhead!" This was aggravating to be sure, but the prophet's reaction can only be described as psychotic: "He cursed them in the name of the LORD. Then two she-bears came out of the woods and mauled forty-two of the boys," presumably to death (2 Kings 2:23–24). Indeed, Alter's translation of the Hebrew gives us "ripped them apart."[1] So strange and unlikely did this story appear that the rabbinic tradition asserted that it never happened.[2] How might we make sense of this bizarre tale? It indicates, to be sure, that prophets are typically opposed, that they customarily endure public taunting and ridicule. Speak to any religious figure today who dares to undertake a ministry in the public forum, and he will assure you that he hears epithets far worse than "baldhead." But even if we grant this, how can we possibly read Elisha's response as anything other than massively disproportionate? A group of boys are mocking you and you respond by calling upon God to murder forty-two of them? As with his master's brutal response to the defeated priests of Baal, we see here the tendency of charismatic religious figures to misuse their power, perhaps to deceive themselves into thinking they are doing God's work when in fact they are protecting their own egos or giving free rein to their distorted passions. As is almost invariably the case with the biblical authors, they undermine their heroes even as they hold them up for admiration. Elisha might be the prophet of the Lord, but he is not the Lord.

ELISHA AND THE SHUNAMMITE WOMAN

In chapter 4, we find a number of miracle stories involving Elisha, which both signal his extraordinary spiritual power and vividly anticipate another prophet from Israel who, some eight centuries later, would perform similar signs. We hear first of the prophet's relationship with a Shunammite woman in whose home he would occasionally stay on his journeys. Because of her kindness to him, Elisha resolved to reward her. When he heard that she was childless, he called her to him and announced, "At this season, in due time, you shall embrace a son," and she did indeed become pregnant and bear a male child (2 Kings 4:16–17). Here, Elisha echoes the

---

1. Robert Alter, *The Hebrew Bible: A Translation with Commentary*, vol. 2, *Prophets* (New York: W.W. Norton, 2019), 534–535.

2. Robert Alter, 534n24.

angelic visitors who predicted in the presence of Abraham that his wife, despite her advanced age, would bear a son, as well as Eli, who assured Hannah of the same. But the supernatural power of Elisha is even more dramatically expressed in an episode that unfolded some years later. The son in question, now a boy, became ill and, after lying helplessly in his mother's lap for several hours, died. Laying his body on the bed in the prophet's room, the mother sent for Elisha, who, after some delay, came to the place. When he saw the boy's dead body, Elisha stretched himself out on top of it, "putting his mouth upon his mouth, his eyes upon his eyes, and his hands upon his hands." Immediately, the body became warm, and the young man, curiously enough, "sneezed seven times" and then opened his eyes, at which point, the boy was returned to his mother (2 Kings 4:34–35).

This story, of course, closely parallels a similar account in 1 Kings regarding Elisha's master, who also revived a young man by stretching out on top of him (1 Kings 17:21). But how can we overlook the detail of the seven sneezes, so unique to this story? Some have attempted to offer naturalistic explanations having to do with respiratory or circulatory ailments, but these strike me as strained, to say the least. More persuasive are the symbolic and spiritual readings that suggest the violent exhalation of air is evocative of real conversion, which is a violent expulsion of bad habits, behavior, and patterns of thinking. As is often the case in the biblical tales, physical death is an icon of spiritual death, and hence physical revival is an icon of spiritual revivification. The number of sneezes, seven, signifies perfection or completion; hence, we might be permitted to interpret this series of convulsions as the thorough conversion from spiritual death to life.

And, of course, how can the Christian reader miss the typological anticipation of Jesus' raising of the daughter of Jairus, the son of the widow of Nain, and Lazarus of Bethany (Mark 5:21–24, 35–43; Luke 7:11–17; John 11:28–34)? All three of those were physical revivals to be sure, but they were also evocative of the act by which Jesus raises us from the death of sin. On Augustine's magnificent reading, the daughter of Jairus, a young girl who died within her own home, represents sin that remains at the level of thought and buried intention; the son of the widow of Nain, who is an adolescent or young man, stands for sin that has made its way into the world through action; and Lazarus, a fully mature adult, whose body has been in the tomb for four days, symbolizes sin that has grown into public scandal and deeply ingrained habit.[3] The point is that Jesus can revive a sinner from any of these states and stages of spiritual dysfunction.

NAAMAN THE SYRIAN

Chapter 5 of 2 Kings conveys the story of Naaman, the commander of the army of the king of Aram, one of Israel's principal enemies. Like the previous account, it is a story of physical healing, but it carries with it a powerful symbolic charge. We are told that Naaman is "a mighty warrior" and "in high favor with his master." He is obviously a man of considerable status and influence in his society. However, he suffered from leprosy, a disease both physically debilitating and deeply embarrassing. In the entourage of Naaman was a young female slave, "captive from the land of Israel," who told her master about a prophet in Samaria who could cure him of his ailment (2 Kings 5:1–3). So, acquiring a letter from the king of Aram, Naaman set out for Israel. What one should notice first is the extraordinary humility demonstrated by this accomplished figure. There would have been absolutely no one lower on the social scale of that time than a slave girl of foreign provenance, and yet the great man abided by her. It would certainly be congruent with biblical intuitions that humility would be a prerequisite for authentic healing at the level of the soul.

Taking with him a treasure trove of goods—presumably to compensate the king of Israel or the prophet himself—Naaman set out. But when he presented his letter of introduction to the king,

3. Augustine, *Tractates on the Gospel of John* 49.3.2–4.

the potentate cried out, "Am I God, to give death or life, that this man sends word to me to cure a man of his leprosy? Just look and see how he is trying to pick a quarrel with me" (2 Kings 5:7). The Israelite strong man likely suspected that his rival was using this visit as a ploy to spy out his territory. At the symbolic level, we are meant to see that the road to healing is always blocked. Our sufferings, both physical and spiritual, take place within and to a large extent are conditioned by the finite, sinful, conflictual world in which we find ourselves, and this means that there will always be obstacles that block the addressing of those sufferings. Crucial to the healing process, therefore, is patience and resilience. Naaman's longsuffering paid off, for the prophet Elisha, having heard of the less than satisfactory audience with the king, invited the visitor to come to him. When the great man arrived at the prophet's home, Elisha did not receive him personally, but rather sent a messenger to instruct Naaman to bathe seven times in the Jordan River. The general was humiliated, for the prophet did not speak to him in person and told him to do something that could have been done, easily enough, back home in his native land. Incensed, Naaman complained, "Are not Abana and Pharpar, the rivers of Damascus, better than all the waters of Israel? Could I not wash in them, and be clean?" (2 Kings 5:12).

Once more, the biblical author is emphasizing the humility required to anyone who desires healing at the spiritual level. If we take Naaman's leprosy as evocative of some malady of the soul, then we understand that his railing against Elisha is expressive of the almost inevitable resistance to healing found in those who are sin-sick. Mollified by members of his entourage, Naaman finally acquiesces and bathes seven times in the Jordan, submitting to what must have seemed to him an arbitrary requirement: Why seven and not six or eight? Upon doing so, he is cured; his "flesh was restored like the flesh of a young boy, and he was clean" (2 Kings 5:14). When Jesus effected a cure of the blind Bartimaeus, he said, "Go; your faith has made you well," insinuating that

Bartimaeus' willingness to submit to grace was essential to his healing (Mark 10:52). Something similar seems to be in play in the story of Naaman, for the cure came only when he, in faith, accepted what the prophet demanded of him. Might we read "faith" here as the existential attitude that is the polar opposite of the prideful self-direction of one's life? The humbling that commenced with the word of the slave girl, and continued through the resistance of the Israelite king and the seemingly aloof instruction offered by Elisha, came to full expression as the great Syrian general washed himself seven times in a foreign river.

It should be to no one's surprise that the Church Fathers, so given to allegorical readings, would see a connection between the non-Israelite who was healed through a bathing process and the sacrament of Baptism by which so many outside of Israel were brought into communion with the Church and who found healing from their sins. Ephrem the Syrian gives voice to a typical patristic reading when he says, "Naaman was sent to the Jordan as to the remedy capable to heal a human being. Indeed, sin is the leprosy of the soul, which is not perceived by the senses, but intelligence has the proof of it, and human nature must be delivered from this disease by Christ's power which is hidden in baptism."[4]

Like the one leper who returned to thank Jesus for his cure (see Luke 17:11–19), Naaman came to Elisha and made this great confession of faith: "Now I know that there is no God in all the earth except in Israel" (2 Kings 5:15). I would insist that this should not be read as self-interested Israelite jingoism, but rather as the drawing out of a crucial implication of the doctrine of creation. Precisely because God is the Creator of all things, his salvific purposes embrace all of humanity, and indeed, as we have frequently seen, all of nature. The source of all finite existence cannot, even in principle, be a tribal deity, for his causal influence extends universally. The choice that God makes vis-à-vis Israel is,

4. John Bergsma and Brant Pitre, *A Catholic Introduction to the Bible*, vol. 1, *The Old Testament* (San Francisco: Ignatius, 2018), 423.

as we have often argued, not for Israel but for the world. Having made his confession of faith, Naaman then offered, from the considerable booty that he had brought, a reward to compensate Elisha, but the prophet was having none of it. So the great Syrian asked instead that the prophet would indulge him and permit him to take two "mule-loads" of Israelite earth back to his native country so that he could properly offer sacrifice to the God of Israel (2 Kings 5:17). According to another very familiar biblical pattern, the healing of body and soul has conduced, in the final analysis, to right worship. The gradual stages of humiliation endured by Naaman have led him, at last, to the radical decentering of the ego that finds expression in orthodoxy.

THE ARMY OF ANGELS

In the next chapter of 2 Kings, we find another story dealing with the king of Aram, this one more conflictual. It seems that this traditional enemy of Israel fell into armed conflict with the chosen people, and he discovered that his private conversations and military instructions were somehow divined by the prophet Elisha. Enraged, he sent a considerable force to the town of Dothan where the prophet was residing and surrounded the city with "horses and chariots . . . and a great army." When Elisha's attendant arose the following morning and saw the enemy encampment, he was terrified and cried out, "Alas, Master! What shall we do?" To this anguished lament, Elisha responded, puzzlingly enough, "Do not be afraid, for there are more with us than there are with them." What he is referring to is the army of angels that he can see but that remain invisible to his attendant. When the prophet prays that his assistant might receive illumination, the young man suddenly perceives that "the mountain was full of horses and chariots of fire all around Elisha" (2 Kings 6:14–17).

Following the course of the biblical narrative, I have mentioned angels a number of times throughout this book, but I have not dwelt upon their nature and purpose. On the biblical reading, angels are creatures of God who share God's purely spiritual manner of being and whose customary habitation is the heavenly realm, around the throne of God. Thomas Aquinas understands them as more intense expressions of finite being, closer, so to speak, to the fire.[5] But they can, when the Creator so desires, condescend to take on visible form in order to communicate to human beings, whence comes the name "angel," which designates messenger. The military manner of the angels' appearance here, which anticipates the *stratias* (army) of angels that manifest themselves during the Christmas account in Luke (Luke 2:13), is worthy of some reflection. For the biblical authors, the physical world is, of course, real and good, a reflection of the Creator. But they also believe in a properly spiritual dimension of existence (customarily designated as "heaven") that is more intensely real, a closer approximation of God's way of being. And this invisible dimension is a source of extraordinary power, greater than any power that the visible world can muster. One might compare Elisha's blithe confidence with that demonstrated by Pope John Paul II in the June of 1979 when he spoke to crowd of a million people in Victory Square in Warsaw. At that moment, Poland was a wholly owned subsidiary of the Soviet Union, which possessed the largest nuclear arsenal in the world and one of the largest armies on the planet. John Paul had absolutely no power in the earthly sense, yet he spoke in that politically hostile capital city of God, of creation and redemption, of human dignity and rights, in a word, of spiritual realities, fully realizing that this move put him in touch with unseen powers. That this event triggered the revolution that eventually brought down the Soviet empire with barely a shot being fired is contested by few serious historians today. Indeed, all visible evidence to the contrary, there were more with him than were with them.[6]

5. Thomas Aquinas, *Summa theologiae* 1.50.1.
6. George Weigel, *Witness to Hope: The Biography of Pope John Paul II* (New York: Harper Perennial, 2005), 291–325.

THE KINGS OF THE NORTH AND THE SOUTH

Chapters 9 through 16 of 2 Kings tell the brutal and dispiriting story of the reigns of the kings of both the northern and southern kingdoms. The violence and idolatry of these monarchs gives evidence of the deep corruption into which the divided nation has fallen. Despite the exertions of Elijah and Elisha, the overwhelming majority of the leaders of this time were desperately out of step with the purpose of God. However, even amidst the chaos, both political and moral, the hand of God can be, at least dimly, discerned. In chapter 9, we hear of Elisha's anointing of Jehu, one-time military commander under King Ahab, as king. What becomes immediately clear is that Jehu's primary kingly task will be settling scores with the clan of Ahab. We recall that Ahab had been described as the very worst king in the history of the nation and that the prophet Elijah had predicted the exceptionally bad end to which Ahab's wife, Jezebel, would eventually come.

Arriving in Jezreel, where Ahab's son, King Joram, is residing and where Ahaziah, the king of Judah, had come to visit, Jehu confronts Joram: "What peace can there be, so long as the many whoredoms and sorceries of your mother Jezebel continue?" (2 Kings 9:22). When Joram attempts to flee, Jehu shoots an arrow through his heart and subsequently deposits the dead king's body on the property of Naboth, whom Jezebel and Ahab had had killed, we recall, in order to obtain that very piece of ground. Then, he seeks after Ahaziah and has him killed as well. Filled with righteous indignation or blood lust (or likely a combination of the two), Jehu then comes to the home of Jezebel. When she looks down upon him from her balcony with contempt, he cries out to two of her eunuchs, "Throw her down." They do so, splattering her blood against the wall and on horses who proceed to trample her remains so that "when they came to bury her, they found no more of her than the skull and the feet and the palms of her hands" (2 Kings 9:33–35).

But Jehu isn't through. Knowing that Ahab's seventy remaining sons still represent a threat, he writes to the elders of Samaria, where the young men are being protected, demanding that they be turned over. Terrified of the man who had already dispatched two kings and a queen, they say that they will do whatever Jehu wanted. So he sends a second letter instructing them to send the heads of the seventy sons to him in Jezreel. "When the letter reached them, they took the king's sons and killed them. . . . They put their heads in baskets and sent them to him at Jezreel" (2 Kings 10:7). Upon receiving the gruesome gift, Jehu, blithely enough, instructs his servants to lay them in two great piles by the city gate so that all the passersby can see them. He then provides the theological gloss on his action: "For the LORD has done what he said through his servant Elijah" (2 Kings 10:10).

To an extent, we can accept this interpretation, for, once again, something like the law of karma does obtain within the biblical universe: sin does have consequences and sinners are often, sooner or later, punished by God. But I wonder whether it might be more fruitful to pursue the hermeneutical line that we have suggested in regard to other similarly brutal scriptural texts. Ahab and Jezebel symbolize the idolatrous practices that had invaded Israel and compromised her spiritual integrity. Their prophets and armies symbolize the manner in which the idolatrous frame of mind works its way into the structures of the society, effecting a systemic corruption. This sort of wickedness cannot be tolerated, and no compromises can be made with it. Rather, it must be eliminated, root and branch. The worship of the true God must be absolute, and therefore, its contrary must be eradicated. The murder, mayhem, mutilated corpses, and piles of severed heads that assault our consciousness as we read this tale are meant to produce the keen sensibility of our need totally to resist evil, to battle it all the way down.

Giving support to this interpretation is the scene that follows immediately after that of the slaughter of the seventy sons of Ahab.

Having arrived in Samaria, the capital of the northern kingdom, Jehu assembled all the inhabitants of the town and told them that he would now outdo Ahab in the worship of Baal: "Summon to me all the prophets of Baal, all his worshippers, and all his priests; let none be missing, for I have a great sacrifice to offer to Baal" (2 Kings 10:19). Once they were all in the temple of the false god, Jehu had special robes brought out for them, and they engaged in their ritual worship, but the king had had the place surrounded with eighty warriors. To them he gave the command: "Come in and kill them; let no one escape" (2 Kings 10:25). Having dispatched all of the people, he then burned the temple and ordered it be converted into a latrine. As always, lack of orthodoxy is the root problem that has to be addressed. But may I also say, as I insisted when looking at both Elijah and Elisha, we also see here the awful fanaticism that has gripped religious people across the ages. Ultimate concern gives rise to what is best in us and what is most depraved in us. The passion to root out bad praise is a holy impulse, but it can turn with remarkable ease into something appalling.

That Jehu's work, though to some degree expressive of the Lord's will, was deeply compromised is made clear in chapters 11 through 16 of 2 Kings. It would be tiresome to rehearse the narrative in detail, but suffice it to say that it is the tale of constant enmity and violence among rival claimants to the thrones of both the northern and southern kingdoms. The Mafia-like machinations of Jehu awakened in response generations of revolutions, insurrections, murders, vengeance, and corruption. With a handful of exceptions among the kings of Judah, all of the monarchs of this period operated at cross-purposes to God and accordingly wreaked havoc in the lands they ruled.

THE ASSYRIAN EXILE

The decisive seventeenth chapter of 2 Kings narrates the manner in which God commenced definitively to deal with the infidelity of Israel. As he often did, in accord with a sort of karmic law, God used a foreign power to punish the chosen nation that had gone after the gods and adopted the customs of foreign peoples. We are told that the king of Assyria, Shalmaneser, came with full force to overthrow Hoshea, the king of Israel. After laying siege to the capital of Samaria for three years (which must have been a brutal business for the people of that unfortunate city), he overthrew the Israelite government and brought the people (undoubtedly, a representative group of them) into exile in Assyria, placing them in distant cities unknown to them. In perfect accord with Deuteronomistic sensibilities, the author tells us exactly why this disaster befell the denizens of the northern kingdom: "They had worshiped other gods and walked in the customs of the nations whom the LORD drove out before the people of Israel. . . . The people of Israel secretly did things that were not right against the LORD their God. They built for themselves high places at all their towns. . . . They set up for themselves pillars and sacred poles on every hill and under every green tree. . . . They served idols. . . . They rejected all the commandments of the LORD their God and made for themselves cast images of two calves . . . and served Baal" (2 Kings 17:7–12, 16). Once more, false worship is the fundamental problem and, once more, God allows Israel to suffer the inevitable consequences of their sin: the loss of the land, which is symbolic of the promise of life to the full. What began with the splitting of Solomon's kingdom in two now continues with the pathetic exile of the ten tribes of the north. If God is a unifying force; sin is always a scattering force.

We recall that one of the marks of the covenant with the Lord is the fruitfulness of the people, the flourishing of family life, the propagation and education of children. Among the crimes that cried out to God and that conduced toward the Assyrian exile was the most wanton abuse of children imaginable—namely, sacrificing them to false gods: "They made their sons and their daughters pass through fire" (2 Kings 17:17). A nation that permits the slaughter of tens of millions of babies through abortion and that countenances the sex trafficking of youngsters, one must admit, is little better.

Compounding the moral and spiritual dysfunction of the situation, the Assyrian king subsequently sent subjects from various parts of his empire to inhabit the cities abandoned by the Israelites. Not knowing the God of Israel, these immigrants naturally worshiped false gods and hence further awakened the ire of the Lord, who sent lions among them to kill them. Alter observes that, from a plethora of biblical evidence, we know that lions were indeed numerous in ancient Israel,[7] but we ought to read this text symbolically as an iteration of the story of the seraph serpents in the desert. Concerned with this dramatic situation, the king of Assyria even sent some Israelite priests, who had been carried off into exile, in order to teach the non-Israelites right worship! This entire scenario—the exile of Israelites, the introduction of foreigners who would intermarry with the remaining population, and the presence of priests who would certainly have had difficulty inculcating the law of Israel in the hearts of a foreign people—goes a long way to explaining why, by the time of Jesus, Samaritans were viewed with such suspicion by pious Jews. Following the Genesis prompt, sin had led to exile and to the spoiling of the garden.

---

7. Robert Alter, *The Hebrew Bible*, 2:584n25.

Ezra and Nehemiah

Though there is an ancient tradition holding that the books of Ezra and Nehemiah were one, written by the same author, scholars today hold this to be unlikely. The literary styles and modes of expression of the two texts are just too different. But they come, to be sure, from the same era and powerfully convey the preoccupations of the Jews returning from Babylon, roughly fifty years after the commencement of their exile. Chief among these concerns was the re-establishment of the people of God, both liturgically and politically. The first of these is associated with Ezra the priest and the second with Zerubbabel, the quasi-Davidic king, and with Nehemiah, the rebuilder of the walls of Jerusalem.

KING CYRUS AND THE RETURN OF THE JEWS

The book of Ezra commences with the evocation of the Persian king Cyrus, who had effected the conquest of Babylon around 539 BC, roughly forty years after the capture of the Jews. As we have often remarked in the course of the commentary, though the focus of the biblical authors is clearly on the people Israel, there is no question that the God of Israel is not a tribal deity, but rather the Creator and sustainer of the entire cosmos and hence the God of every nation. In accord with his universal providence, God, we are told, "stirred up the spirit of King Cyrus of Persia" (Ezra 1:1), inspiring him to permit the Jews to return to their capital and rebuild their great temple. God can use any vessel he chooses, and his purpose ultimately is the renewal and salvation of the world. Therefore, we should not be surprised by this gracious intervention of a foreign potentate, one who held the Jews captive. Further, we should, by now, not be surprised to know that God has, despite much evidence to the contrary, refused to give up on his chosen people.

And so we are told that the families belonging to the two southern tribes, Judah and Benjamin, began to make their way back to Jerusalem, carrying with them much of the wealth that was absconded two generations before by Nebuchadnezzar: "gold basins, thirty; silver basins, one thousand; knives, twenty-nine; gold bowls, thirty; other silver bowls, four hundred ten; other vessels, one thousand; the total of the gold and silver vessels was five thousand, four hundred" (Ezra 1:9–11). We are also given an exhaustive list of the Israelite families, groups, and clans that made their way to the capital, led by Zerubbabel, a descendant of David, whose name means "seed of Babylon" or "planted in Babylon." This Jewish leader, bearing a Persian name, clearly represents this generation of Jews who nevertheless were culturally and linguistically formed in a foreign land and who now face the challenge of discovering their religious identity anew.

The first step in that direction was the erection of an altar on the site of the ruined temple, so that sacrifice to the Lord might be offered. In fairly short compass, the returned exiles managed to assemble the materials necessary for a reconstruction of the sanctuary, and in a manner altogether reminiscent of their ancestors at the time of Solomon, they even brought in cedar trees from Lebanon to the port at Joppa. When the foundations for the new place of worship were laid, the people broke into songs of thanksgiving to God, but some of the elders, who remembered the splendor of Solomon's edifice, wept at the comparative inadequacy of the new building.

After facing down irrational but fierce opposition from some of those who had inhabited the area before the exiles came back, the Jews, with the approval of a second Persian King, Darius, continued to work on the temple. When they finished their labors, they "celebrated the dedication of this house of God with joy," sacrificing "one hundred bulls, two hundred rams, four hundred lambs, and as a sin offering for all Israel, twelve male goats" (Ezra 6:16–17). Once again, the sacrifices recommended in Exodus, Leviticus, and Deuteronomy, expressive of the people's radical dependence upon God, stood at the heart of Israelite religious consciousness.

It should also be noted, however, that the smoke indicative of the divine presence, which descended upon the Solomonic temple centuries before, quite noticeably did not fill the holy place this time. What would perdure even to the time of Jesus was the nagging suspicion that this "second" temple, though the place of right praise, was never quite what the Lord intended. As we shall see, the prophet Ezekiel, writing around the time of the exile, imagined the divine presence leaving the sacred precincts and moving eastward away from the temple. Nowhere in the Old Testament do we ever find an account of the return of the Lord to the place that he had abandoned, though we might well have expected it in Ezra's narrative of the rededication. Given this rather strange background, the texts in the New Testament dealing with the various ways that Jesus entered the temple take on a profound significance. They are not simply about an itinerant rabbi making his way into the holy precincts to preach and pray; they are about the glory of the God of Israel finally coming back to his earthly dwelling. What did not happen at the time of Zerubbabel indeed happened, centuries later, in and through the Messiah.

EZRA THE PRIEST

As chapter 7 of the book of Ezra begins, we have moved several decades forward from the temple dedication, and we come to the decisively important moment of the arrival of Ezra himself. We are instructed that this man, a respected figure in the court of King Artaxerxes (the third Persian beneficiary of the Jews mentioned in this text), was a direct descendant of Aaron himself, the first high priest. And his task, to which Artaxerxes appointed him, was similar to Aaron's—namely, to instruct the returned exiles in the Law of the Lord and to instill in them the moral and liturgical demands implicit in the Law. What Zerubbabel accomplished (at least to a degree) politically, Ezra will seek to accomplish religiously. Chapter 7 includes an extraordinary letter that Artaxerxes gave to Ezra, commissioning him and setting out the parameters of his responsibility. To his Jewish colleague, the king provides "all the silver and gold that you shall find in the whole province of Babylonia" in order to offer proper adornment to the temple and fitting praise to God (Ezra 7:16). He goes so far as to say, "Whatever else is required for the house of your God, which you are responsible for providing, you may provide out of the king's treasury" (Ezra 7:20). Finally, Artaxerxes specifies that it will be unlawful to impose any "tribute, custom, or toll on any of the priests, the Levites, the singers, the doorkeepers, the temple servants, or other servants of this house of God" (Ezra 7:24). The reader can only share the astonishment that Ezra himself expresses in his text: "Blessed be the LORD, the God of our ancestors, who put such a thing as this into the heart of the king to glorify the house of the LORD in Jerusalem" (Ezra 7:27). God has undoubtedly used foreign potentates to humiliate and punish Israel, but sometimes he uses them to reward his chosen people. Once more, the utter universality of God's providence is on display, as well as the total compliance of the human will under God's influence. Just as God made the world *ex nihilo*, he can remake a human heart from the nonbeing of sin.

Ezra then endeavored to continue the liturgical life of Israel in the temple, but he was informed that many of the returned exiles had rendered themselves impure by marrying women from the environing tribes—"Canaanites, the Hittites, the Perizzites, the Jebusites, the Ammonites, the Moabites, the Egyptians, and the Amorites" (Ezra 9:1). The pedantic listing of the alien peoples is, of course, an echo of what we find in Exodus, Deuteronomy, Joshua, and Samuel. The intermarrying has led to a moral compromise as the people of God came to adopt the practices of these foreigners, leading Ezra to cry out: "The land that you are entering to possess is a land unclean with the pollutions of the peoples of the lands, with their abominations. They have filled it from end to end with their uncleanness" (Ezra 9:11). Sensing their leader's anguish, a number of the Jews vowed that they would send away their foreign wives and their children as well.

Certainly, in light of our contemporary sensibilities, this vow seems rash, even cruel, especially in regard to the dismissal of the children, but we should appreciate this move as in creative tension with the universalism just referenced. Israel is indeed for the world, and the God of Israel is lord of all the nations, but in order for the holy people to do its work, it must have moral and spiritual integrity. The introduction of errant belief and practice into Israelite life will result in the dimming of the very light meant to attract all the world. Bede the Venerable gives voice to the patristic interpretive consensus when he remarks that Ezra's anguished cry here on account of the sins of the people is a type of Christ, who offered up priestly sacrifice on behalf of the sinful human race.[1]

With this political, liturgical, and moral purification undertaken under the direction of Zerubbabel and Ezra, the nation is now ready for the physical restoration of Jerusalem, which will be led by the figure who stands at the heart of the next book of the Scriptures—namely, Nehemiah.

NEHEMIAH

The book of Nehemiah is quite distinctive in the biblical literature in the measure that it represents a straightforwardly autobiographical voice. For the most part, this book is the first-person musing of Nehemiah himself. We discover that, while he was functioning as a high-level advisor to King Artaxerxes in Susa, Nehemiah heard of the sorry state of the city of Jerusalem to which many of the exiles had returned. Though the temple had been reconstructed,

1. Bede, *On Ezra and Nehemiah* 2.12.

the walls and the gate were still in ruins from the Babylonian siege and capture in 587 BC. Nehemiah's immediate response is not to ask Artaxerxes for help or to rouse his own people to action; rather, he prays to the God of Israel, and his prayer reveals that he understood with remarkable clarity the basic Deuteronomistic moral dynamic that governs God's relationship to his chosen people. As long as they followed the commands of the Lord, God would keep them safe; but if they strayed from those precepts, God would disperse them: "If you are unfaithful, I will scatter you among the peoples" (Neh. 1:8). What this Jewish man, high in the officialdom of Persia, realized is that the broken walls amounted themselves to a kind of scattering, for they permitted any and all passersby to infiltrate the holy city and compromise its integrity.

One day, Artaxerxes noticed that Nehemiah was sad and so inquired, "Why is your face sad, since you are not sick? This can only be sadness of the heart" (Neh. 2:2). His cupbearer confessed the source of his melancholy and then, after a brief silent prayer, asked the king for permission to journey to Jerusalem and undertake the task of rebuilding its walls. With astonishing generosity, the Persian monarch once again shows favor to God's chosen people, giving Nehemiah safe passage, as well as access to the materials he would need to accomplish the mission. Upon arriving in the holy city, Nehemiah conducts an inspection of the walls, and, having procured the aid of some officials of the city, he commences to organize a team to repair the walls. After only a few months, and despite the opposition of some enemies of the people, the basic work is done.

It would be useful to pause at this point and reflect upon the symbolic significance of the rebuilt walls. We recall that Eden itself is presented in the book of Genesis as a walled garden, a place with its own strictly defined identity, but we recall as well that the purpose of the original inhabitants of that "paradise" was to carry the beauty of that place out to the rest of creation. That rhythm of over and against the world for the sake of the world has, as we've frequently seen, been reiterated up and down the biblical text. Sometimes the needful thing is the re-establishment of identity through Law, ritual, language, ethical practice, and above all, right worship; and sometimes, the needful thing is outward expansion. Nehemiah correctly discerned that, at his particular historical moment, the former was called for.

Considerable light is shed if we consider Nehemiah's project in ecclesiological terms. The Church, which is the descendant of the people Israel—grafted onto Israel, in Paul's language (Rom. 11:17–24)—must be defined over and against the sinful world and the merely secular society. It indeed has its own language, custom, liturgical sensibility, manner of thinking, codes of behavior, etc. If the walls of the Church are broken down, then any influence from the environing culture can enter into its life, leading eventually to the compromising of its identity and mission. On the other hand, if those walls are too high and too thick, and if they accordingly permit no intercourse with the world outside, then the Church loses its ultimate *raison d'être*. Thus, sometimes in the life of the Church, the walls must be built up. One thinks perhaps of St. Benedict's establishment of monasticism in the Western Church or of the hunkering down of the Church during times of persecution. Other times, the knocking down of those walls, what Hans Urs von Balthasar called "the razing of the bastions,"[2] is a desideratum in the life of a community with a missionary purpose. Even Balthasar's Reformed colleague, Karl Barth, who could never have been accused of underplaying the importance of Christian distinctiveness, said that the Christian church is never meant to crouch defensively "behind Chinese walls."[3] Those caught in the strictures of ideologies of either the left or the right often do not see that there is no one answer to the question of walls.

2. Hans Urs von Balthasar, *Razing the Bastions*, trans. Brian McNeil (San Francisco: Ignatius, 1993).

3. Karl Barth, *The Humanity of God*, trans. Thomas Wieser and John Newton Thomas (Louisville: Westminster John Knox, 1960), 18.

The eighth chapter of the book of Nehemiah is the high point of the text, the hinge upon which it turns. We hear again of Ezra the priest, who at the prompting of the people themselves, commenced to read aloud the Torah, "the law of Moses." We are told that all the men and women of the city, as well as those children old enough to understand, gathered at the so-called "Water Gate" of the town and, from dawn until midday, listened to Ezra's recitation. When he had finished, they raised their hands and answered, "Amen, Amen," and then they bowed down to worship (Neh. 8:3, 6). In these two moves—hearing the Word and worshiping the one who spoke it—they gave expression to their essential identity as the people Israel. Nehemiah tells us that, upon hearing the Torah, the people wept, so moved were they to discover once again who they were. If we interpret walls in only a negative way, we forget this fundamental biblical truth that the flourishing of the people is tied, at least to a degree, to their sense of identity and distinctiveness.

Chapter 9 of Nehemiah is reminiscent of Stephen's speech in the seventh chapter of the Acts of the Apostles, for both are eloquent and remarkably pithy summaries of God's dealing with his chosen people. Moving from creation itself, to the call of Abraham through slavery in Egypt and Exodus, to the conquest of the Promised Land and the exile, Ezra provides the narrative identity of Israel. They are a nation defined not by land primarily, nor by ideas, nor by common culture, but by the manner in which God dealt with them. It is, accordingly, in telling a story of God's fidelity that Israel discovers its identity. What follows, in chapters 10, 11, and 12, is a thorough listing of the officials, Levites, and priests who formally subscribed to the story so delineated. As the walls defined the city, so the covenant narrative defined the people. Zerubbabel and Nehemiah built up the former, and Ezra ratified the latter.

After hearing this densely textured story of building, repairing, repenting, listening, and worshiping, how could we not think of the liturgy, that primal act, that source and summit of the Christian life,[4] which takes place within the walls of a church building and which involves the confession of sin, the hearing of the Word of God, and the fervent adoration of the Lord? From the time that Israel petitioned Pharaoh to be allowed to worship the Lord in the desert, through the Sinai stipulations, the building of the tabernacle, the dance of David before the ark of the covenant, the construction of Solomon's temple, all the way to the reconstruction of that temple at the time of Ezra and Nehemiah, Israel had celebrated its identity as a priestly people, a nation uniquely qualified to give God the praise that he desired and deserved. So the new Israel of the Church continues to express its life liturgically through the orthodoxy of its belief and practice.

However, as we have come to expect, this tale of restoration and liturgical rectitude does not end well. It is as though, by an irresistible instinct, the biblical authors feel compelled to remind us that, prior to the definitive action of God, nothing in the affairs of Israel will ever be flawless. Nehemiah notices that the people of Judah are regularly violating the command not to work on the sabbath, "treading wine presses on the sabbath, and bringing in heaps of grain and loading them on donkeys; and also wine, grapes, figs, and all kinds of burdens" (Neh. 13:15). Moreover, many sons of Israel are marrying the daughters of the surrounding tribes and peoples, imitating thereby the sin of Solomon. So Nehemiah takes matters rather dramatically into his own hands: "And I contended with them and cursed them and beat some of them and pulled out their hair" (Neh. 13:25). As he builds a physical wall around Jerusalem, he is endeavoring to construct a spiritual wall around the moral and liturgical practices of Israel. But per usual, we have, in the narrative of God's people, one step forward and at least two backward—prompting an even more ardent expectation of the one who would, in time, fulfill the promises made to Israel.

4. Vatican Council II, *Lumen Gentium* 11, *The Word on Fire Vatican II Collection*, ed. Matthew Levering (Park Ridge, IL: Word on Fire Institute, 2021), 59–61.

Tobit

The book of Tobit—accepted by Roman Catholics and Eastern Orthodox as canonical but regarded as deuterocanonical by Jews and
Protestants—is an extraordinary text, by turns funny, theologically
profound, ethically instructive, absurd, and deeply moving. A good
deal of its theological profundity has to do with divine providence,
the reliable yet quirky and unpredictable way that God guides his
creatures, both human and nonhuman, to do his work. It is, at
the same time, a warmly human story and a triumphant tale of
divine activity. And despite its relative brevity and somewhat comic
quality, it is a book with remarkable allusive power, hearkening
back to many stories from the Old Testament and looking forward
to many central themes of the New Testament.

The principal character of the book—and indeed the one
who directly narrates the first part of it—is Tobit, an Israelite of
the tribe of Naphtali who had been taken into captivity during
the Assyrian exile in the late eighth century BC and who lives in
Nineveh. Tobit tells us that though his family had broken with
the house of David and the worship in the Jerusalem temple, he
had remained faithful to that ancient tradition. While his relatives
worshiped the calf that Jeroboam had erected in the north after
the splitting of the kingdoms in two, Tobit continued to journey
to David's city and offer firstfruits in the temple. He also tells us
that he faithfully practiced various works of piety, giving money to
the poor, offering assistance to widows, and following the dietary
laws of the Torah. Even after he and his family were carried off

to Assyria, he continued to honor the God of Israel, practicing what the later tradition would term the "corporal works of mercy," including and especially burying the dead. This loving act put him at cross purposes with the king of Assyria, for Tobit was burying some whom the king had purposely put to death. In consequence, the faithful Israelite ran away and suffered the confiscation of his property. When a king more agreeable to Tobit commenced to reign, Tobit returned to his home and family and continued the practice of burying the bodies of his fellow Israelites. On one occasion, Tobit interred a body and then lay down to sleep by the wall of a courtyard, leaving his face uncovered on account of the heat. While he slumbered, sparrows, who were perched on the wall above him, left their droppings on his eyes, causing Tobit to go blind. Despite all the efforts of physicians, he failed to recover his sight. Finally, due to a petty dispute, he fell out with his wife, Anna, who upbraided him for his lack of charity.

We see in this somewhat homely tale an anticipation of the book of Job, for we find an utterly faithful, even heroic, follower of the God of Israel who experiences not blessing, as we might expect from the promises made in the book of Deuteronomy, but rather blindness, exile, loss of property, and alienation from his family. The prayer that Tobit offers in the wake of this loss shows him to be, like Job, a symbol of Israel itself, the specially chosen people who nevertheless experience myriad sorrows: "Do not punish me for my sins and for my unwitting offenses and those that my ancestors committed before you. They sinned against you, and disobeyed your commandments. So you gave us over to plunder, exile, and death" (Tob. 3:3–4). Though he is acknowledging at least hidden faults or those committed by his forebears, he begs, finally, for release: "Command, O Lord, that I be released from this distress; release me to go to the eternal home" (Tob. 3:6). Behind the pious language is the quasi-suicidal desire of the suffering Tobit that his life might come to an end. The "How long, O Lord?" of Israel is encapsulated in this man's painful prayer.

Then we are told that on the very same day that Tobit uttered his prayer, a woman by the name of Sarah was offering a prayer even more desperate and heartfelt. Her backstory is one of the most extraordinary of any biblical figure. She had been married to seven men in succession, each of whom died on his wedding night before he could consummate the marriage. A demon by the name of Asmodeus had ruthlessly put these men to death, but her family and acquaintances blamed her. Driven to despair, she, like Tobit, contemplated suicide, but she thought better of it and instead cried out to the Lord, "Blessed are you, merciful God! Blessed is your name forever. . . . And now, Lord, I turn my face to you, and raise my eyes toward you. . . . Why should I still live? But if it is not pleasing to you, O Lord, to take my life, hear me in my disgrace" (Tob. 3:11–12, 15). Her name ties her to Abraham's wife, who remained childless until extreme old age, and the fervor of her prayer calls to mind Hannah, who was similarly childless.

The narrator then tells us that both of these prayers were heard and that God sent the angel Raphael (whose name means "God heals") to bring comfort to both Tobit and Sarah. We will see in the intertwining of these two stories a peculiar mark of the divine providence. A gift that God gives to one will prove to be a benefit for another. Thomas Aquinas compares the providential God to a king, who arranges, by means of separate commands, for two of his charges to meet, so that what appears to the two as coincidence is actually the result of the king's intention.[1] So from the vantage point of his unconditioned causality, God can influence the nexus of conditioned causality in a noninvasive manner and in such a way that a grace to one becomes a grace for another.

At this point in the narrative, Tobit resolves to send his son Tobias to collect some money that Tobit had left in trust with a man in the town of Media. This commissioning of Tobias gives Tobit the opportunity to share some fundamental moral instruction.

---

1. Thomas Aquinas, *Summa theologiae* 1.22.2 ad 1; 1.116.1.

Very much in accord with his own predilections, the father tells the son to attend to basic works of charity and justice: "To all those who practice righteousness give alms from your possessions, and do not let your eye begrudge the gift when you make it," and "Do not turn your face away from anyone who is poor, and the face of God will not be turned away from you" (Tob. 4:6–7). The law of the gift—namely, that one's being increases in the measure that one gives it away—can become a mere abstraction unless and until it is instantiated concretely. The actual offer of alms serves that purpose. Moreover, in the remarkable observation regarding the face of God in the face of the poor, we find an anticipation of Emmanuel Levinas' fundamental moral theology, according to which moral obligation arises, not so much from the intuition of legal norms, but from the face of the sufferer who stands before us.[2] In the unconditioned demand occasioned by that particular person's need, the infinity of God opens up.

This speech of Tobit is also well known for containing the first biblical formulation of what would come to be called "the golden rule," though expressed in a form more negative than positive. Instead of the more familiar "Do unto others as you would have them do unto you," we find "Watch yourself, my son, in everything you do, and discipline yourself in all your conduct. And what you hate, do not do to anyone" (Tob. 4:14–15). In either the positive or negative formulation, this rule serves to de-center the ego by means of empathy. Within a purely Nietzschean will-to-power context, all that finally matters is what is to the benefit of the agent.[3] But to sense in the other the very same impulses and aversions that one senses in oneself is to move, *ipso facto*, out of the space of mere self-regard. It is to move in the direction of willing the good of the other and not simply willing the other as a good for oneself. It is to

2. Emmanuel Levinas, *Totality and Infinity: An Essay on Exteriority*, trans. Alphonso Lingis (Pittsburgh, PA: Duquesne University Press, 1969).

3. Friedrich Nietzsche, *The Will to Power*, ed. Walter Kaufman, trans. Walter Kaufman and R.J. Hollingdale (New York: Vintage Books, 1968).

break free of the black hole of an egotism that would draw all things into itself. And this psychological and spiritual transformation is the condition for the possibility of fulfilling the concrete commands regarding gift-giving that we have already specified.

Having received instruction from his father, Tobias sets out to retrieve the money that Tobit had left in Media. Not knowing the precise route, he seeks out someone who knows the way and happens upon a man who is in fact the angel Raphael in disguise. With the full support of his father, Tobias sets out with Raphael to Media. On the way, they camp by the banks of the river Tigris, and when Tobias goes down to the water to bathe, a "large fish leaped up from the water and tried to swallow the young man's foot" (Tob. 6:3). But the angel encourages him, "Catch hold of the fish and hang on to it!" (Tob. 6:4). Then, he instructs him to eviscerate the animal and extricate its gall, heart, and liver, since they would be useful for medicine. Lest this seem simply fantastical, let us remember the symbolic significance of water and water creatures in the biblical context. In the book of Genesis, God brings order out of the watery chaos; that *tohu wabohu* returned in the flood of Noah; it re-presented itself as well in the waters of the Red Sea that blocked the escape of the children of Israel from Egypt. And water-creatures Behemoth and Leviathan, in the book of Job, are evocative of the forces within the created order that only God can master. Further, in the book of the prophet Isaiah, we hear that "the LORD with his cruel and great and strong sword will punish Leviathan the fleeing serpent, Leviathan the twisting serpent, and he will kill the dragon that is in the sea" (Isa. 27:1). Therefore, this great fish who emerges suddenly and dangerously from the river Tigris is symbolic of the cosmic negative, what Karl Barth called *das Nichtige*, the nothingness, that which is death-dealing and dangerous in the extreme.[4] The crucially important lesson contained in this episode is that this power ought not to be simply

4. Karl Barth, "God and Nothingness," in *Church Dogmatics*, ed. G.W. Bromiley and T.F. Torrance, vol. 3.3, *The Doctrine of Creation, Sections 50–51* (London: T&T Clark, 2010), 1–78.

destroyed or run from, but rather mastered and then, in a limited way, taken in. One thinks here of the way in which the phobic is encouraged not to hide from his fear but to look at it and thereby to disempower it. And once the negative is conquered in that sense, it becomes, ironically, a source of strength and healing.

In very short order, Tobias discovered precisely how the fish organs that he had preserved would disclose their healing power, for Raphael told him of Sarah. When the angel insisted that Tobias marry this girl, the young man responded, "I have heard that she already has been married to seven husbands and they died in the bridal chamber" (Tob. 6:14). But Raphael informed him that when the fish's liver and heart are burned as a sort of incense, they will give off an odor that will chase away the demon who had killed the seven husbands. And so, they came to the town of Ecbatana, where Sarah lived with her father, Raguel, a relative of Tobit, and her mother, Edna. Overjoyed to receive a kinsman, Raguel was even more delighted when he heard that Tobias wanted to marry Sarah. At the same time, the father felt obligated to rehearse the sad tale of the seven previous husbands. So, filled with both hope and trepidation, Tobias and Sarah entered into a marriage contract according to the Law of Moses. When, after a festive dinner, Tobias and Sarah repaired to the bedroom, the young man remembered the words of Raphael and placed the fish's liver and heart on the fire, and the foul odor did indeed drive Asmodeus away, significantly to Egypt, the land of slavery and sin from which Israel had escaped. Wonderfully, we are told that Raphael, manifesting his full angelic power and geographic range, followed the demon and bound him hand and foot. We are quite clearly meant to see a recapitulation of the Exodus here.

Before they sleep together, Tobias leads Sarah in a prayer that is so beautiful that it has found its way into the matrimonial liturgy of the Catholic Church. Indeed, if Catholics have heard anything of the book of Tobit, they probably heard it at a wedding. Tobias begins, "Blessed are you, O God of our ancestors. . . .

You made Adam, and for him you made his wife Eve as a helper and support. . . . You said, 'It is not good that the man should be alone'" (Tob. 8:5–6). In still another striking allusion to the biblical tradition, Tobias and Sarah are presented here as a sort of new Adam and new Eve, and their sexual congress as a kind of new creation. The parallels with the first couple are striking. Whereas Adam fails to protect Eve from the wiles of the serpent, Tobias protects Sarah from Asmodeus; whereas in the Genesis account, the evil one triumphs, in Tobit the evil spirit is exiled and held bound; whereas Adam and Eve fall into spiritual death and are expelled from the garden, Tobias is saved from death and Sarah brought back to spiritual health. Tobias' prayer ends as follows: "I now am taking this kinswoman of mine, not because of lust, but with sincerity. Grant that she and I may find mercy and that we may grow old together" (Tob. 8:7). That Tobias is physically attracted to Sarah is made plain in a number of places in the story, but it is significant indeed that, on their wedding night, he places his carnal desire for her within the wider context of "sincerity" and "mercy." In this, we see a biblical ground for much of the Church's teaching on sexuality, which consistently wants to bring the sexual impulse under the aegis of love—which is to say, intentionally willing the good of the other. There is nothing puritanical or anti-sex in either the biblical or Catholic imagination, but there is an insistence that sex must be expressive of love if it is to be integral. It is noteworthy that, after their prayer, Tobias and Sarah simply go to sleep and do not immediately consummate their marriage, emphasizing the primacy of love over sex, even within the confines of marriage.

Finally, to fulfill the purpose of God's providential design, Tobias, Sarah, and Raphael return to Nineveh in order to heal the blindness of Tobit. While they are still a long way off, Anna, Tobias' mother, catches sight of her son, runs up to him, and throws her arms around him. How can the reader of the Gospels possibly miss an overtone here of the return of the prodigal son?

When Tobit comes stumbling out of the house, his son runs up to him and immediately applies the gall of the fish to his father's eyes, making them sting. Next, he manages to peel "white films from the corners of his eyes" (Tob. 11:13), and Tobit, for the first time in years, sees his son. God's complete healing intention achieved, everyone settles in for a seven-day wedding feast. So that the human beings involved might realize the remarkable manner in which God used secondary causality in the attainment of his end, Raphael then reveals his angelic identity, specifying that he was the one who conveyed the prayers of Tobias and Sarah before the throne of God and the messenger sent to affect the double healing: "I am Raphael, one of the seven angels who stand ready and enter before the glory of the Lord" (Tob. 12:15). That there are purely spiritual creatures at a higher pitch of existence, who dwell in the presence of God and who serve as messengers and servants here below in the working out of God's providence, is a commonplace in the Bible. In point of fact, angels are mentioned 273 times in the Old and New Testaments. Given the wild fecundity of God's creativity evident in the visible order, why should we be surprised that there might be an equally extravagant creativity on display in the invisible order?

When Raphael disappears into the heavens, Tobit sings one of the most remarkable songs in the entire Scripture. The Church so reverences these verses that it places a substantial portion of Tobit's exultation within the Liturgy of the Hours. It serves as an exuberant summary of God's dealing with his holy people and a hopeful anticipation of the ultimate trajectory of the history of salvation.

The first truth that Tobit proclaims is that God's providence is such that it embraces both darkness and light, both suffering and joy: "For he afflicts, and he shows mercy; he leads down to Hades in the lowest regions of the earth, and he brings up from the great abyss" (Tob. 13:2). Again, we find something of the book of Job here. It is decidedly not the case that God is providently present when we are fortunate and somehow absent when we are not. Both are ingredient in his plan, the first directly willed and the second allowed. Thomas Aquinas, in answer to the objector who said that if God is infinitely good, evil would be destroyed, put it this way: God is so benevolent that he can permit evil so as to bring about a good that could never have been realized otherwise. Sometimes, indeed, we can see the logic of this permission, but very often we cannot—which seems to be the central theme of the book of Job—but whether we understand it or not, God's providence obtains.

Next, Tobit gives a specific example of this providential permission of evil: "Acknowledge him before the nations, O children of Israel; for he has scattered you among them. He has shown you his greatness even there" (Tob. 13:3–4). On the one hand, Israel was scattered for its wickedness, but on the other hand, even this scattering served to bring the light of the God of Israel to far-flung lands. And there will be an end to the punishment, once the children of Israel turn back to the Lord: "He will gather you from all the nations among whom you have been scattered. If you turn to him with all your heart and with all your soul, to do what is true before him, then he will turn to you and will no longer hide his face from you" (Tob. 13:5–6). Echoing the prophet Isaiah here, Tobit anticipates the blessed era when the Messiah would repristinate the temple, deal with the enemies of the nation, and above all, bring the tribes back from exile. As we have seen throughout this commentary, the conviction of the biblical authors is that only a properly united Israel would serve adequately as a signal to the rest of the world.

And we hear precisely of this hope as Tobit continues his prayer of praise: "O Jerusalem, the holy city, he afflicted you for the deeds of your hands, but will again have mercy on the children of the righteous. . . . A bright light will shine to all the ends of the earth; many nations will come to you from far away . . . bearing gifts in their hands for the King of heaven" (Tob. 13:9,

11). Tobit explicitly references the prophet Isaiah, who imagined the day when "all the nations shall stream" toward "the mountain of the Lord's house" (Isa. 2:2)—which is to say, Zion. In Tobit's language: "For Jerusalem will be built as his house for all ages. . . . The gates of Jerusalem will be built with sapphire and emerald, and all your walls with precious stones." Moreover, "the streets of Jerusalem will be paved with ruby and with stones of Ophir" (Tob. 13:16). Given the fact, of course, that the actual city of Jerusalem would meet with a far less glorious fate, and given the charged symbolic language of the book of Revelation, so redolent of this final speech of Tobit, Christians will interpret his words as applying, not so much to David's city on Mt. Zion, but rather to the ultimate goal of the spiritual journey, the heavenly Jerusalem.

Thus it is that this tale of an Israelite exile ends with the vibrant hope that all exile will end within the confines of the city on high.

Judith

That the book of Judith is not meant to be taken as a strictly literal, historical account of events is signaled at the very commencement of the work, for the author tells us that Nebuchadnezzar was ruling over the great city of Nineveh. Anyone even vaguely acquainted with the history of Israel would have known that Nebuchadnezzar was in fact the king of Babylon at the time of the exile of the southern tribes and that Nineveh was a threat to Israel long before the time of Nebuchadnezzar. The anachronism, therefore, indicates that we are dealing here with something of an archetypal tale of the struggle between the people of God and her enemies, a theme that echoes, as we've seen, up and down the Old Testament. This line of interpretation finds further confirmation in that the name of the central character, Judith, means simply "a Jewess." Hence, the heroine of the tale should rightly be read as a sort of embodiment of the Jewish people in their seemingly never-ending struggle against her adversaries.

The story begins, in the manner of many biblical accounts, with a mighty potentate asserting his authority. Putting us in mind of Pharaoh enslaving the Israelites or of Augustus ordering a census of the entire empire, Nebuchadnezzar, we are told, commands all of his vassal states, both east and west, to aid him in his battle against the Median capital of Ecbatana. His subordinates in the east acquiesce, but those in the west do not; so after making short work of Ecbatana, the king resolves to settle accounts with his uncooperative western allies, assembling an army overwhelming in size and strength and tapping his top general, Holofernes, to command it. And so Holofernes "mustered the picked troops by divisions as his lord had ordered him to do, one hundred twenty thousand of them, together with twelve thousand archers on horseback, and he organized them as a great army is marshaled for a campaign. He took along a vast number of camels and donkeys and mules for transport, and innumerable sheep and oxen and goats for food; also ample rations for everyone, and a huge amount of gold and silver from the royal palace" (Jth. 2:15–18). This crushing host, this enormous and well-provisioned army, is one more biblical iteration of the forces of the world that stand opposed to God's creative intentions. Adam himself was meant to be a king, capable of defending the garden against intruders and then going on march effectively to Edenize the world. His failure, and the ongoing failure of Israel's kings, goes hand in hand with the increasing power of sin. Hence, we have Israel against the flood, against the Egyptians, against the Amalekites, against the Assyrians, against the Babylonians, and here against the army of Nebuchadnezzar. The detailed description of the king's host calls to mind the equally comprehensive accounting of Goliath's battle gear in 1 Samuel. As the latter sets up the encounter with David, so the former prepares us for Nebuchadnezzar's confrontation with Judith.

In the company of his stupendous array, Holofernes moves through Nebuchadnezzar's western provinces with dispatch and cruelty, a blitzkrieging General Sherman: "He ravaged Put and Lud . . . and destroyed all the fortified towns along the brook Abron. . . . He also seized the territory of Cilicia and killed everyone who resisted him. . . . Then he went down into the plain of Damascus during the wheat harvest, and burned all their fields and destroyed their flocks and herds and sacked their towns and ravaged their lands and put all their young men to the sword" (Jth. 2:23–27). As the general moves through the western territories, he not only reestablishes the king's political authority but also tears down any religious shrines, insisting that Nebuchadnezzar alone should be worshiped as a god. With that move, we are meant to see the spiritual meaning of this invasion: when the power of the world is at full tide, orthodoxy is supplanted, for sin is always correlate to false praise. And thus, it is no wonder that the people of Israel and Judah are terrified at Holofernes' approach.

At the prompting of Joakim, the high priest in Jerusalem at the time, people in the hill country prepare militarily to meet the threat, but "every man of Israel cried out to God with great fervor, and they humbled themselves with much fasting" (Jth. 4:9). Even, we are told, wives, children, and cattle put on sackcloth, and hordes of worshipers come to the temple, "praying fervently to the God of Israel not to allow their infants to be carried off and their wives to be taken as booty, and the towns they had inherited to be destroyed" (Jth. 4:12). When Holofernes hears of the Israelite military preparations, he is incensed and wonders why this people, of all the nations of the west, choose to stand against him. At this point, one of his allies, Achior by name, endeavors to inform him of the peculiar history of the nation opposing his might. He rehearses all of the vicissitudes of Israelite history, from Abraham to the present day, insisting that as long as they remain faithful to their God, they find protection. He concludes, in fine Deuteronomistic fashion, "So now, my master and lord, if there is any oversight in this people and they sin against their God and we find out their offense, then we can go up and defeat them. But if they are not a guilty nation, then let my lord pass them by; for their Lord and God will defend them" (Jth. 5:20–21). Achior finishes his speech in a manner practically guaranteed to annoy Holofernes and his entourage. If, he argues, they go out against faithful Israel, they will "become the laughingstock of the whole world" (Jth. 4:21). Predictably infuriated, the general's attendants call for Achior's immediate execution, but Holofernes decides to delay the matter somewhat, sending his former advisor to Bethulia, one of the fortified hill cities, confident that he will die with its hapless defenders. Giving full voice to the manic fury of the opponents of God, the general sums up, "We will overwhelm them; their mountains will be drunk with their blood, and their fields full of their dead. Not even their footprints will survive our attack" (Jth. 6:4).

With that, the Assyrian commander lays siege to Bethulia and cuts off its water supply. In their desperation, the people cry out to their leader, Uzziah, who begs them to pray and to wait for five days. If, he says, after that time there is no relief, he will agree to surrender to the Assyrians and accept enslavement for his people rather than see them destroyed. At this desperate juncture, the heroine of the story is finally introduced: "Now in those days Judith heard about these things" (Jth. 8:1). She is described as a widow and as a very pious daughter of Israel, and as exceptionally beautiful. Of those three descriptors, perhaps the most important theologically is widow, for this archetypal Jewess represents the nation that had lost its king, the son of David, at the time of the exile. And if we follow the prompts of Isaiah, Ezekiel, and the Psalms, the Davidic king would function as the means by which the God of Israel himself would succeed in shepherding his people. Therefore, Judith might be construed as the faithful remnant of Israel longing for reunion with its heavenly bridegroom from whom she has been estranged. A major obstacle to this marriage, of course, is that Israel could be conquered and co-opted by foreign potentates such as Nebuchadnezzar and his servant. We shall watch this marriage dynamic at play in Judith's cunning seduction of Holofernes.

Before Judith confronts the great enemy of Israel, she delivers herself of a rather remarkable disquisition on the mystery of God's purpose, one that is perfectly congruent with the musings of both Isaiah and Job on the same matter. She upbraids the rulers of Bethulia for putting God to the test, essentially giving him five days to act. We cannot, she argues, even fathom the depths of the human heart or ever fully understand mere human motivation; therefore, how could we possibly expect to comprehend the ways and purposes of God? The Lord might save the city in five days, and he might not, but in either case, he knows what he is about, and it does not belong to the people of the city to "try to bind the purposes of the Lord our God" (Jth. 8:16). Rather, our task is to pray and to wait.

Then, Judith introduces a category that is employed by a number of biblical authors in a variety of contexts, namely, that of the trial—not our trial of God, but rather his of us. In a lyrical passage, which has found its way into the Liturgy of the Hours, Judith encourages her countrymen: "In spite of everything, let us give thanks to the Lord our God, who is putting us to the test as he did our ancestors. Remember what he did with Abraham, and how he tested Isaac, and what happened to Jacob in Syrian Mesopotamia. . . . For he has not tried us with fire, as he did them, to search their hearts, nor has he taken vengeance on us; but the Lord scourges those who are close to him in order to admonish them" (Jth. 8:25–27). Though in recent years, biblical interpreters have had almost an allergic reaction to this kind of thinking, it is difficult to deny its presence in the Bible itself. And there are a number of aspects of it that we could bring to light. First, it seems undoubtedly the case that certain powers of ours would not be called forth unless we passed through some sort of test or trial. Many would confess that intense suffering or an acute threat brought out the best in them. Why else would we bring prospective athletes through the rigors of practice or prospective soldiers through the ordeal of boot camp? A second perspective is that love itself requires a kind of test. If, as we have argued, love is willing the good of the other, a person could truly know that he *loves* another, and not his own good through the other, if and only if he has strongly felt the tug in the direction of his own ego. Finally, a trial is necessary to effect a distinction between loving God for his own sake and loving him for the sake of the consolations that he provides. Many of the spiritual masters teach that, at the commencement of a person's relationship with God, she often enjoys good feelings in association with prayer and the works of love. But in time, these consoling emotions are withdrawn, not because God is fickle, but rather because he wants the person to love *him* and not the goods that he might offer. That this removal of consolations constitutes a test or a trial is obvious to anyone who has endeavored to walk the spiritual path. For the most terrible biblical instance of this sort of trial, one should consult the story of the binding of Isaac. Therefore, Judith effects a reversal: while Israel was putting God to the test, she insists that God is putting his people to the test.

She then blithely tells the people of Bethulia that she is about to do something that will liberate her people, but that they shouldn't inquire of her as to the details. They should only have confidence that, on her own, she will take vengeance on the enemies of the people. It would be impossible to miss the overtone here of David going out, unarmored and weaponless, against Goliath. In fact, David's magnificent "You come to me with sword and spear and javelin; but I come to you in the name of the LORD of hosts" (1 Sam. 17:45) is echoed in the prayer that Judith utters before she sets out: "Here now are the Assyrians . . . priding themselves in their horses and riders, boasting in the strength of their foot soldiers, and trusting in shield and spear, in bow and sling. They do not know that you are the Lord who crushes wars" (Jth. 9:7). A Christian cannot help but see an anticipation of the naked and defenseless Jesus, nailed to the cross and facing down the institutional and military might of Rome. God does not conquer through the weapons of the world, but rather through the instrumentality of those who trust radically in him.

So Judith and her maid go out from Bethulia and are soon captured by Assyrian patrols. Judith tells them that she has a message for Holofernes that will prove beneficial to him. Captivated by her words and especially by her extraordinary beauty, they convey the Hebrew woman into the presence of the great general. Holofernes and his entire court are similarly smitten by her loveliness, and they are further impressed by the wisdom and elegance of her speech. As in the stories of Joseph, Moses, and Daniel, we find a Jew behind enemy lines, a child of Israel who manages to outwit the enemies of God and undermine them from within. Four days later, Holofernes holds a banquet for his personal entourage, but also invites Judith to join them. Dressing herself in her finest robes, she comes into the presence of the general, "and his passion was aroused, for he had been waiting for an opportunity to seduce her from the day he first saw her" (Jth. 12:16). The Assyrian commander proceeds to drink more than he had ever drunk before, and, by the end of the evening, he is spread out on his bed, asleep and thoroughly intoxicated. Seizing the opportunity, Judith takes Holofernes' sword down from the wall and, having invoked the aid of the Lord, swings twice at his neck, cutting off his head. Once again, in the grossest manner possible, this archetypal story echoes that of David.

Upon returning to Bethulia, Judith, to the astonishment of the townspeople, removes the head from a bag and shouts, "See here, the head of Holofernes, the commander of the Assyrian army. . . . The Lord has struck him down by the hand of a woman" (Jth. 13:15). Then, she calmly instructs the elders to hang the grisly trophy from the parapet of the wall. When the Assyrians rise the next morning and discover the headless body of their commander, they fall into grief and confusion, "and their loud cries and shouts rose up throughout the camp" (Jth. 14:19). In their panic, they flee "by every path across the plain and through the hill country" (Jth. 15:2), and the Israelites follow them, cutting them down and seizing the cities and towns formerly held by the Assyrians. Finally, in the manner of Miriam, Hannah, and David, Judith delivers herself of a hymn of praise and thanksgiving: "Begin a song to my God with tambourines, sing to my Lord with cymbals. Raise to him a new psalm; exalt him, and call upon his name" (Jth. 16:1). According to the familiar pattern, the mighty works of God on behalf of his people are followed by a liturgical act of praise on the part of those whom the Lord had liberated. Unlike the other peoples of the world, Israel finds itself not in its own accomplishments, but rather in surrender to God and worship of him. Indeed, the book of Judith tells us that, just after the heroine's song, the people flock to Jerusalem and offer "their burnt offerings, their freewill offerings, and their gifts" (Jth. 16:18). Judith herself dedicates to the temple all of the possessions of Holofernes that she had managed to acquire, including the canopy from his bedchamber.

Faithful to Israel's traditions, trusting in the power and providence of God, dedicated to the praise of the Lord in the temple, Judith is evocative of Israel itself, as we saw, but also of the Church, the spotless Bride of Christ. We might be even more specific and say that she evokes the "fighting Church," which battles the powers of darkness up and down the ages, even as she waits for the definitive victory of the King. Jesus told his followers that the gates of hell will not prevail against the Church, implying that his people are on the march, battering down the gates of the enemy's city. In light of that image, Judith, who proactively hung the head of her enemy from the walls of her city, is richly symbolic of the Church Militant.

Esther

The brief but powerful book of Esther poses a number of anomalies and challenges to the interpreter. First, like the Song of Solomon, the original text contains absolutely no mention of God, a curiosity that led some rabbis in the early centuries of the common era not to consider it part of the scriptural canon. It was only in the Septuagint translation into Greek that several texts, more explicitly theological in nature, were inserted. Secondly, nothing obviously miraculous or obviously "supernatural" takes place in the story, contributing to the sense that it is a more or less secular narrative. Third, it oscillates oddly between the utterly grave and the comical. On the one hand, it centers around an attempt by a powerful enemy to commit genocide against the Jews; on the other hand, it has many of the literary qualities of a fairy tale, marked by mockery and farcical reversals of fortune. Once again, I see it as belonging very much to the familiar biblical genre of what we might call "Jews behind enemy lines," echoing motifs in the stories of Joseph, Moses, Daniel, and Judith. Speaking most generally, the book of Esther is still another meditation on the theme of Israel in relation to the Gentile nations.

The story is set in the time of the Persian king Ahasuerus, more commonly known as Xerxes, when many Jews, descendants of the original Babylonian exiles, were present throughout the sprawling Persian empire. We are informed that the king, in order to display his wealth and splendor, held a banquet for his nobles that lasted, incredibly enough, one hundred and eighty days—more than

half the year! At the culmination of this marathon celebration,
he sponsored seven days of intense celebration in his capital city
of Susa, at which there were "couches of gold and silver on a mosaic pavement of porphyry, marble, mother-of-pearl, and colored
stones" and at which "drinks were served in golden goblets . . . and
the royal wine was lavished according to the bounty of the king"
(Esther 1:6–7). One has the distinct impression that Ahasuerus
was not exactly a hardworking monarch and that his kingdom
was not being very effectively governed.

On the final day of this culminating banquet, he gave orders
that his queen, the lovely Vashti, should be paraded before his
guests so that everyone could appreciate her beauty. Some scholars suggest that the implication is that she was asked to appear
nude, which helps to explain her negative reaction: "But Queen
Vashti refused to come at the king's command" (Esther 1:12). At
this, Ahasuerus became enraged and, after consulting with his
advisors, determined that Vashti, having insulted both the king
and the entire nation, should be put away and another queen
found. Accordingly, he arranged for "beautiful young virgins"
(Esther 2:2) to be brought before him from all corners of his
empire and endeavored, through what appears to have been a sort
of sexual trial, to see who would appeal to him the most. Among
those introduced to the king was Esther, the comely adopted
daughter of Mordecai, a Jew who lived in Susa and who was a
descendent of a member of the house of Benjamin carried off in
the Nebuchadnezzar exile. Ahasuerus was smitten by Esther, and
she "won his favor and devotion" so thoroughly that the king
elevated her to royal status (Esther 2:17). It would be impossible
for any attentive biblical reader to miss the overtones of the Joseph
and Moses stories, in which a Jew, against all expectations, is
raised to prominence in a foreign setting. What those previous
tales have primed us to expect, of course, is that Esther's elevation
is a consequence of divine providence and is meant to be of benefit
to suffering Israel.

The tale turns dark indeed when we hear that the king has promoted "Haman son of Hammedatha the Agagite" (Esther 3:1) to a position of supreme importance among the royal advisors. Once again, the attentive student of the Bible will not miss the almost tossed-off reference to Haman's provenance as a descendant of Agag, the king of the Amalekites, Israel's long-standing enemy, the tribe that the God of Israel, we were told in Exodus, would battle down through the ages (Exod. 17:16). Though the prophet Samuel "hewed Agag in pieces" (1 Sam. 15:33) many centuries before, this offspring of the Amalekite leader is about to wreak havoc upon God's chosen race. Informed that Mordecai, the new queen's relative, refused to bow to Haman in accord with a royal decree, Haman inquired as to why. When told that it was on account of Mordecai's Jewish identity, he lashes out with unspeakable violence, plotting to wipe out all Jews throughout the Persian empire. In light of the awful violence against the Jewish race on display throughout history but especially in the last century, we are positively chilled to hear Haman's explanation, given in the presence of the king: "There is a certain people scattered and separated among the peoples in all the provinces of your kingdom; their laws are different from those of every other people, and they do not keep the king's laws. . . . If it pleases the king, let a decree be issued for their destruction" (Esther 3:8–9). In consequence, letters go out in the name of Ahasuerus to all his governors and satraps, in a variety of languages, instructing them "to destroy, to kill, and to annihilate all Jews, young and old, women and children, in one day, the thirteenth day of the twelfth month . . . and to plunder their goods" (Esther 3:13). That this wanton slaughter would take place *in the course of a single day* shows the sheer ferocious barbarity of what is being proposed.

Shocked by the decree, Jews throughout the Persian empire go into mourning, and Mordecai, clothed in sackcloth, walks through the streets of the capital "wailing with a loud and bitter cry" (Esther 4:1). Sensing the movement of divine providence that had placed his adopted daughter in a position of enormous influence, Mordecai inquires of her to petition the king on behalf of her people. Knowing that she would be executed were she to dare to enter the king's presence without being summoned, Esther nevertheless resolves to go before Ahasuerus: "If I perish, I perish!" (Esther 4:16). So the queen comes into the presence of the king, and he graciously agrees to grant her any request. She asks that Ahasuerus and Haman would come to a banquet that she would prepare. Haman readily agrees but remains chagrined that Mordecai continues to protest in sackcloth outside the palace. Consequently, Haman's wife suggests that a gallows fifty cubits high should be constructed so that the annoying man might be hanged from it.

On the second day of the celebration, the king finally inquires of Esther what her request might be, blithely informing her that he would grant it "even to the half of my kingdom" (Esther 7:2). The queen tells of her heartbreak at the mortal threat to herself and her people, and the king demands to know who is responsible for this. (Admittedly, this is a little strange, since Haman had announced his anti-Jewish decree in the presence of the Ahasuerus.) But his possibly feigned ignorance allows Esther to deliver herself of her dramatic *j'accuse*: "A foe and enemy, this wicked Haman!" (Esther 7:6). With that, the infuriated king storms out and commences to pace in the palace garden, giving Haman the opportunity to throw himself at Esther's feet and beg for mercy. A farcical element of the story is that, upon his return, finding Haman groveling on the couch of the queen, Ahasuerus indignantly shouts, "Will he even assault the queen in my presence, in my own house?" (Esther 7:8). With that, one of the king's eunuchs helpfully points out that the very gallows that Haman had had built for Mordecai would be the perfect instrument on which to kill the wicked man himself. "So they hanged Haman on the gallows that he had prepared for Mordecai. Then the anger of the king abated" (Esther 7:10).

Subsequent to the death of her tormentor, Esther is given Haman's house, and she, in turn, gives it to Mordecai. Then, with the approval of the king, a decree goes out giving Jews the right to defend themselves against any militia that would come against them and to plunder their attackers' goods. And so, under the direction of Mordecai, Jews across the Persian empire put to death those who are seeking their destruction. We are told that they "killed seventy-five thousand of those who hated them" (Esther 9:16). Thus, the great reversal is fully accomplished, the wheel of fortune thoroughly turned, and as a result, a day of festival and rejoicing is established among the Jews. Many scholars suggest that the book of Esther was written to provide a justification for the feast of Purim on the Jewish calendar.

Though this text is quite short and though, as we saw, in its original Hebrew version, God is not even mentioned, there are a number of theological themes that it contains, first and most obviously that of divine providence. The various odd twists and turns of the narrative, the distinctive interplay of the characters, and the unlikely reversals all reveal the God who clandestinely but surely works his purpose out within human affairs. The ardent prayers of both Mordecai and Esther herself correspond to the God who cares, in very particular ways, for his chosen people. That threats to Israel do not dissipate as promptly and thoroughly as they do in this tale is apparent not only from the brutal facts of history but also from the Bible itself. We will see how the book of Job in particular undermines any simplistic confidence in a Deuteronomistic reading of history. However, the book of Esther requires us to say that God's providence, though sometimes strange in its expression, never fails.

A second theological motif is that of the demonic opposition to God. As we remarked, Haman is identified as a descendent of Agag the Amalekite, the king of a tribe against which Israel would be destined to fight throughout the ages. He stands, therefore, for those spiritual powers (often expressed through avatars in the visible order) who hound both the old and the new Israel throughout history. His deeply irrational but brutal assault on the Jews of the Persian empire anticipates the myriad ways that the dark powers have harried the people of God. That he calls Hitler vividly to mind is, given this context, altogether appropriate.

A third theme is that of Christological typology, specifically the manner in which the tormented Mordecai anticipates the tormented Christ. A Syriac father known as Aphrahat makes the comparison explicitly: "Mordecai was also persecuted as Jesus was persecuted. Mordecai was persecuted by the wicked Haman; and Jesus was persecuted by the rebellious people. Mordecai by his prayer delivered his people from the hands of Haman; and Jesus by his prayer delivered his people from the hands of Satan. . . . Mordecai trod on the neck of Haman . . . and as for Jesus, his enemies shall be put under his feet."[1]

Finally, we might draw attention to the comparison between Esther and the Virgin Mary, who are both powerful intercessors on behalf of their people. Pope St. John Paul II brought this motif to light: "Esther did not kill the enemy but, by playing the role of mediator, interceded for those who were threatened with destruction."[2] He goes on to observe that, throughout the Old Testament, powerful women act as agents of salvation, thus anticipating Mary's great and definitive role as intercessor for the entire human race. Though Esther most certainly invoked the mercy of Ahasuerus, her primary intervention was her impassioned prayer to the God of Israel. Because a great woman begged, the Jews were delivered. At the close of the Hail Mary, the prayer invokes the aid of the greatest woman: "Holy Mary, Mother of God, pray for us sinners, now and at the hour of our death."

1. Aphrahat, *Demonstrations* 21.20, in *Old Testament V: 1–2 Kings, 1–2 Chronicles, Ezra, Nehemiah, Esther*, ed. Marco Conti and Gianluca Pilara, Ancient Christian Commentary on Scripture (Downers Grove, IL: InterVarsity, 2008), 389.

2. John Paul II, *Theotokos: Woman, Mother, Disciple: A Catechesis on Mary, Mother of God* (Boston: Pauline Books and Media, 2000), 74.

1 and 2 Maccabees

The two books of Maccabees provide a fascinating glimpse into the history of Israel between the establishment of the second temple and the coming of Jesus. Roughly 75 percent of these texts consist of descriptions of political machinations and military maneuvers of long-forgotten potentates. There is, to speak honestly, something rather tiresome about these lengthy narratives. That said, there is substantial material in these texts that is of great interest theologically and that has significantly impacted the spiritual and theological tradition. What I shall do in this chapter is focus on those moments and leave much of the military and political business aside.

As we get underway, it is important to point out that the two books of Maccabees are not like the two books of Samuel or the two volumes of Kings—which is to say, a subdivision of one extended narrative. 1 and 2 Maccabees are discrete texts written by different authors with entirely different styles and purposes. In fact, most scholars agree that, though we have these books only in the Septuagint, 1 Maccabees was likely written originally in Hebrew and 2 Maccabees originally in Greek.[1] Moreover, they cover more or less the same time period but tell the story from their unique perspectives. In the course of this chapter, we shall dip into both books and consider four pivotal theological themes—namely, the relation between Israel and other cultures, the doctrine of *creatio*

---

1. John Bergsma and Brant Pitre, *A Catholic Introduction to the Bible*, vol. 1, *The Old Testament* (San Francisco: Ignatius, 2018), 506–507.

ex nihilo, the problem of the resurrection of the body, and finally, the much-contested matter of praying for the dead.

ISRAEL AND SURROUNDING CULTURES

One could argue that the master theme of both books is the play between Israel and environing cultures that threaten its integrity. To be sure, any reader of the Bible is familiar with this motif, for it is on display practically everywhere in the Torah and the historical books. How many times does God warn Israel not to succumb to the practices and beliefs of foreign people? How often do the authors of Exodus, Leviticus, Numbers, and Deuteronomy call the nation to careful adherence to the dietary, moral, and liturgical laws upon which the Lord has insisted? During the time of the conquest, how often was Israel instructed to eliminate, even to the point of putting the ban on entire peoples, those who stood athwart Israel's purpose? At the same time, did we not notice, again and again, that an integral and purified Israel exists not for its own sake but for the sake of the world? This tension, never adequately resolved in the history of God's chosen people, is the dominant theme of the Maccabees books.

The narrative centers on the oppressive reign of Antiochus IV Epiphanes, a descendent of one of Alexander the Great's generals, who was asserting a Hellenizing political and cultural influence on the people of Judea. After conquering Jerusalem itself, Antiochus ravaged the temple, stripping it of its decoration and taking its furnishings for his own use. Then, he destroyed David's city by fire and subsequently rebuilt it as his own fortification. From this power base, he dominated the surrounding territories, destroying books of the Law, killing young men who were circumcised and murdering mothers who dared to circumcise their sons, building gymnasiums and other centers of Hellenistic culture, compelling Jews to eat pork in violation of the dietary laws of the Torah, etc. The second book of Maccabees relates an episode from this period. Eleazar, an elderly man and a deeply respected scribe of Israel, is being forced to eat swine's flesh, but he refuses, spitting out the meat. When friends and colleagues urge him to compromise, pretending to eat the forbidden food, Eleazar objects: "Such pretense is not worthy of our time of life . . . for many of the young might suppose that Eleazar in his ninetieth year had gone over to an alien religion" (2 Macc. 6:24). Accordingly, the old man goes to his death rather than giving in.

It is during this awful period that Mattathias and his five sons—John, Simon, Eleazar, Jonathan, and Judas, called "Maccabeus" (the hammer)—assert themselves. When officials of Antiochus come to their town of Modein to enforce the new regulations, the father speaks up: "We will not obey the king's words by turning aside from our religion to the right or to the left" (1 Macc. 2:22). Then, when a Jew comes forward to offer the prescribed sacrifice, Mattathias is filled with righteous indignation and kills him as well as the presiding officer. With that, he and his sons take to the hills, and like David before them, they gather an army of oppressed and disaffected Israelites to their cause. At the death of Mattathias, Judas the Hammer becomes the military commander and leads the ragtag band to a series of unlikely victories against imperial forces of far greater size. They come at last to Jerusalem and overwhelm the enemy defenses. Surveying the desolate sanctuary of the temple, the profaned altar, and the ruined courtyard and priestly chambers, they tear their clothes and weep. Next, like Ezra and Nehemiah before them, they engage in a great project of construction and purification: "They took unhewn stones, as the law directs, and built a new altar like the former one. They also rebuilt the sanctuary and the interior of the temple and consecrated the courts. They made new holy vessels, and brought the lampstand, the altar of incense, and the table into the temple" (1 Macc. 4:47–49).

The formal dedication of the repristinated temple, which took place on the morning of the twenty-fifth day of the ninth month of the Hebrew calendar, is the event commemorated, to this day,

THE GREAT STORY OF ISRAEL

on the Feast of Hanukkah. Following the celebration, Judas and the whole assembly of Jerusalem fortify Mt. Zion "with high walls and strong towers all around, to keep the Gentiles from coming and trampling them down as they had done before" (1 Macc. 4:60). Once again, Israelite national and religious identity is secured over and against those outsiders who would compromise them. So far, so familiar. But what about the vocation of Israel to the nations? Is there not a danger that, crouching behind its defensive walls, it will not be the magnet to the world that it is meant to be? How can the contemporary Christian reader of the Maccabees books not remark the irony that the very culture whom Israel so strongly opposed became, in time, a prime, even privileged, vehicle by which the Christian faith understood itself and propagated itself to the wider world? To be sure, there was a sharp clash between Greek values and Jewish dietary and liturgical law, but in the Christian dispensation, Hellenistic thought was gratefully assimilated. One thinks, of course, of the extensive use of Plato's epistemology and metaphysics in so many of the Fathers of the Church—Origen, Pseudo-Dionysius, Gregory of Nyssa, and Augustine, to name just a few—and of Thomas Aquinas' creative appropriation of the thought of Alexander the Great's tutor, Aristotle. But more generally, one can observe, with Joseph Ratzinger, that as Christianity moved into the wider Greco-Roman world, it quite consciously opted for "logos" over "mythos"—that is to say, for a distinctively philosophical manner of thinking rather than a mythological one.[2] That move would have been unthinkable apart from the Hellenizing culture in which the early Church operated.

We notice something similar in the political order as well. In the course of his struggles with the Seleucid Empire, Judas Maccabeus himself turned happily to Rome, which was at that time an emerging power, and made alliances with it. It is easy enough to

2. Joseph Ratzinger, *Introduction to Christianity*, 2nd ed., trans. J.R. Foster (San Francisco: Ignatius, 2004), 137–150.

see that this opening led, in time, to Herod's ambiguous dealings with the Roman Empire and eventually to Roman dominance of Israel. On the other hand, who can doubt that the new Israel, the Church, benefitted enormously from the Roman cultural/political order, which permitted the ready communication of the Gospel message? Thus, as so often in the biblical texts, the poles of identity and relevance emerge, or perhaps better stated, the tension inherent in the idea of a chosen people comes into play: Israel is uniquely elected among all the peoples of the world, not for itself, but for the world. Therefore, the Maccabees were right in a sense to oppose themselves to Hellenization, lest Israel simply devolve into an echo of the surrounding and dominant culture. But can we see how, in God's providence, the eventual cooperation with the Hellenizers and the Romans would serve God's purposes as well? John Henry Newman taught that the Church, moving its way through various cultures, is something like a foraging animal moving its way through its environment. If the animal is utterly unresistant to the world in which it finds itself, it will be, in short order, dead; and if the animal is completely resistant to its world, it will meet the same fate. Rather, a healthy animal resists what it must, even as it assimilates what it can—resistance and openness existing in a permanently tensive relationship. So it goes with the Church vis-à-vis its cultural milieu. A conservatism so absolute that it permits no intercourse with the culture kills the organism of the Church, just as surely as does a liberalism that allows for no distinctiveness.

CREATION AND RESURRECTION

From a theological standpoint, the seventh chapter of 2 Maccabees is exceptionally important, and the narrative that it contains is one of the most powerful and compelling in the entire Old Testament. It concerns a mother and her seven sons during the time of the most intense persecution of Israel by Antiochus. Under arrest and threatened with torture by whips and thongs, the woman and the young men are told that they must eat pork. One of the sons, acting as spokesman for the entire family, tells his tormentors, "What do you intend to ask and learn from us? For we are ready to die rather than transgress the laws of our ancestors" (2 Macc. 7:2). Hearing this, the king (presumably Antiochus himself) flies into a rage and commands that the spokesman's tongue be excised and his scalp sheared off and his hands and feet cut off—all in the presence of his mother and brothers. After he dies, the brothers are, one by one, subjected to similar threats and tortures, but each one nobly resists. The second victim shouts to his persecutor: "You accursed wretch, you dismiss us from this present life, but the King of the universe will raise us up to an everlasting renewal of life, because we have died for his laws" (2 Macc. 7:9). And the third, when told to stretch out his hands that they might be sliced off, blithely remarks, "I got these from Heaven, and because of his laws I disdain them, and from him I hope to get them back again" (2 Macc. 7:11).

As we saw earlier in our discussion of Saul's conversation with the seer of Endor, the most common Old Testament conception of the afterlife—if such a conception were entertained, which was not always the case—was shadowy *Sheol*. The pathetic shade of Samuel, whom the seer called out of that dark place, was certainly not enjoying anything like "renewal of life"—just the contrary. Yet it is precisely that "everlasting renewal" that the tortured son in 2 Maccabees is anticipating. And to make matters even more precise, his brother looks forward to getting back again from the Lord the very hands that were lopped off by his executioner. The point is that, by this stage of Jewish history, a real bodily resurrection is, at least for some, the object of eschatological hope. Clearly, for the seven sons in this story, death is not followed by either nonexistence or a pathetic half-existence, but rather by elevation, perfection, renewal. By the first century, the party of the Pharisees embraced just this sort of conception of the afterlife, holding that the righteous dead will be bodily raised at the end of time. They were, of course, opposed by the Sadducees, who held, it seemed, to the classically Jewish idea that death is simply the end. Christians find this matter enormously interesting, precisely because of the Resurrection of Jesus from the dead. The claim of the first witnesses to the risen Christ is that what was expected of all the righteous at the end of time had happened to a particular person within time. They absolutely did not maintain that Jesus' soul had gone to heaven (according to the rather Greek conception), nor that he had journeyed to depressing *Sheol*, nor that he had been reincarnated (another theory entertained apparently by some Jews); rather, they proclaimed that the selfsame Jesus, who had been nailed to a Roman cross, had been raised bodily from the dead—and not in the manner of Lazarus or the daughter of Jairus, who came back to life only to die again. As the young man in 2 Maccabees hoped, the risen Jesus received his body in an elevated, transfigured, perfected state—a spiritual body, in the language of St. Paul (1 Cor. 15:44).

The other great theological theme that emerges in this seventh chapter is curiously related to the one just under consideration. The only time that the doctrine of "creation from nothing" is explicitly mentioned in the entire Scripture is in this narrative. Exhorting the last of her sons, the mother says, "I beg you, my child, to look at the heaven and the earth and see everything that is in them, and recognize that God did not make them out of things that existed. And in the same way the human race came into being" (2 Macc. 7:28). In referencing heaven and earth, she means the whole of finite reality, both visible and invisible, and therefore she is saying, to put it in more philosophical language, that God is responsible for the being of everything that is not God. He has made all of it, indeed, not "out of things that existed"—that is to say, not in the manner of a maker who fashions a new form of existence out of pre-existing matter. The Creator whom she praises has produced, therefore, the very being of finite things, and this means that there is literally nothing that stands between finite existence and the Creator, no ontological buffer between the giver and receiver of being. There is no place to stand in order to assess God objectively, for whatever is in the subjectivity of the observer has been created by God.

Accordingly, as we saw in our consideration of the opening verses of the book of Genesis, creation cannot take place within the framework of time, for time itself must be a creature; nor does it happen within the theater of space, for space, too, is created. It is, as Thomas Aquinas specified, not a change, for change presupposes a substrate that remains the same from the commencement to the termination of the change. But there is nothing outside of God that is "prior" to the act of creation or that could receive it. Thus, as Aquinas memorably puts it, creation is "a kind of relation to the Creator with freshness of being" (*quaedam relatio ad Creatorem cum novitate essendi*).[3] To put this abstract language in more spiritual terms, the fact of creation means that we cannot finally relate to God in a standard "creature to creature" manner, as though we must establish a relationship to a being that is extrinsic to us. The creature *is* a relationship to the Creator, and hence, as Meister Eckhart put it, we do not so much climb the holy mountain to access a distant God, but rather we "sink" into God.[4] In this same Thomist vein, Thomas Merton characterized contemplative prayer as finding the place in us where we are here and now being created by God.[5]

I mentioned that this high theological idea is related to that of the resurrection of the body, and this is why. The same God who made (and indeed *makes*) the whole of a person through creation can certainly remake the whole of a person even after the death of the body through that same creative power. The young man under torture can express his trust that God will give him back his hands, precisely because God made those hands *ex nihilo* in

3. Thomas Aquinas, *Quaestiones disputatae de potentia Dei* 3.3, in *Quaestiones disputatae*, vol. 2, ed. P. Bazzi (Turin: Marietti, 1949).

4. Meister Eckhart, "Sermon Thirty-One," in *The Complete Mystical Works of Meister Eckhart*, trans. Maurice O'Connell Walshe (New York: Crossroad, 2009), 188.

5. See Thomas Merton, *New Seeds of Contemplation* (New York: New Directions, 1961), 1–5.

the first place. If God were a limited cause, operating within the nexus of similarly limited causes, there would be a restriction in the range of his efficacy. And if that were true, we might be forgiven for saying that God cannot restore to being and to life those of his creatures who have died. But if God is truly the Creator of all things, then there is no limitation to his power to give rise to existence, and hence there is a metaphysical ground for our hope in the resurrection of the body.

A final theological matter that I should like to consider is related to the idea of resurrection from the dead, and it emerges in the twelfth chapter of 2 Maccabees. We are told that Judas Maccabeus has gone out against the army of Gorgias, the governor of Idumea. In the aftermath of the battle, he and his men venture onto the field to gather up the bodies of their slain. They find, to their dismay, under the tunics of each of the dead, amulets and sacred tokens dedicated to idols, and they conclude that this sin is the reason that those soldiers had died. They bless God for bringing this truth to light, and then "they turned to supplication, praying that the sin that had been committed might be wholly blotted out." Subsequently, Judas takes up a sizeable collection, which he sends to Jerusalem to "provide for a sin offering" on behalf of the dead. The author adds the editorial comment that this was an honorable thing to do, "taking account of the resurrection" (2 Macc. 12:42–43). For indeed, if death was simply the end or if the dead go into hopeless *Sheol*, then praying for them would be pointless.

And it would, by the same token, be equally pointless if the dead were utterly in the presence of God (where they would need no prayers) or utterly in alienation from God (where the prayers would have no effect). Therefore, the impulse to pray that the sins of the dead might be addressed rests necessarily on the assumption that there exists a third state of being intermediate between "heaven" and "hell." In this condition, the dead evidently are not beyond hope, yet they require some sort of purification. What we have in this simple story is the ground for the Catholic doctrine of purgatory, according to which there is a sort of "school of souls" in which some who have died in friendship with God, but yet imperfect in capacity to love, are prepared for complete union with the Lord. In their document on the Church, *Lumen Gentium*, the fathers of the Second Vatican Council defend the teaching on purgatory and make explicit reference to 2 Maccabees: "Fully conscious of this communion of the whole Mystical Body of Jesus Christ, the pilgrim Church from the very first ages of the Christian religion has cultivated with great piety the memory of the dead, and 'because it is a holy and wholesome thought to pray for the dead that they may be loosed from their sins' (2 Macc. 12:45), also offers suffrages for them."[6]

As I bring this chapter—and indeed this entire volume—to a close, might I draw our attention again to the heroic mother of the seven sons? Like Judith and Esther, she could be construed as an embodiment of Israel itself. Under terrible persecution, she confesses the faith in the one Creator God that was bequeathed to the chosen people. Over and against the enemies of the nation, she declares what is most distinctive in Israelite religion: "Hear, O Israel: The LORD is our God, the LORD alone" (Deut. 6:4). For the one who created the whole of contingent reality from nothing is not one being among many and therefore can have no competitors. However, in asserting what is most peculiar to Israel, she implicitly asserts what brings all people together. For all things, all peoples, all nations are equally grounded in the creative love of God and are, for that very reason, connected to one another by a bond deeper than those of family, culture, or country. Thus, this unnamed heroine might function as a symbol of Israel, chosen out of the world precisely for the sake of the world.

---

6. *Lumen Gentium* 50, in *The Word on Fire Vatican II Collection*, ed. Matthew Levering (Park Ridge, IL: Word on Fire Institute, 2021), 114.

Bibliography

Alter, Robert. *The Hebrew Bible: A Translation with Commentary*, vol. 1, *The Five Books of Moses*. New York: W.W. Norton, 2019.

——. *The Hebrew Bible: A Translation with Commentary*, vol. 2, *Prophets*. New York: W.W. Norton, 2019.

Ambrose. *Concerning Widows*. Translated by H. de Romestin, E. de Romestin, and H.T.F. Duckworth. In Nicene and Post-Nicene Fathers, Second Series, vol. 10, ed. Philip Schaff and Henry Wace. Buffalo, NY: Christian Literature, 1896. newadvent.org.

——. *Exposition on the Christian Faith*. Translated by H. de Romestin, E. de Romestin, and H.T.F. Duckworth. In Nicene and Post-Nicene Fathers, Second Series, vol. 10, ed. Philip Schaff and Henry Wace. Buffalo, NY: Christian Literature, 1896. newadvent.org.

——. *Exposition of the Holy Gospel According to Saint Luke*. Translated by Theodosia Tomkinson. Etna, CA: Center for Traditionalist Orthodox Studies, 1998.

Anderson, Carl and Jose Granados. *Called to Love: Approaching John Paul II's Theology of the Body*. New York: Doubleday, 2009.

Anselm. *Proslogion*. In *Anselm: Monologion and Proslogion*, trans. Thomas Williams, 91–118. Indianapolis, IN: Hackett, 1996.

Aphrahat. *Demonstrations*. In Ancient Christian Commentary on Scripture, vol. 5, *1–2 Kings, 1–2 Chronicles, Ezra, Nehemiah, Esther*, ed. Marco Conti. Downers Grove, IL: InterVarsity, 2008.

Aristotle. *Metaphysics*. Translated by C.D.C. Reeve. Indianapolis, IN: Hackett, 2016.

——. *Nicomachean Ethics*. Translated by C.D.C. Reeve. Indianapolis, IN: Hackett, 2014.

Augustine. *The City of God, Books VIII–XVI*. Edited by Hermigild Dressler. Translated by Gerald G. Walsh and Grace Monahan. Washington, DC: The Catholic University of America Press, 1952.

———. *Confessions*. Edited by Michael P. Foley. Translated by F.J. Sheed. Park Ridge, IL: Word on Fire Classics, 2017.

———. *Expositions on the Psalms*. In Ancient Christian Commentary on Scripture, vol. 4, *Joshua, Judges, Ruth, 1–2 Samuel*, ed. John R. Franke. Downers Grove, IL: InterVarsity, 2005.

———. *Expositions on the Psalms*. Translated by A. Cleveland Coxe. In Nicene and Post-Nicene Fathers, First Series, vol. 8, ed. Philip Schaff. Buffalo, NY: Christian Literature, 1888. newadvent.org.

———. *Quaestiones in Heptateuchum*. In *Patrologia cursus completus*, series Latina, edited by J.-P. Migne, 34:547–824. Paris, 1865.

———. *Questions on Judges*. In Ancient Christian Commentary on Scripture, vol. 4, *Joshua, Judges, Ruth, 1–2 Samuel*, ed. John R. Franke. Downers Grove, IL: InterVarsity, 2005.

———. *Tractates on the Gospel of John*. Translated by John W. Rettig. Washington, DC: The Catholic University of America Press, 1993.

Balthasar, Hans Urs von. *Razing the Bastions*. Translated by Brian McNeil. San Francisco: Ignatius, 1993.

———. *Theo-Drama: Theological Dramatic Theory*, vol. 4, *The Action*. San Francisco: Ignatius, 1994.

Barth, Karl. "God and Nothingness." In *Church Dogmatics*, vol. 3, *The Doctrine of Creation*, ed. G.W. Bromiley and T.F. Torrance, 1–78. London: T&T Clark, 2010.

———. *The Humanity of God*. Translated by Thomas Wieser and John Newton Thomas. Louisville, KY: Westminster John Knox, 1960.

Bede. *On Ezra and Nehemiah*. In Ancient Christian Commentary on Scripture, vol. 5, *1–2 Kings, 1–2 Chronicles, Ezra, Nehemiah, Esther*, ed. Marco Conti. Downers Grove, IL: InterVarsity, 2008.

Benedict XVI. *Jesus of Nazareth: From the Baptism in the Jordan to the Transfiguration*. Translated by Adrian J. Walker. New York: Doubleday, 2007.

Bergsma, John and Brant Pitre. *A Catholic Introduction to the Bible*, vol. 1, *The Old Testament*. San Francisco: Ignatius, 2018.

Burrell, David B. *Aquinas: God and Action*. Notre Dame, IN: University of Notre Dame Press, 1979.

Caesarius of Arles. *Sermons*, vol. 2, *81–186*. Translated by Mary Magdaleine Mueller. Washington, DC: The Catholic University of America Press, 1964.

Catechism of the Catholic Church. New York: Image Books, 1995.

Dauphinais, Michael and Matthew Levering. *Holy People, Holy Land*. Grand Rapids, MI: Brazos, 2005.

Denzinger, Heinrich et al. *Compendium of Creeds, Definitions, and Declarations on Matters of Faith and Morals*. 43rd ed. San Francisco: Ignatius, 2012.

Ephrem the Syrian. *Hymns on Paradise*. Translated by Sebastian Brock. Crestwood, NY: St. Vladimir's Seminary Press, 1990.

Gambero, Luigi. *Mary and the Fathers of the Church: The Blessed Virgin Mary in Patristic Thought*. Translated by Thomas Buffer. San Francisco: Ignatius, 1999.

Girard, René. *The Scapegoat*. Translated by Yvonne Freccero. Baltimore, MD: Johns Hopkins University Press, 1986.

———. *Things Hidden Since the Foundation of the World*. Translated by Stephen Bann and Michael Metteer. Stanford, CA: Stanford University Press, 1987.

Gregory of Nyssa. *The Life of Moses*. Edited and translated by Abraham J. Malherbe and Everett Ferguson. Mahwah, NJ: Paulist, 1978.

Gregory the Great. *Forty Gospel Homilies*. Translated by David Hurst. Kalamazoo, MI: Cistercian, 1990.

———. *Morals on the Book of Job*. In Ancient Christian Commentary on Scripture, vol. 4, *Joshua, Judges, Ruth, 1–2 Samuel*, ed. John R. Franke. Downers Grove, IL: InterVarsity, 2005.

Guardini, Romano. *The Spirit of the Liturgy*. Translated by Ada Lane (New York: Crossroad, 1998).

Hegel, Georg Wilhelm Friedrich. *Lectures on the Philosophy of Religion*. Edited and translated by E.B. Speirs. London: Kegan Paul, Trench, Trübner & Co., 1895.

Irenaeus. *Against Heresies*. Translated by Alexander Roberts and William Rambaut. In Ante-Nicene Fathers, vol. 1, ed. Alexander Roberts, James Donaldson, and A. Cleveland Coxe. Buffalo, NY: Christian Literature, 1885. newadvent.org.

Isidore of Seville. *On Ruth*. In *Medieval Exegesis in Translation: Commentaries on the Book of Ruth*, ed. and trans. Lesley Smith. Kalamazoo, MI: Medieval Institute, 1996.

Jerome. *Letters*. Translated by W.H. Fremantle, G. Lewis, and W.G. Martley. In Nicene and Post-Nicene Fathers, Second Series, vol. 6, ed. Philip Schaff and Henry Wace. Buffalo, NY: Christian Literature, 1893. newadvent.org.

John Chrysostom. *Homilies on the Gospel of Saint Matthew*. Translated by George Prevost and M.B. Riddle. In Nicene and Post-Nicene Fathers, First Series, vol. 10, ed. Philip Schaff. Buffalo, NY: Christian Literature, 1888. newadvent.org.

John of the Cross. *John of the Cross: Selected Writings*. Edited and translated by Kieran Kavanaugh. Mahwah, NJ: Paulist, 1987.

John of Damascus. *Three Treatises on the Divine Images*. Translated by Andrew Louth. Crestwood, NY: St. Vladimir's Seminary Press, 2003).

John Paul II. "General Audience: The Boundary Between Original Innocence and Redemption." September 26, 1979. vatican.va.

———. *Love and Responsibility*. Translated by H.T. Willetts. San Francisco: Ignatius, 1993.

———. *Theotokos: Woman, Mother, Disciple: A Catechesis on Mary, Mother of God*. Boston: Pauline Books and Media, 2000.

Kierkegaard, Søren. *Fear and Trembling*. In *Fear and Trembling / Repetition*, ed. and trans. Howard V. Hong and Edna H. Hong, 1–124. Princeton, NJ: Princeton University Press, 1983.

Kugel, James L. *The Bible as It Was*. Cambridge, MA: The Belknap Press of Harvard University Press, 1997.

Leo the Great. *Sermons*. Translated by Jane Patricia Freeland and Agnes Josephine Conway. Washington, DC: The Catholic University of America Press, 1996.

Levinas, Emmanuel. *Totality and Infinity: An Essay on Exteriority*. Translated by Alphonso Lingis. Pittsburgh, PA: Duquesne University Press, 1969.

Meister Eckhart. "Sermon Thirty-One." In *The Complete Mystical Works of Meister Eckhart*, trans. Maurice O'Connell Walshe. New York: Crossroad, 2009.

Merton, Thomas. *New Seeds of Contemplation*. New York: New Directions, 1961.

Moses Maimonides. "The Laws of Injury and Damages." In *Mishneh Torah: Sefer Neziki (The Book of Damages)*, trans. Eliyahu Touger. Brooklyn, NY: Moznaim, 1997.

Newman, John Henry. *An Essay in Aid of a Grammar of Assent*. Edited by I.T. Ker. Oxford: Clarendon, 1985.

———. *An Essay on the Development of Christian Doctrine*. Park Ridge, IL: Word on Fire Classics, 2017.

Nietzsche, Friedrich. *The Will to Power*. Edited by Walter Kaufman. Translated by Walter Kaufman and R.J. Hollingdale. New York: Vintage Books, 1968.

Noth, Martin. *The Deuteronomistic History*. Sheffield, UK: JSOT, 1981.

———. *The History of Israel*. London: SCM, 1983.

O'Connor, Flannery. "An Interview with Flannery O'Connor." In *Conversations with Flannery O'Connor*, ed. Rosemary M. Magee, 58–60. Jackson: University Press of Mississippi, 1987.

Ordway, Holly and Daniel Seseske, eds., *Ignatian Collection*. Park Ridge, IL: Word on Fire Classics, 2020.

Origen. *Homilies on Exodus*. In *Homilies on Genesis and Exodus*, ed. Hermigild Dressler, trans. Ronald E. Heine, 227–387. Washington, DC: The Catholic University of America Press, 1982.

———. *Homilies on Joshua*. Edited by Cynthia White. Translated by Barbara J. Bruce. Washington, DC: The Catholic University of America Press, 2002.

———. *Homilies on Judges*. In *Origen: Spirit and Fire: A Thematic Anthology of His Writings*, ed. Hans Urs von Balthasar, trans. Robert J. Daly. Washington, DC: The Catholic University of America Press, 1984.

———. *Homilies on Judges*. Translated by Elizabeth Ann Dively Lauro. Washington, DC: The Catholic University of America Press, 2010.

———. *Homilies on Leviticus*. Edited by Thomas P. Halton. Translated by Gary Wayne Barkley. Washington, DC: The Catholic University of America Press, 1990.

———. *Homilies on Numbers*. Edited by Christopher A. Hall. Translated by Thomas P. Scheck. Downers Grove, IL: IVP Academic, 2009.

Otto, Rudolf. *The Idea of the Holy*. 2nd ed. Translated by John W. Harvey. Oxford: Oxford University Press, 1958.

Placher, William C. "Contemporary Confession and Biblical Authority." In *To Confess the Faith Today*, ed. Jack L. Stotts and Jane Dempsey Douglass, 64–81. Louisville, KY: Westminster / John Knox, 1990.

Plato. *Complete Works*. Edited by John M. Cooper. Indianapolis, IN: Hackett, 1997.

Ratzinger, Joseph. *Introduction to Christianity*. 2nd ed. Translated by J.R. Foster. San Francisco: Ignatius, 2004.

Sacks, Jonathan. "The Meanings of Shema." https://www.rabbisacks .org/covenant-conversation/vaetchanan/the-meanings-of-shema/.

Salvian the Presbyter. *The Governance of God*. In *The Writings of Salvian, the Presbyter*, trans. Jeremiah F. O'Sullivan, 21–232. Washington, DC: The Catholic University of America Press, 1947.

Schleiermacher, Friedrich. *On Religion: Speeches to Its Cultured Despisers*. Translated by John Oman. London: Kegan Paul, Trench, Trübner & Co., 1893.

Sokolowski, Robert. *The God of Faith and Reason: Foundations of Christian Theology*. Washington, DC: The Catholic University of America Press, 1995.

Spinoza, Baruch. *Ethics*. In *The Collected Works of Spinoza*, vol. 1, trans. Edwin Curley, 408–446. Princeton: Princeton University Press, 1985.

Steinsaltz, Adin Even-Israel, ed. *Koren Talmud Bavli: Noé Edition*, vol. 23, *Bava Kamma Part 1*. Jerusalem: Koren, 2016.

Tan, Randall K., David A. deSilva, and Isaiah Hoogendyk, eds. *The Lexham Greek-English Interlinear Septuagint: H.B. Swete Edition*. Bellingham, WA: Lexham, 2012.

Teresa of Avila. *The Interior Castle*. Translated by Kieran Kavanaugh and Otilio Rodriguez. Mahwah, NJ: Paulist, 1979.

Thomas Aquinas. *Quaestiones disputatae de potential Dei*. In *Quaestiones disputatae*, vol. 2, ed. P. Bazzi. Turin: Marietti, 1949.

———. *Summa contra Gentiles*, book 3, *Providence Part 1*. Translated by Vernon J. Bourke. Notre Dame, IN: University of Notre Dame Press, 1975.

———. *Summa theologiae*. In *Sancti Thomae de Aquino Opera Omnia*, Leonine ed., 4:25. Rome, 1882.

———. *Summa theologiae, Prima Pars 1–49*. Translated by Fr. Laurence Shapcote. Lander, WY: The Aquinas Institute for the Study of Sacred Doctrine, 2012.

———. *Summa theologiae, Prima Secundae 1–70*. Translated by Fr. Laurence Shapcote. Lander, WY: The Aquinas Institute for the Study of Sacred Doctrine, 2012.

Tillich, Paul. *Die religiöse Deutung der Gegenwart; Schriften zur Zeitkritik*. Stuttgart: Evangelisches Verlagswerk, 1968.

———. *Systematic Theology*. Vol. 1. Chicago: University of Chicago Press, 1973.

Vatican Council II. *Lumen Gentium*. In *The Word on Fire Vatican II Collection*, ed. Matthew Levering, 43–149. Park Ridge, IL: Word on Fire Institute, 2021.

Weigel, George. *Witness to Hope: The Biography of Pope John Paul II*. New York: Harper Perennial, 2005.

Wright, N.T. *Jesus and the Victory of God*. Minneapolis, MN: Fortress, 1996.

———. *The New Testament and the People of God*. Minneapolis: Fortress, 1992.

———. *Scripture and the Authority of God: How to Read the Bible Today*. San Francisco: HarperOne, 2013.

Index